Collins

Collins

Italian

Phrasebook
and Dictionary

T0204662

Italian Phrasebook and Dictionary

Other languages in the
Collins Phrasebook and Dictionary series:
French, German, Greek, Japanese, Mandarin,
Polish, Portuguese, Spanish, Turkish.

HarperCollins Publishers
Westerhill Road, Bishopbriggs,
Glasgow G64 2QT

www.collinslanguage.com

First published 2004
This edition published 2008

Reprint 10 9 8 7 6 5 4 3 2

© HarperCollins Publishers 2004, 2008

ISBN 978-0-00-726454-4

Typeset by Davidson Pre-Press Graphics Ltd,
Glasgow

Printed in Malaysia for Imago

Your *Collins Italian Phrasebook and Dictionary* is a handy, quick-reference guide that will help make the most of your stay abroad. Its clear layout will save valuable time when you need that crucial word or phrase. Download free all the essential words and phrases you need to get by from www.collinslanguage.com/talk60. These hour long audio files are ideal for practising listening comprehension and pronunciation. The main sections in this book are:

Everyday Italy – photoguide
Packed full of photos, this section allows you to see all the practical visual information that will help with using cash machines, driving on motorways, reading signs, etc.

Phrases
Practical topics are arranged thematically with an opening section, Key talk containing vital phrases that should stand you in good stead in most situations. Phrases are short, useful and each one has a pronunciation guide so that there is no problem saying them.

Eating out
This section contains phrases for ordering food and drink (and special requirements) plus a photoguide showing different places to eat, menus and practical information to help choose the best options. The menu reader allows you to work out what to choose.

Grammar
There is a short Grammar section explaining how the language works.

Dictionary
And finally, the practical 5000-word English–Italian and Italian–English Dictionary means that you won't be stuck for words.

So, just flick through the pages to find the information you need and listen to the free audio download to improve your pronunciation.

Useful websites

Accommodation

www.travel.it
www.abouthotel.com
www.venere.com
www.agriturist.it (staying in
the countryside on a farm)

Culture & Activities

www.operabase.com
www.teatroallascala.org
(La Scala)
www.hostetler.net
(info on Italian festivals)

Currency Converters

www.x-rates.com

Driving

www.autostrade.it
(Italian motorways)
www.drivingabroad.co.uk
www.quattroruote.it/infotrafic
(Italian road and traffic info)

Facts

www.cia.gov/library/publications
/the-world-factbook

Foreign Office Advice

www.fco.gov.uk/travel
www.dfat.gov.au (Australia)
www.voyage.gc.ca (Canada)

Health advice

www.dh.gov.uk/travellers
www.thetraveldoctor.com
www.smartraveller.gov.au
(Australia)
www.phac-aspc.gc.ca (Canada)

Internet Cafés

www.cybercafes.com

Passport Office

www.ukpa.gov.uk
www.passports.gov.au (Australia)
www.pptc.gc.ca (Canada)

Pets

www.defra.gov.uk/animalh/
quarantine

Sightseeing

www.doge.it (Venice guide)
www.enit.it (official site of Italian
state tourist board)
www.initaly.com
www.italytour.com
www.romeguide.it
www.uffizi.firenze.it
(Uffizi, Florence)

Transport

www.europeanrailguide.com
www.trenitalia.com
(Italian railways)
www.aeroporti.com
(Italian airports)

Weather

www.bbc.co.uk/weather

Italian isn't hard to pronounce once you've learned a few basic rules. We've tried to make it as clear as possible by splitting up words to make them easy to read, but don't pause too long between syllables.

Longer words are usually stressed on the next to last syllable, but we show all stressed syllables in **bold type**, so you won't be caught out by any exceptions.

The spellings **c** and **ch** might confuse you, because **c** is sometimes pronounced like English **ch** as in church, while the Italian **ch** is pronounced like the English **k** (see the English for kilo and the Italian **chilo**). So **c'è** (there is) is pronounced like English 'check' without the final k sound, while **che?** (what?) is pronounced kay. The rule to remember is that **c** followed by **e** or **i** makes it a soft **ch** sound. But **c** followed by **a**, **o** or **u** has a hard **k** sound:

chiave kee-**a**-vay (key)	**cibo chee**-bo (food)
chiesa kee-**ay**-za (church)	**cena chay**-na (dinner)

The letter **g** behaves in a similar way. When followed by **a**, **o** or **u**, **g** will be hard. When followed by **e** or **i**, it will be soft. The word for lake is **lago**, for lakes the word is **laghi**. The **h** has been added to keep the **g** hard. So when you see a **ch** or **gh** combination in Italian, remember to make the **c** and **g** hard.

Sometimes Italian has two distinctive vowel sounds next to each other eg. **dei** pronounced **day**-ee. These sounds merge with each other, so don't separate them with a long pause.

Finally, pronounce all r's when you see them in Italian words. Basic rules to remember are:

Italian	sounds like	example	pronunciation
a	c**a**t	**pasta**	**pas**-ta
e	b**e**t/d**ay**	**letto/per**	**let**-to/payr
i	m**ee**t	**vino**	**vee**-no
o	g**o**t	**botta**	**bot**-ta
u	b**oo**t	**luna**	**loo**-na
gli	mi**lli**on	**figlio**	**feel**-yo
sc (before **e/i**)	**sh**op	**sci**	shee
sc (before **a/o/u**)	**sc**an	**scarpa**	**skar**-pa

Everyday photoguide

Everyday Italy

Open Small shops tend to close between 1 and 3.30pm, but stay open later till about 7.30pm.

Closed Don't be fooled by the **ch**, it's pronounced kee-**oo**-zo.

Opening Hours
Orario = timetable
Apertura = opening

ENTRATA

Entrance Look out for the words **entrata libera** which means free entry.

Orario Sportello means counter opening hours (i.e. open to public).

FUORI SERVIZIO

Out Of Order

CASSA

Pay Here

USCITA

Exit Uscita is also used for exit on motorways.

Forbidden Another word for forbidden is **divieto di...**

Danger

Symbol for the **euro**. Italy is in the eurozone.

Prices The word for price is **prezzo** (singular) and **prezzi** (plural). **Metà prezzo** means half price.

Prices are generally written with a comma. The price here is 5 euros: **virgola** = comma **punto** = full stop

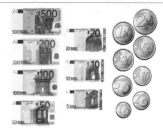

The euro is the currency of Italy. It breaks down into 100 euro cents. Notes: 5, 10, 20, 50, 100, 200, 500. Coins: 1 and 2 euros, 1, 2, 5, 10. 20 and 50 cents. Although coins are officially **cent**, Italians call them **centesimi** chen-**tay**-zee-mee, a more familiar Italian term. Euro is pronounced **ay**-oo-ro. It stays the same in the plural. Euro notes are the same throughout Europe. The backs of coins carry different designs from each of the member European countries.

Banca Popolare di Sondrio

Banca Italy has many regional banks such as **Banca Popolare di Sondrio**; nationwide banks include **UniCredit Banca** and **Banca Nazionale del Lavoro**.

Cash machines (ATM) (**Bancomat**) are common. Banks have a double-door system with metal detectors. Press a button and wait for the green light to enter.

Cash machines (ATM) operate as at home.
cancella = cancel last part of transaction
annulla = cancel whole of transaction
esegui = proceed

Service is usually included in a restaurant bill so tipping is discretionary. However, it is usual to leave a small tip. In busy bars there will often be a saucer to leave loose change.

Often attached to a bar and sell stamps, cigarettes bus and lottery tickets, etc. It is a good place for an early morning cup of coffee.

Receipt **richiesta scontrino** = request for receipt.
Scontrino is a good word to remember. You get this in bars when you pay for your order in advance.
Ricevuta is a receipt in restaurants, taxis, clothes shops, etc.

When friends or family meet up, they usually kiss each other on the cheeks. Among friends you hear **ciao** for hi and bye, but for people you come across in the street, use **buon giorno** or **buona sera** (late pm/eve). If you are unsure whether to use **ciao**, **salve** is always a good option.

CARABINIERI

Police In small towns you find **carabinieri**, and in larger towns, **polizia**. You must report any crimes to them.

Automatic machines take both coins and notes

AFFITTASI

For Rent

Agriturism is popular. You get away from it all on a farm, visit **www.agriturist.it**.

The tourist office has guides to hotels and campsites.

Tourist Information The tourist office is known as the **Ufficio turistico**. They have maps and brochures in English.

Hotel Hotels are known as **albergo** (**alberghi** in plural) or hotel (the h is not sounded).

For Sale 'Sold' in Italian is **venduto** ven-**doo**-to.

AUTONOLEGGIO

Car Hire Noleggio = rental, hire.

Chiuso per ferie dall'11 al 18 Agosto.

Closed For Holidays Italians take their main holiday in the first 3 weeks in August. The weekend of the 15th August is a public holiday **Ferragosto**. Avoid travelling at the start and end of this period (especially by car).

Paper Recycling Bin

bagno

Bathroom

Rubbish Rubbish isn't collected from houses, you have to take it to refuse points. There are banks for recycling glass, plastic, paper etc.

toilette

Toilet Some bars (particularly in cities) will lock their toilet and you will have to ask for a key.

Swimming pool It's obligatory to wear swimming caps in public pools. You can usually buy or borrow one at the pool.

Not Drinking Water The word for water is **acqua** (ak-wa). **Non bere acqua** = don't drink water.

Ladies = Donne Ladies and gents toilets are generally shown with a pictogram.

Gents = Uomini WC is also known as **gabinetto**.

Timetables

ORARIO DAL 26 GIUGNO AL 1° OTTOBRE

Timetable

dal = from **al** = to

Giorni		Days
lunedì	loo-ned-**ee**	Monday
martedì	mar-ted-**ee**	Tuesday
mercoledì	mer-ko-led-**ee**	Wednesday
giovedì	jov-ed-**ee**	Thursday
venerdì	ven-er-**dee**	Friday
sabato	**sa**-bat-o	Saturday
domenica	dom-**en**-ee-ka	Sunday

In Italian, unlike English, neither months or days start with a capital letter.

ORARIO ESTIVO

Summer Timetable

mattino

Morning

pomeriggio

Afternoon

Giornaliere

Daily

Settimanale

Weekly

oggi

Today

domani

Tomorrow

Mesi		Months
gennaio	jen-**na**-yo	January
febbraio	feb-**ra**-yo	February
marzo	**mar**-tso	March
aprile	a-**pree**-lay	April
maggio	**mad**-jo	May
giugno	**joon**-yo	June
luglio	**lool**-yo	July
agosto	a-**gos**-to	August
settembre	set-**tem**-bray	September
ottobre	ot-**tob**-ray	October
novembre	nov-**em**-bray	November
dicembre	dee-**chem**-bray	December

Tickets

CORSE BATTELLO - SCHIFF - BATEAU - SCHIP								BELLAGIO - LECCO	
Annotazioni		③ feriale	sabato e festivi		festiva	Rapido festiva		③ feriale	sabato e festivi
N° CORSE		181	283	85	287	SR253	87	189	289
BELLAGIO *part.*		6.40	8.20	11.45	12.45	14.34	16.50	18.05	18.05
Lierna "		I	8.38	I				I	18.23
Limonta "		6.57	8.46	12.02				18.22	18.31
Vassena "		7.09	8.58	12.14				18.34	18.43

Timetable feriale = weekdays (Monday to Friday)
sabato e festivi = Saturday and Sunday holidays

Self-service You can purchase tickets from machines rather than queueing. Note you can also validate train tickets in the yellow slot rather than on the platforms (where you might miss the validating machine).

Ticket Office

VILLA VALMARANA «AI NANI»
INGRESSO
alla **PALAZZINA**
ed alla **FORESTERIA**
N° 4489
singolo
€5

Entrance Ticket
biglietto d'ingresso

part. ore 19.28
arr. ore 23.45

part. ore =
partenza alle ore ...
= departure at ... hours
arr. ore =
arrivo alle ... ore =
arrival at ... hours

Getting around

Taxi You can call for taxis (usually on freephone numbers).

Official taxis are white. You can find them at stations and taxi stands. People do not usually hail them in the street. It is always better to use official ones as private operators (blue limousines) might charge more.

Pedestrian Area

Other Routes

Pictograms are increasingly used on signs (hospital, post office and police).

Centro
Town centre – note the pictogram used.

MUSEI CIVICI

Local Museums

Town Hall

piazza Nuova

Square = **piazza**

Cathedral Duomo = Cathedral

150 m a destra

150m on right
a sinistra = on left

City buses are generally orange. You enter from the back and validate your ticket at the machine as you enter. In rural areas shops near the bus stop sell bus tickets and are likely to shut for lunch from 1–3.30pm.

Bus stops often have the time-table and stops en route. Bus stop = **la fermata dell'autobus**.

You must validate your ticket before boarding the train.

Station Stations are well sign-posted.

Departure Board

Metro The symbol for the metro system (**metropolitana**) is **M**.

Category Of Train The red IC stands for InterCity. The different colours indicate the 'speed' of trains: red = fastest and usually most expensive. Always check if you need to pay a supplement.

Driving

Roundabouts Beware! New roundabouts follow the same rules as UK – stop and give way to vehicles already on it. Old roundabouts are the opposite – you can drive straight onto them and cars on it have to give way to you. The problem is telling which system operates! Watch out carefully for give way signs and don't trust other drivers. Italians don't use indicators properly.

Parking Sign
More and more pictograms are being used on signs.

Pictograms
Parking disk required
1 ora = 1 hour
crossed mallets = work days Mon-Sat
cross = Sunday

eccetto

The word **eccetto** means 'except for'.

Some areas have a scratch and display card, place it on your windscreen.

Spaces Careful!
libero means spaces not that it's free.
Completo = full

giorni feriali = week days (inc. Sat.)
dalle 9.00 = from 9am
alle 20.00 = to 8pm

Motorways are sign-posted green with **A** for **Autostrada**. Blue signs indicate main routes. White signs indicate local destinations.

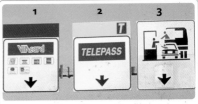

There are different lanes for paying.
1 Viacards can be bought at newsagents. You can also pay by credit card.
2 Telepass, the in-car device. Avoid this lane.
3 Cash payment only. The amount is displayed at the pay booth.

Stop Payment Station

Price List Servito means that you are served. Prices are slightly higher than self-service.

Self Service Petrol
Benzina = petrol
Payment machines take 5, 10 and 20 euro notes. Don't choose too much petrol as you don't get money back.

Recommended Speed 70kph Speed limits are 130kph on motorways, 110 or 90kph on dual carriageways, 90kph on ordinary roads, 50kph in built-up areas. When raining the limits of 130/110kph are lowered by 20kph.
rallentare = slow down

Shopping

saldi fine stagione

End Of Season Sale

Duty Pharmacy
If the address of the duty pharmacy (**farmacia di guardia**) is not displayed, ask at the local police station. Details will be printed in the local paper.

Confezione = packet or pack. Here the offer is for 3 packets of **tortellini** for 5 euro.

You need euro coins to release the shopping trolley.

STANDA
SUPERMERCATI
**Orario continuato
8.00 - 20.00**

Standa is one of Italy's biggest supermarket chains. **Orario continuato** means that it doesn't close for lunch like most of the smaller shops. Sunday opening is becoming more common in Italy.

Reductions

Pharmacy You can recognise the pharmacy by the green cross. If you're worried about a medical condition, ask the pharmacist for advice. They are medically trained and often able to supply suitable medication. If you need over-the-counter medicine (for headaches, etc), you may find them in some of the big supermarkets.

ALIMENTARI
PANE VINO LIQUORI L.MARCONI.

Grocers An **Alimentari** usually sells bread (**pane**) and wine (**vino**). It generally opens early selling fresh bread and shuts between 1–4pm.

Weighing Machine In the supermarket, fruit and vegetables must be weighed and stickered. Either you or an attendant can do it.

Pane = bread
Panini = rolls
pane integrale = wholemeal bread
pane di segale = rye bread.
Bread is sold by the weight.

In supermarkets you generally get a ticket at busy counters.

Fats grassi = fats

Milk Look for the colour-coding for milk (**latte**). Blue is whole milk (**intero**), pink semi-skimmed (**parzialmente scremato**). Skimmed is **scremato**.

Water Look out for the colour-coding for **acqua minerale** (mineral water). The word for sparkling is **frizzante** or **gassata** and the word for still is **naturale**.

Keeping in touch

Post Office The **Posta** has a yellow and blue logo. Most open in the morning until 2pm Monday to Friday and until 12 noon on Saturdays.

famiglia Galli
via A. Volta, 16
20132 Milano
Italy

Addressing an envelope to family friends; road & house no.; postcode & town; country.

Stamps for postcards and letters are the same (0.60€) within Europe. There is no longer any **posta prioritaria**.
Ultimo ritiro = last collection.
Festivi = Sundays and holidays.

Tourist offices have internet access for €1 per 30 mins and wi-fi access if you are in a hotspot zone. By law you must register, so bring your passport.

Most phoneboxes take: **monete** = coins
schede = phonecards
carte = credit cards

Numero verde = freephone. Numbers begin – 800. Landline numbers begin – 0 (the area code) and mobile numbers begin – 3.

Phonecard Italian phonecards (**schede telefoniche**) are sold

for 5 or 10€. With some you must tear off (**strappare**) the perforated corner; with others you dial a number and key in the pin number on the card (you scratch to reveal it).

Key talk

Key talk

• It is customary to use the polite form **lei** and surname with people you've just been introduced to, unless it's clear you're going to establish a friendly relationship. In that case the informal **tu** form and first name will be used.
• The easiest way to ask for something is to name it and add 'please', **per favore**.

yes	sì	see
no	no	no
that's fine	va bene	va **ben**-ay
please	per favore	payr fa-**vo**-ray
thank you	grazie	**grat**-see-ay
don't mention it	prego	**pray**-go
hello	buon giorno	bwon **jor**-no
hi/bye	ciao	chow
goodbye	arrivederci	ar-ree-ve-**der**-chee
good night	buona notte	**bwo**-na **not**-tay
good afternoon/ evening	buona sera	**bwo**-na **say**-ra
that's very kind	molto gentile	**mol**-to jen-**tee**-lay
excuse me/sorry	scusi	**skoo**-zee
excuse me (to get past people)	permesso	payr-**mes**-so

• Here is an easy way to ask for something ... just add **per favore**

| a/an... | un... ('il' and 'lo' words) | oon... |
| an ice cream | un gelato | oon jay-**la**-to |

2 ice creams	due gelati	**doo**-ay jay-**la**-tee
a...	una... ('la' words)	**oo**-na...
a beer	una birra	**oo**-na **beer**-ra
2 beers	due birre	**doo**-ay **beer**-ray
a beer and two ice creams, please	una birra e due gelati, per favore	**oo**-na **beer**-ra ay **doo**-ay jay-**la**-tee, payr fa-**vo**-ray

- **Salve** meaning 'hello' is less casual than **ciao**.
- When entering a shop, bar or approaching someone, greet them with **buon giorno** (or **buona sera** from late afternoon).
- There are masculine and feminine endings. 'I'm clever' for a man is **sono bravo**, for a lady **sono brava**.

I'd like...	vorrei...	vor-**ray**-ee...
we'd like...	vorremmo...	vor-**rem**-mo...
I'd like an ice cream	vorrei un gelato	vor-**ray**-ee oon jay-**la**-to
we'd like to go to Pisa	vorremmo andare a Pisa	vor-**rem**-mo an-**da**-ray a **pee**-za
do you have...?	avete...?	a-**vay**-tay...?
do you have any milk?	avete del latte?	a-**vay**-tay del **lat**-tay?
do you have stamps?	avete dei francobolli?	a-**vay**-tay **day**-ee fran-ko-**bol**-lee?
do you have a map?	avete una carta?	a-**vay**-tay **oo**-na **kar**-ta?
do you have fruit?	avete della frutta?	a-**vay**-tay **del**-la **froot**-ta?
how much is it?	quanto costa?	**kwan**-to **kos**-ta?
how much does ... cost?	quanto costa il/la...?	**kwan**-to **kos**-ta eel/la...?

how much is the wine?	quanto costa il vino? **kwan**-to **kos**-ta eel **vee**-no?
how much is the ticket?	quanto costa il biglietto? **kwan**-to **kos**-ta eel beel-**yet**-to?
how much is a kilo?	quanto costa al chilo? **kwan**-to **kos**-ta al **kee**-lo?
how much is each one?	quanto costa l'uno? **kwan**-to **kos**-ta **loo**-no?

- You can use **ha**? or **avete**? for 'do you have?' Both are equally polite. '**H**' isn't sounded in Italian.
- Local dialects are quite different from 'proper' Italian. **Andiamo a casa** (let's go home) in the Como dialect is **'ndem a ca**. Even if you know Italian, you might have difficulty understanding dialects!

where is...?	dov'è...? dov-**e**...?
where are...?	dove sono...? **dov**-ay **so**-no...?
where is the toilet?	dov'è la toilette? dov-**e** la twa-**let**?
where are the children?	dove sono i bambini? **dov**-ay so-no ee bam-**bee**-nee?
is there?	c'è...? che...?
are there...?	ci sono...? chee so-no...?
there is no...	non c'è... non che...
is there a restaurant?	c'è un ristorante? che oon ree-sto-**ran**-tay?
where is there a chemist?	dove c'è una farmacia? **dov**-ay che **oo**-na far-ma-**chee**-a?
are there any children?	ci sono dei bambini? che so-no **day**-ee bam-**bee**-nee?
is there a swimming pool?	c'è una piscina? che **oo**-na pee-**shee**-na?

there is no hot water	non c'è acqua calda
	non che **ak**-wa **kal**-da
there is no bread	non c'è pane
	non che **pa**-nay
I need...	ho bisogno di...
	o bee-**zon**-yo dee...
I need a doctor	ho bisogno di un medico
	o bee-**zon**-yo dee oon **med**-ee-ko
I need to phone	ho bisogno di telefonare
	o bee-**zon**-yo dee te-le-fo-**na**-ray

● To catch someone's attention, begin your request with **scusi**.
● If you are in a busy street, or market, you can push your way through politely with the word **permesso**.
● You also use **permesso** when entering someone's home. It is a polite custom.

can I...?	posso...?
	pos-so...?
can we...?	possiamo...?
	pos-see-**a**-mo...?
where can I...?	dove posso...?
	dov-ay **pos**-so...?
can I pay?	posso pagare?
	pos-so pa-ga-ray?
can we go in?	possiamo entrare?
	pos-see-**a**-mo en-**tra**-ray?
where can I buy bread?	dove posso comprare il pane?
	dov-ay **pos**-so kom-**pra**-ray eel **pa**-nay?
where can I get tickets?	dove posso trovare i biglietti?
	dov-ay **pos**-so tro-**va**-ray ee beel-**yet**-tee?
when?	quando?
	kwan-do?
at what time...?	a che ora...?
	a kay **o**-ra...?
when does it leave?	quando parte?
	kwan-do **par**-tay?

when does it arrive?	quando arriva?
	kwan-do ar-**ree**-va?
when does it open?	a che ora apre?
	a kay **o**-ra **a**-pray?
when does it close?	a che ora chiude?
	a kay **o**-ra kee-**oo**-day?
yesterday	ieri
	ye-ree
today	oggi
	od-jee
tomorrow	domani
	do-**ma**-nee
this morning	stamattina
	sta-mat-**tee**-na
this afternoon	oggi pomeriggio
	od-jee po-may-**reed**-jo
tonight	stasera
	sta-**say**-ra
is it open?	è aperto?
	e a-**payr**-to?
is it closed?	è chiuso?
	e kee-**oo**-zo?

- **Signor** (Mr) is used mainly with name and surname (e.g. **signor Carlo Rossi** or **signor Rossi**), but it can also be used with first name only (e.g. **signor Carlo**).
- **Signora** (Mrs/Ms) is used the same way as **signor**.
- **Signorina** (Miss) is becoming 'politically incorrect'. Women should all be called **signora**, regardless of age or marital status.

how are you?	come sta?
	ko-may sta?
fine, thanks, and you?	bene, grazie, e Lei?
	be-nay, **grat**-see-ay, ay lay?
my name is...	mi chiamo...
	mee kee-**a**-mo...

what is your name?	**come si chiama?**
	ko-may see kee-**a**-ma?
I didn't understand	**non ho capito**
	non o ka-**pee**-to
do you speak English?	**parla inglese?**
	par-la een-**glay**-zay?
Italy is very beautiful	**l'Italia è molto bella**
	lee-**tal**-ya e **mol**-to **bel**-la
I love Italian food	**mi piace molto la cucina italiana**
	mee pee-**a**-chay **mol**-to la koo-**chee**-na ee-tal-**ya**-na
Italian people are very kind	**gli Italiani sono molto gentili**
	lee ee-tal-**ya**-nee so-no **mol**-to jen-**tee**-lee
I'd like to come back	**vorrei ritornare**
	vor-**ray**-ee ree-**tor**-na-ray
you're very kind	**è molto gentile**
	e **mol**-to jen-**tee**-lay
I enjoyed myself very much	**mi sono divertito(a) moltissimo**
	mee **so**-no dee-ver-**tee**-to(a) mol-**tees**-see-mo
can I have your address?	**potrei avere il suo indirizzo?**
	po-**tray**-ee a-**vay**-ray eel **soo**-o een-dee-**reet**-so?
see you next year!	**all'anno prossimo!**
	al-**lan**-no **pros**-see-mo!

Money

Money – changing

● Italy is in the eurozone. Euro, pronounced **ay**-oo-ro, stays the same in the plural.
● Cent is **centesimo** (chen-**tay**-zee-mo) singular and **centesimi** (chen-**tay**-zee-mee) plural.
● Banks are generally open Monday to Friday, 8.30am to 1.30pm, and for one hour in the afternoon which can vary from city to city. In many tourist areas they are open from 8.30am to 4.00pm.

where is there a cash machine (ATM)?	**dove c'è un bancomat?** **dov**-ay che oon **ban**-ko-mat?
where can I change money?	**dove posso cambiare i soldi?** **dov**-ay **pos**-so kam-bee-**a**-ray ee **sol**-dee?
where is the bank?	**dov'è la banca?** **dov**-ay la **ban**-ka?
when does the bank open?	**quando apre la banca?** **kwan**-do **a**-pray la **ban**-ka?
when does the bank close?	**quando chiude la banca?** **kwan**-do kee-**oo**-day la **ban**-ka?
where is the bureau de change?	**dov'è il cambio?** **dov**-ay eel **kam**-bee-yo?
I want to cash these traveller's cheques	**vorrei cambiare questi travellers cheque** vor-**ray**-ee kam-bee-**a**-ray **kwes**-tee travellers cheque
what is the rate?	**quant'è il cambio?** kwan-**te** eel **kam**-bee-yo?
for pounds/dollars	**per sterline/dollari** payr ster-**lee**-nay/payr **dol**-la-ree

| I want to change ... pounds/dollars | **vorrei cambiare ... sterline/dollari** |
| | vor-**ray**-ee kam-bee-**a**-ray ... ster-**lee**-nay/dol-**la**-ree |

Money – spending

• Credit cards and debit cards are widely accepted.
• Cash machines (ATM), known as **Bancomat** in Italy, are widespread and you will be able to use English instructions. It avoids wasting time in bank queues.
• Remember to take your bank's phone number in case of problems.

how much is it?	**quanto costa?**
	kwan-to **kos**-ta?
where do I pay?	**dove devo pagare?**
	dov-ay **day**-vo pa-**ga**-ray?
I want to pay	**vorrei pagare**
	vor-**ray**-ee pa-**ga**-ray
how much do I have to pay?	**quanto devo pagare?**
	kwan-to **day**-vo pa-**ga**-ray?
can I pay by credit card?	**posso pagare con la carta di credito?**
	pos-so pa-**ga**-ray kon la **kar**-ta dee **kray**-dee-to?
I want to pay with euros	**vorrei pagare con euro**
	vor-**ray**-ee pa-**ga**-ray kon **ay**-oo-ro
with Swiss francs	**kon franchi svizzeri**
	kon **fran**-kee **sveet**-ser-ee
do you accept traveller's cheques?	**accettate i travellers cheques?**
	a-chet-**ta**-tay ee travellers cheques?
put it on my bill	**lo metta sul mio contro**
	lo **met**-ta sool **mee**-o **kon**-to
how much is it...?	**quanto costa...?**
	kwan-to **kos**-ta...?

per person	**per persona**
	payr per-**so**-na
per night	**per notte**
	payr **not**-tay
per kilo	**al chilo**
	al **kee**-lo
I need a receipt	**ho bisogno di una ricevuta**
	oh bee-**zon**-yo dee **oo**-na ree-chay-**voo**-ta
do I need to pay a deposit?	**devo dare una caparra?**
	day-vo dar-ay **oo**-na ka-**par**-ra?
pay at the cash desk	**paghi alla cassa**
	pag-ee **al**-la **kas**-sa

Getting around

Airport

• Signs are generally in Italian and English.
• Research the best way of getting to and from the airport using **www.aeroporti.com/aeroporti.html**.
• If you are staying in a hotel, they will organise your trip to the airport.
• You can find internet access at airports.

to the airport, please	**all'aeroporto, per favore** al-la-**ay**-ro-**por**-to, payr fa-**vo**-ray
how do I/we get into town?	**scusi, come si va in città?** **skoo**-zee, **ko**-may see va een cheet-**ta**?
where do I get the bus into town?	**dove prendo l'autobus per la città?** **dov**-ay **pren**-do **low**-to-boos payr la cheet-**ta**?
how much is it...?	**quanto costa...?** **kwan**-to **kos**-ta...?
to the centre/ to the airport	**per il centro/per l'aeroporto** payr eel **chen**-tro/payr la-ay-ro-**por**-to
where is the check-in for...?	**scusi, dov'è il check-in per...?** **skoo**-zee, dov-**e** eel check-in payr...?
which gate is it for the flight to...?	**qual è l'uscita per il volo per...?** kwal e loo-**shee**-ta payr eel **vo**-lo payr...?
boarding will take place at gate number...	**l'imbarco sarà all'uscita numero...** leem-**bar**-ko sa-**ra** al-loo-**shee**-ta **noo**-may-ro...
the last call	**l'ultima chiamata** **lool**-tee-ma kee-a-**ma**-ta
the flight is delayed	**il volo è in ritardo** eel **vo**-lo e een ree-**tar**-do

Customs and passports

● ●

● EU citizens with nothing to declare can use the blue customs channels.
● There's no restriction in quantity or value of goods purchased by travellers in another EU country, provided they are for their own personal use (this covers gifts). Check guidelines on customs. **www.hmrc.gov.uk**.

I have nothing to declare	**non ho niente da dichiarare** non o nee-**en**-tay da deeya-**ra**-ray
here is...	**ecco...** **ek**-ko...
my passport	**il mio passaporto** eel **mee**-o pas-sa-**por**-to
do I have to pay duty on this?	**devo pagare la dogana per questo?** **day**-vo pa-**ga**-ray la do-**ga**-na payr **kwes**-to?
it's for personal use	**è per uso personale** e payr **oo**-zo per-so-**na**-lay
we are on our way to... (if in transit through country)	**siamo in transito per...** see-**a**-mo een tran-zee-to payr...
this is the baby's passport	**questo è il passaporto del(la) bambino(a)** **kwes**-to e eel pas-sa-**por**-to **del**(-la) bam-**bee**-no(a)
I'm British (m/f)	**sono inglese** **so**-no een-**glay**-zay
American (m/f)	**Americano(a)** a-mer-ee-**ka**-no(a)
Australian (m/f)	**australiano(a)** ow-stra-lee-**a**-no(a)
I bought it in...	**l'ho comprato in...** lo kom-**pra**-to een...
here's the receipt	**ecco la ricevuta** **ek**-ko la ree-**chay**-voo-ta

Asking the way – questions

• •

• You can ask the way simply by asking **scusi, per andare a...?** (how do I get to...?)
• Tourist offices have free maps and leaflets in English.
• Learn the words for 'near', **vicino** (vee-**chee**-no) and 'far' **lontano** (lon-**ta**-no).

excuse me	**scusi**
	skoo-zee
where is...?	**dov'è...?**
	dov-**e**...?
how do I get to...?	**per andare a...?**
	payr an-**da**-ray a...?
where is the nearest...?	**dov'è il/la ... più vicino(a)?**
	dov-**e** eel/la ... pee-**yoo** vee-**chee**-no(a)?
is this the right way to...?	**questa è la strada giusta per...?**
	kwes-ta e la **stra**-da **joos**-ta payr...?
the...	**il/la...**
	eel...
is it far?	**è lontano(a)?**
	e lon-**ta**-no(a)?
can I walk there?	**si può andare a piedi?**
	see pwo an-**da**-ray a pee-**ay**-dee?
is there a bus that goes there?	**c'è un autobus che ci va?**
	che oon **ow**-to-boos kay chee va?
we're looking for...	**stiamo cercando...**
	stee-**a**-mo cher-**kan**-do...
we're lost	**ci siamo persi**
	chee see-**a**-mo **per**-see
can you show me on the map?	**mi può indicare sulla cartina?**
	mee pwo een-dee-**ka**-ray **sool**-la kar-**tee**-na?

Asking the way – answers

- Key words – 'right' **destra** (**des**-tra), 'left' **sinistra** (see-**nees**-tra).
- Learn 'crossroads' **l'incrocio** (leen-**kroch**-o), 'square' **piazza** (py**at**-sa), 'centre of town' **centro** (**chen**-tro), 'exit' **uscita** (oo-**shee**-ta) and 'follow' **seguire** (seg-**wee**-ray).
- If you're not sure of the reply, say **non ho capito** (non o ka-**pee**-to), 'I didn't understand'.

keep going straight ahead	**continui sempre dritto** kon-**tee**-noo-ee **sem**-pray **dreet**-to
you have to turn round	**deve tornare indietro** **day**-vay tor-**na**-ray een-dee-**ay**-tro
turn...	**giri...** **jee**-ree...
right	**a destra** a **des**-tra
left	**a sinistra** a see-**nee**-stra
go...	**vada...** **va**-da...
towards...	**verso...** **ver**-so...
keep going...	**continui...** kon-**tee**-noo-ee...
as far as...	**fino a...** **fee**-no a...
take...	**prenda...** **pren**-da...
the first road on the right	**la prima strada a destra** la **pree**-ma **stra**-da a **des**-tra
the second road on the left	**la seconda strada a sinistra** la sek-**on**-da **stra**-da a see-**nee**-stra
cross...	**attraversi...** at-tra-**ver**-see...

the square	**la piazza**
	la pee-**at**-sa
it's after the traffic lights	**è dopo il semaforo**
	e **do**-po eel se-**ma**-fo-ro

Bus

• •

• Tickets must be stamped on board in a machine which is usually beside the front or rear doors on buses.
• Tickets can be bought at newsstands, tobacconists and bars displaying the bus company logo.
• In Milan and Rome tickets can be used on bus and metro and are valid for 75 minutes.
• In Rome you can buy a special tourist pass valid for three days. In Milan 24- and 48-hour tickets are available as well as a book (**carnet**) of ten tickets (which works out cheaper).

where is the bus station?	**dov'è la stazione degli autobus?**
	dov-**e** la stats-**yo**-nay **del**-yee **ow**-to-boos?
I want to go...	**vorrei andare...**
	vor-**ray**-ee an-**da**-ray...
to the station	**alla stazione**
	al-la stats-**yo**-nay
to the museum	**al museo**
	al moo-**zay**-o
to Piazza Cavour	**a Piazza Cavour**
	a pee-**at**-sa ka-**voor**
to the Vatican	**al Vaticano**
	al va-tee-**ka**-no
does this bus go to...?	**questo autobus va a...?**
	kwes-to **ow**-to-boos va a...?
what bus do I take?	**quale autobus devo prendere?**
	kwa-lay **ow**-to-boos **dev**-o **pren**-der-ay?
where does the bus go from?	**da dove parte l'autobus?**
	da **dov**-ay **par**-tay **low**-to-boos?

how frequent are the buses?	**ogni quanto ci sono gli autobus?**
	on-yee **kwan**-to chee so-no lee **ow**-to-boos?
can you please tell me when to get off?	**può dirmi quando devo scendere?**
	pwo **deer**-mee **kwan**-do **day**-vo **shen**-der-ay?

Metro

••

• Only Milan and Rome have metro systems. Tickets can also be used on buses and are valid for 75 minutes.
• Tourist passes and blocks of tickets are available in both cities.
• In the metro system, tickets can be stamped only once. So while you could come out and go on a bus with the same ticket, you couldn't use it again for another metro trip.

where is the metro station?	**dov'è la stazione della metro?**
	dov-**e** la stats-**yo**-nay **del**-la met-ro?
a block of tickets, please	**un carnet di biglietti, per favore**
	oon kar-**nay** dee beel-**yet**-tee, payr fa-**vo**-ray
do you have a metro map?	**avete una piantina della metro?**
	a-**vay**-tay **oo**-na pee-an-**tee**-na **del**-la **met**-ro?
a 24-hour ticket	**un biglietto da ventiquattro ore**
	oon beel-**yet**-to da vent-tee-**kwat**-tro **o**-ray
48-hour	**da quarantotto ore**
	da kwar-ant-**ot**-to **o**-ray
I want to go to...	**vorrei andare a...**
	vor-**ray**-ee an-**da**-ray a...
can I go by metro?	**si può andare con la metro?**
	see pwo an-**da**-ray kon la **met**-ro?
do I have to change?	**devo cambiare?**
	dev-o kam-bee-**a**-ray?
where?	**dove?**
	dov-ay?
which line do I take?	**quale linea prendo?**
	kwa-lay **lee**-nay-a **pren**-do?
which is the station...?	**qual è la stazione per...?**
	kwal e la stats-**yo**-nay payr...?

Train

• •

• Italy has a highly efficient national rail network. Check offers and info on **www.trenitalia.com**.
• The highspeed tilting train (**pendolino**) and other fast trains (like the **Alta Velocità Eurostar**) must be booked in advance.
• Tickets must be validated before boarding the train. Machines are yellow and located at the beginning of the platform or in yellow slots at the automatic ticket machines.

where is the station?	**dov'è la stazione?**
	dov-**e** la stats-**yo**-nay?
to the main station, please	**alla stazione centrale, per favore**
	al-la stats-**yo**-nay chen-**tra**-lay, payr fa-**vo**-ray
a single to...	**una sola andata per...**
	oon an-**da**-ta payr...
2 singles to...	**due andate per...**
	doo-ay an-**da**-tay payr...
a return to...	**un'andata e ritorno per...**
	oon an-**da**-ta ay ree-**tor**-no payr...
2 returns to...	**due andata e ritorno per...**
	doo-ay an-**da**-ta ay ree-**tor**-no payr...
a child's return to...	**un'andata e ritorno ridotto per...**
	oon an-**da**-ta ay ree-**tor**-no ree-**dot**-to payr...
1st/2nd class	**prima/seconda classe**
	pree-ma/se-**kon**-da **klas**-say
is there a supplement to pay?	**c'è un supplemento da pagare?**
	oon soop-play-**men**-to da pa-**ga**-ray?
is my pass valid for this journey?	**è valida la tessera per questo viaggio?**
	e **va**-lee-da la **tes**-ser-a payr **kwes**-to vee-**ad**-jo?
must I book in advance?	**la prenotazione è obbligatoria?**
	la pren-o-tats-**yo**-nay e ob-blee-ga-**tor**-ya

- All fast trains require a supplement. Buy it before boarding as it costs more on the train. The overhead departure board indicates if a **supplemento** is required.
- A Swiss Pass must be bought before arriving in Switzerland. Check **www.raileurope.com**.
- Remember to validate tickets for both outward and return trips.

I want to book...	**voglio prenotare...**
	vol-yo pren-o-**ta**-ray...
a seat	**un posto**
	oon **pos**-to
a couchette	**una cuccetta**
	oo-na koo-**chet**-ta
where?	**dove?**
	dov-ay?
do I have to change?	**devo cambiare?**
	dev-o kam-bee-**a**-ray?
how long is there for the connection?	**quanto tempo c'è per la coincidenza?**
	kwan-to **tem**-po che payr la ko-een-chee-**dent**-sa?
which platform does it leave from?	**da quale binario parte?**
	da **kwa**-lay bee-**nar**-yo **par**-tay?
does the train to ... leave from this platform?	**il treno per ... parte da questo binario?**
	eel **tray**-no payr ... **par**-tay da **kwes**-to bee-**nar**-yo?
is this the train for...?	**è questo il treno per...?**
	e **kwes**-to eel **tray**-no payr...?
where is the left-luggage?	**dov'è il deposito bagagli?**
	dov-**e** eel de-**po**-zee-to ba-**gal**-yee?
is this seat taken?	**è occupato?**
	e ok-koo-**pa**-to?

Taxi

• •

• Get a taxi from a taxi stand – generally located at stations or call a radio taxi.
• Taxis are white and it's better to use these as other private operators (blue limousines) might charge more.
• To go from Fiumicino airport to the centre of Rome or from Malpensa to Milan the price should be around 80 euros.

to the airport, please	**all'aeroporto, per favore** al-la-ay-ro-**por**-to, payr fa-**vo**-ray
please take me to this address	**per favore mi porti a questo indirizzo** payr fa-**vo**-ray mee **por**-tee a **kwes**-to een-dee-**reet**-so
how much will it cost?	**quanto verrà a costare?** **kwan**-to ver-**ra** a kos-**ta**-ray?
it's too much	**è troppo** e **trop**-po
how much is it to the centre?	**quanto costa per il centro?** **kwan**-to **kos**-ta payr eel **chen**-tro?
where can I get a taxi?	**dove posso trovare un taxi?** **dov**-ay **pos**-so tro-**va**-ray oon **tak**-see?
please order me a taxi	**per favore mi chiami un taxi** payr fa-**vo**-ray mee kee-**a**-mee oon **tak**-see
can I have a receipt?	**posso avere una ricevuta?** **pos**-so a-**vay**-ray **oo**-na ree-chay-**voo**-ta?
I've nothing smaller	**non ho moneta** non o mon-**ay**-ta
keep the change	**tenga il resto** **ten**-ga eel **res**-to

Boat

• In the city of Venice, public transport is by waterbus (**vaporetto**).
• Tickets may be purchased in advance at landing stages or from some tobacconists, shops and bars.
• Purchase is also possible on board at an extra cost.
• 24- and 72-hour tickets are available.
• Tickets must be punched before boarding.
• In Switzerland the Swiss Pass includes travel on some lake steamers.

1 ticket	**un biglietto**
	oon beel-**yet**-to
2 tickets	**due biglietti**
	doo-ay beel-**yet**-tee
single	**andata**
	an-**da**-ta
round trip	**andata e ritorno**
	an-**da**-ta ay ree-**tor**-no
where does the vaporetto leave from?	**da dove parte il vaporetto?**
	da **dov**-ay **par**-tay eel va-por-**et**-to?
is there a tourist ticket?	**c'è un biglietto turistico?**
	che oon beel-**yet**-to too-**rees**-tee-ko?
are there any boat trips?	**ci sono delle gite in battello?**
	chee so-no **del**-lay **jee**-tay een bat-**tel**-lo?
when does the boat leave?	**quando parte il battello?**
	kwan-do **par**-tay eel bat-**tel**-lo?
do you have a time table?	**ha l'orario?**
	a lo-**rar**-yo?
is there a restaurant on board?	**c'è un ristorante a bordo?**
	che oon rees-to-**ran**-tay sool bat-**tel**-lo?
can we hire a boat?	**possiamo noleggiare una barca?**
	pos-see-**ya**-mo no-led-**ja**-ray **oo**-na **bar**-ka?

Car

Driving

- Headlights must be kept on during the day on motorways and all roads outside towns.
- When raining (i.e. when windscreen wipers in use), speed limits of 130 and 110kph are lowered by 20kph.
- Fines are high if you drive 11kph or more over the limit.
- Carry your passport at all times, even if you're a passenger.
- Surface parking in the centre of Milan and Rome almost always requires payment of a fee: either with a ticket bought in cash at a **parchimetro** or with a scratch card called **gratta e sosta** that can be purchased at tobacconists, newsstands or from parking attendants.

can I park here?	**posso parcheggiare qui?**
	pos-so par-ked-**ja**-ray kwee?
do I need to pay to park here?	**questo parcheggio è a pagamento?**
	kwes-to par-**ked**-jo e a pa-ga-**men**-to?
do I need a parking disk?	**è necessario il disco orario?**
	e ne-ches-**sar**-yo eel **dee**-sko o-**rar**-yo?
where can I park?	**dove posso parcheggiare?**
	dov-ay **pos**-so par-ked-**ja**-ray?
is there a car park?	**c'è un parcheggio?**
	che oon par-**ked**-jo?
where can I get a parking disk?	**dove posso trovare un disco orario?**
	dov-ay **pos**-so tro-**va**-ray oon **dee**-sko o-**rar**-yo?
how long can I park here?	**per quanto tempo posso parcheggiare qui?**
	payr **kwan**-to **tem**-po **pos**-so par-ked-**ja**-ray kwee?

we're going to....	andiamo a...
	an-dee-**a**-mo a...
what's the best route?	qual è la strada migliore?
	kwal e la **stra**-da meel-**yo**-ray?
is the pass open?	il passo è aperto?
	eel **pas**-so e a-**payr**-to?
how do I get to the motorway?	scusi, per andare sull'autostrada?
	skoo-zee, payr an-**da**-ray sool-**low**-to-stra-da?
which exit is it for...?	qual è l'uscita per...?
	kwal e loo-**shee**-ta e payr...?

Petrol

• •

• Petrol stations have both manned and self-service pumps. Prices are lower for self-service pumps.
• If you choose a manned pump, make sure that the attendant doesn't fill you up with unwanted special fuels that cost more (BlueAgip, V-power etc.). Don't accept oil checks, etc – you might be charged for ones that aren't required.
• Outside opening times most petrol stations switch on the automatic pumps. Make sure you have 10, 20 and 50 euro notes on you, but also ATM cards are widely accepted. No change is given so be careful how much fuel you put in.

is there a petrol station near here?	c'è una stazione di servizio qui vicino?
	che **oo**-na stats-**yo**-nay dee ser-**veets**-yo kwee vee-**chee**-no?
fill it up, please	il pieno, per favore
	eel pee-**ay**-no, payr fa-**vo**-ray
unleaded	senza piombo
	sent-sa pee-**om**-bo
diesel	gasolio
	ga-**zol**-ee-o
...euro-worth of petrol	...euro di benzina
	...**ay**-oo-ro dee ben-**tsee**-na

where is the air line?	**dov'è l'aria compressa?**
	dov-ay **la**-ree-a kom-**pres**-sa?
please check...	**per favore controlli...**
	payr fa-**vo**-ray kon-**trol**-lee...
the tyre pressure	**la pressione delle gomme**
	la pres-**yo**-nay **del**-lay **gom**-may
the oil	**l'olio**
	lol-ee-o
the water	**l'acqua**
	lak-wa
can I pay by credit card?	**posso pagare con la carta di credito?**
	pos-so pa-**ga**-ray kon la **kar**-ta dee **kray**-dee-to?
everything is ok	**tutto a posto**
	toot-to a **pos**-to
which pump?	**quale pompa?**
	kwa-lay **pom**-pa?

Problems/breakdown

* *

- Motorways have emergency phones every 2km. The police will automatically know your location if you use them.
- Visibility Vests are now compulsory in Italy. If you break down and have to get out, you must put on this fluorescent waistcoat that should be carried in all vehicles.
- If you need the police dial 113 (motorways) or 112 (elsewhere).

my car has broken down	**la mia macchina è in panne**
	la **mee**-a **mak**-kee-na e ee **pan**-nay
I'm on my own (female)	**sono da sola**
	so-no da **so**-la
there are children in the car	**ci sono bambini nella macchina**
	chee so-no bam-**bee**-nee **nel**-la **ma**-kee-na
where is the nearest garage?	**dov'è il garage più vicino?**
	dov-**e** eel ga-**raj** pee-**yoo** vee-**chee**-no?
is it serious?	**è una cosa seria?**
	e **oo**-na **ko**-za **say**-ree-a?

42

can you repair it?	**può ripararlo?**
	pwo ree-pa-**rar**-lo?
when will it be ready?	**quando sarà pronta?**
	kwan-do sa-**ra pron**-ta?
how much will it cost?	**quanto costerà?**
	kwan-to kos-tay-**ra**?
the car won't start	**la macchina non parte**
	la **ma**-kee-na non **par**-tay
I have a flat tyre	**ho una gomma a terra**
	o **oo**-na **gom**-ma a **ter**-ra
the engine is overheating	**il motore si surriscalda**
	eel mo-**to**-ray see soor-rees-**kal**-da
the battery is flat	**la batteria è scarica**
	la bat-tay-**ree**-a e **ska**-ree-ka
can you replace the windscreen?	**può cambiare il parabrezza?**
	pwo kam-bee-**a**-ray eel pa-ra-**brey**-dz-za?

Car hire

- To avoid problems, book a car in advance. If you buy your air ticket on the internet, many airlines also offer car hire.
- All hire cars have air conditioning.
- Remember to find out where the nearest petrol station is for returning a full tank.
- Check that the fluorescent waistcoats and parking disk are in the car.
- The word for 'hire' is **noleggio** (no-**led**-jo).

I want to hire a car	**vorrei noleggiare una macchina**
	vor-**ray**-ee no-led-**ja**-ray oo-na **ma**-kee-na
for one day	**per un giorno**
	payr oon **jor**-no
for ... days	**per ... giorni**
	payr ... **jor**-nee

does the price include fully comprehensive insurance?
il prezzo è inclusivo della polizza kasco?
eel **prets**-so e een-kloo-**see**-vo **del**-la po-**leet**-sa **kas**-ko?

I want...
vorrei...
vor-**ray**-ee...

a large car
una macchina grande
oo-na **ma**-kee-na **gran**-day

a small car
una macchina piccola
oo-na **ma**-kee-na **peek**-kol-la

an automatic
una automatica
oo-na ow-to-**ma**-tee-ka

must I return the car here?
devo riportare la macchina qui?
dev-o ree-por-**ta**-ray la **ma**-kee-na kwee?

by what time?
per che ora?
payr kay **o**-ra?

where is the nearest petrol station?
dov'è il distributore più vicino?
dov-**e** eel dees-tree-boo-**tor**-ay pee-**yoo** vee-**chee**-no?

I'd like to leave it in...
vorrei lasciarla a...
vor-**ray**-ee la-**shar**-la a...

where are the documents?
dove sono i documenti?
dov-ay so-no ee do-koo-**men**-tee?

Shopping

Shopping – holiday

- Opening times vary enormously depending on the area you are in and the time of year, but generally shops close between 1 and 3.30pm and stay open till about 7.30pm. In some high streets and malls the shops stay open at lunchtime.
- If you want to go shopping, you are best to avoid tourist areas.
- Street markets are good places for clothes, food and antiques.
- Shops, including the big malls, close on Monday mornings.

do you sell...?	**vendete...?**
	ven-**day**-tay...?
stamps	**francobolli**
	fran-ko-**bol**-lee
batteries for this	**pile per questo**
	pee-lay payr **kwes**-to
where can I buy...?	**dove posso comprare...?**
	dov-ay **pos**-so kom-**pra**-ray...?
a colour film	**una pellicola a colori**
	oo-na pel-**lee**-ko-la a ko-**lo**-ree
10 stamps	**dieci francobolli**
	dee-**ay**-chee fran-ko-**bol**-lee
for postcards	**per cartoline**
	payr kar-to-**lee**-nay
to Britain	**per la Gran Bretagna**
	payr la gran bre-**tan**-ya
a miniDV for this video camera, please	**un miniDV per questa videocamera, per favore**
	oon mee-nee dee-**vee** payr **kwes**-ta vee-**day**-o-ka-**may**-ra, payr fa-**vo**-ray

I'm looking for a present	**sto cercando un regalo**
	sto cher-**kan**-do oon ray-**ga**-lo
have you something cheaper?	**ha qualcosa di meno caro?**
	a kwal-**ko**-za dee **may**-no **ka**-ro?
it's a gift	**è un regalo**
	e oon ray-**ga**-lo
please wrap it up	**può incartarlo, per favore**
	pwo een-kar-**tar**-lo, payr fa-**vo**-ray
is there a market?	**c'è un mercato?**
	che oon mer-**ka**-to?
which day?	**quale giorno?**
	kwa-lay **joor**-no?

Shopping – clothes

• There are some good Italian department stores: **Upim**, **Coin** and **Standa**. In Milan there is **La Rinascente**.
• Big malls are open all day until late (about 10pm).
• If you are interested in designer clothes then you have to stay in the centre of towns. But good deals can be found in factory outlets. Ask at tourist info centres.

can I try this on?	**posso provarlo?**
	pos-so pro-**var**-lo?
I like it	**mi piace**
	mee pee-**a**-chay
it's too big	**è troppo grande**
	e **trop**-po **gran**-day
have you a smaller one?	**ne ha uno più piccolo?**
	ne a **oo**-no pee-**yoo peek**-ko-lo?
it's too small	**è troppo piccolo**
	e **trop**-po **peek**-ko-lo
have you a larger one?	**ne ha uno più grande?**
	ne a **oo**-no pee-**yoo gran**-day?
it's too expensive	**è troppo caro**
	e **trop**-po **ka**-ro

I'll take this one	**prendo questo** **pren**-do **kwes**-to
can you give me a discount?	**mi può fare uno sconto?** mee pwo **fa**-ray **oo**-no **skon**-to?
I take a size ... shoe	**porto il numero...** **por**-to eel **noo**-may-ro...
what size are you?	**che taglia porta?** kay **tal**-ya **por**-ta?
what shoe size do you take?	**che numero di scarpe porta?** kay **noo**-may-ro dee **skar**-pay **por**-ta?

Shopping – food

• •

• Smaller shops generally close between 1 and 3.30pm.
• Supermarkets are open all day Monday–Saturday. Some of them also open on Sundays.
• Supermarkets include **Standa**, **Bennet**, **Esselunga**, **Iper**, **Ipercoop** etc.
• You will need euro coins to release the shopping trolley.

where can I buy...?	**dove posso comprare...?** **dov**-ay **pos**-so kom-**pra**-ray...?
fruit	**della frutta** **del**-la **froot**-ta
bread	**del pane** del **pa**-nay
milk	**del latte** del **lat**-tay
where is the supermarket?	**dov'è il supermercato?** dov-**e** eel **soo**-per-mer-**ka**-to?
where is the market?	**dov'è il mercato?** dov-**e** eel mer-**ka**-to?
when is the market?	**quando c'è il mercato?** **kwan**-do che eel mer-**ka**-to?
it's me next	**tocca a me** **tok**-ka a me

that's enough	**basta così**
	bas-ta ko-**zee**
6 bread rolls	**sei panini**
	say-ee pa-**nee**-nee
a ciabatta	**una ciabatta**
	oo-na cha-**bat**-ta
a litre of...	**un litro di...**
	oon **lee**-tro dee...
milk	**latte**
	lat-tay
beer	**birra**
	beer-ra
mineral water	**acqua minerale**
	ak-wa mee-nay-**ra**-lay
a bottle of...	**una bottiglia di...**
	oo-na bot-**teel**-ya dee...
wine	**vino**
	vee-no
still water	**acqua naturale**
	ak-wa na-too-**ra**-lay
sparkling water	**acqua gassata**
	ak-wa gas-**za**-ta
a can of...	**una lattina di...**
	oo-na lat-**tee**-na dee...
coke	**coca**
	ko-ka
tonic water	**acqua tonica**
	ak-wa **ton**-ee-ka

• Fruit and veg must be weighed and stickered before taking it to the check-out. In some places you do it yourself, in others an assistant does it for you.
• Bread is generally bought daily.
• You need to pay for plastic bags. They are usually found next to the checkout.

100 grams/4oz of...	**un etto di...**
	oon **et**-to dee...
salami	**salame**
	sa-**la**-may
grated parmesan	**parmigiano grattugiato**
	par-mee-**ja**-no grat-too-**ja**-to
cooked ham	**prosciutto cotto**
	pro-**shoot**-to **kot**-to
Parma ham	**prosciutto crudo**
	pro-**shoot**-to **kroo**-do
250 grams/	**due etti e mezzo di...**
half a pound of...	**doo**-ay **et**-tee ay **med**-zo dee...
butter	**burro**
	boor-ro
cheese	**formaggio**
	for-**mad**-jo
a kilo of...	**un chilo di...**
	oon **kee**-lo dee...
potatoes	**patate**
	pa-**ta**-tay
apples	**mele**
	may-lay
two slices of pizza	**due fette di pizza**
	doo-ay **fet**-tay dee **peet**-sa
three pieces	**tre pezzi di focaccia**
of focaccia	tray **fet**-tay dee fo-**ka**-cha
a portion of...	**una porzione di...**
	oo-na ports-**yo**-nay dee...
Russian salad	**insalata russa**
	een-sa-**la**-ta **roos**-sa
lasagne	**lasagne**
	la-**zan**-yay
a packet of...	**un pacchetto di...**
	oon pak-**ket**-to dee...
biscuits	**biscotti**
	bee-**skot**-tee

sugar	**zucchero**
	tsook-kay-ro
a tin of tomatoes	**una scatola di pelati**
	oo-na **ska**-to-la dee pel-**a**-tee
a jar of honey	**un vaso di miele**
	oon **va**-zo dee mee-**ay**-lay
can I help you?	**mi dica?**
	mee **dee**-ka?
anything else?	**altro?**
	al-tro?
is that everything?	**è tutto?**
	e **toot**-to?

Daylife

Sightseeing

• The Italian Tourist Office website is **www.enit.it**.
• It is sometimes necessary to book tickets in advance (e.g. for the **Musei Vaticani** in Rome or to see **Il Cenacolo**, Leonardo's Last Supper, in Milan).
• If visiting churches or religious sites, remember that these are primarily places of worship, so no shorts or bare shoulders.

where is the tourist office?	**scusi, dov'è l'ufficio turistico?** **skoo**-zee, dov-**e** loof-**fee**-cho too-**rees**-tee-ko?
we want to visit...	**vogliamo visitare...** vol-**ya**-mo vee-zee-**ta**-ray...
have you any leaflets?	**ha degli opuscoli?** a **del**-yee o-**poos**-ko-lee?
do you have a town guide?	**ha una guida della città?** a **oo**-na **gwee**-da **del**-la cheet-**ta**?
in English	**in inglese** een een-**glay**-zay
we'd like to go to...	**vorremmo andare a...** vor-**rem**-mo an-**da**-ray a...
are there any excursions?	**ci sono delle gite?** chee **so**-no **del**-lay **jee**-tay?
when does it leave?	**quando parte?** **kwan**-do **par**-tay?
where does it leave from?	**da dove parte?** da **dov**-ay **par**-tay?
how much is it to get in?	**quanto costa l'ingresso?** **kwan**-to **kos**-ta leen-**gres**-so?

is it open to the public?	è aperto al pubblico?
	e a-**payr**-to al poob-**blee**-ko?

Beach

• •

• Beaches are crowded in July, August and summer weekends.
• Every resort must have at least one beach where you can go without paying.
• If you want an umbrella, chairs, changing cabins, lifeguard, bars, etc, then go to a **bagno**. These can be really nice, but fees can be quite high.

can you recommend a quiet beach?	ci può consigliare una spiaggia tranquilla?
	chee pwo kon-seel-**ya**-ray **oo**-na spee-**ad**-ja tran-**kweel**-la?
is there a swimming pool?	c'è una piscina?
	che **oo**-na pee-**shee**-na?
can we swim in the lake?	si può fare il bagno nel lago?
	see pwo **fa**-ray eel **ban**-yo nel **la**-go?
is the water clean?	l'acqua è pulita?
	lak-wa e poo-**lee**-ta?
is the water deep?	l'acqua è profonda?
	lak-wa e pro-**fon**-da?
is the water cold?	l'acqua è fredda?
	lak-wa e **fred**-da?
is it dangerous?	c'è pericolo?
	che pe-**ree**-ko-lo?
are there currents?	ci sono correnti?
	chee so-no kor-**ren**-tee?
where can we...?	dove si può...?
	dov-ay see pwo...?
windsurf	fare windsurf
	fa-ray **weend**-surf
waterski	fare sci nautico
	fa-ray shee **now**-tee-ko

hire a beach umbrella	**noleggiare un ombrellone**
	no-led-**ja**-ray oon om-brel-**lo**-nay

Sport

....

• Tourist offices are the places to ask about sport.
• Football matches usually start at 3pm on Sundays, but in winter they start at 2.30 or even 2pm. There are also matches on Saturdays (at 6pm and 8.30pm) and on Sundays at 8.30pm.
Visit **www.calciofans.com**.
• It is compulsory to wear a swimming cap in public pools, even outdoor ones. It is usually possible to buy or borrow a cap from the reception.

where can we...?	**dove si può...?**
	dov-ay see pwo...?
play tennis	**giocare a tennis**
	jo-**ka**-ray a **ten**-nees
play golf	**giocare a golf**
	jo-**ka**-ray a golf
hire bikes	**noleggiare biciclette**
	no-led-**ja**-ray bee-chee-**klet**-ay
go fishing	**pescare**
	pes-**ka**-ray
go riding	**andare a cavallo**
	an-**da**-ray a ka-**val**-lo
how much is it...?	**quanto costa...?**
	kwan-to **kos**-ta...?
per hour	**all'ora**
	al-**lo**-ra
per day	**al giorno**
	al **jor**-no
how do I book a court?	**come si prenota il campo da tennis?**
	ko-may see pren-**o**-ta eel **kam**-po da **ten**-nees?
can I hire...?	**posso noleggiare...?**
	pos-so no-led-**ja**-ray...?

racquets	le racchette
	lay rak-**ket**-tay
golf clubs	le mazze da golf
	lay **mat**-say da golf
is there a football match?	c'è una partita di calcio?
	che **oo**-na par-**tee**-ta dee **kal**-cho?
where is there a sports shop?	dove c'è un negozio di articoli sportivi?
	dov-ay che oon nay-**gots**-yo dee ar-**tee**-ko-lee spor-**tee**-vee?

Skiing

● Ski resorts and runs get very busy. It is vital that skiers and snowboarders behave in such a manner so as not to cause any danger to others. Italy has begun to impose codes of conduct with fines for breaking them.

● Children up to 14 years of age must wear a protective helmet.

can I hire skis?	posso noleggiare gli sci?
	pos-so no-led-**ja**-ray lee shee?
how much is a pass?	quanto costa lo skipass?
	kwan-to **kos**-ta lo skee-pass?
I'm a beginner	sono un principiante
	so-no oon preen-cheep-**yan**-tay
which is an easy run?	qual è una pista facile?
	kwal e **oo**-na **pees**-ta **fa**-chee-lay?
what is the snow like today?	com'è la neve oggi?
	ko-**me** la **nev**-ay **od**-jee?
is there a map of the ski runs?	avete una piantina delle piste?
	a-**vay**-tay **oo**-na pee-an-**tee**-na **day**-lay **pees**-tay?
my skis are...	i miei sci sono...
	ee mee-**ay**-ee shee so-no...
too long	troppo lunghi
	trop-po **loon**-gee

too short	troppo corti
	trop-po **kor**-tee
my bindings are...	i miei attacchi sono...
	ee mee-**ay**-ee at-**tak**-kee so-no...
too loose	troppo larghi
	trop-po **larg**-ee
too tight	troppo stretti
	trop-po **stret**-tee
where can we go cross-country skiing?	dove si può andare a fare sci di fondo?
	dov-ay see pwo an-**da**-ray a **fa**-ray shee dee **fon**-do?
is there any danger of avalanches?	c'è pericolo di valanghe?
	che pe-**ree**-ko-lo dee va-**lan**-gay?

Nightlife

Nightlife – popular

• The best bars, restaurants and nightclubs are usually in town centres, whereas large discos can be outside towns along main roads. Check the local paper.
• To see what locals do, simply go to the trendy areas of a town and watch.
• When you go to a disco, the entrance fee usually includes one drink.

what is there to do at night?	**che cosa c'è da fare di sera?** kay **ko**-za che da **fa**-ray dee **say**-ra?
can you recommend a good place/bar?	**mi può consigliare un buon locale/bar?** me pwo-kon-seel-**ya**-ray oon bwon lo-**ka**-lay/bar?
can you recommend a good disco?	**mi può consigliare una buona discoteca?** mee pwo kon-seel-**ya**-ray **oo**-na **bwo**-na dee-sko-**te**-ka?
is it expensive?	**è caro?** e **ka**-ro?
where do local people go at night?	**dove va la gente del posto di sera?** **dov**-ay va la **jen**-tay del **pos**-to dee **say**-ra?
is it in a safe area?	**è in una zona sicura?** e een oona **zo**-na see-**koo**-ra?
are there any concerts?	**ci sono concerti?** chee so-no kon-**cher**-tee?
do you like dancing?	**ti piace ballare?** tee pee-**a**-chay bal-**la**-ray?
I like dancing	**mi piace ballare** mee pee-**a**-chay bal-**la**-ray

do you want to dance?	**vuoi ballare?**
	vwoy-ee bal-**la**-ray?
what's your name?	**come ti chiami?**
	ko-may tee kee-**a**-mee?
I'm Marco	**mi chiamo Marco**
	mee kee-**a**-mo **mar**-ko

Nightlife – cultural

• Always check the local newspaper to find what's on.
• There is usually one cheap night for films, but it varies from town to town (in Milan it is Wednesdays).
• The opera season runs Oct–June (though **La Scala** starts in December). Visit **www.teatroallascala.org**.
• Check out Italian festivals on **www.hostetler.net**.
• Watch out for signs advertising local festivals, generally called **sagre**, where you can eat cheaply (usually outdoors on rough tables) tasting the culinary specialities of the area and dancing to live music.

is there a list of cultural events?	**c'è un programma degli spettacoli?**
	che oon pro-**gram**-ma **del**-yee spet-**ta**-ko-lee?
are there any local festivals?	**ci sono delle sagre locali?**
	chee so-no **del**-lay **sag**-ray lo-**ka**-lee?
we'd like to go...	**vorremmo andare...**
	vor-rem-mo an-**da**-ray...
to the theatre	**a teatro**
	a tay-**a**-tro
to the opera	**all'opera**
	al-l**o**-pay-ra
to the ballet	**al balletto**
	al bal-**let**-to
to a concert	**a un concerto**
	a oon kon-**cher**-to
what's on?	**che cosa c'è?**
	kay **ko**-za che?

do I need to book?	**devo prenotare?**
	day-vo pren-o-**ta**-ray?
how much are the tickets?	**quanto costano i biglietti?**
	kwan-to **kos**-ta-no ee beel-**yet**-tee?
2 tickets...	**due biglietti...**
	doo-ay beel-**yet**-tee...
for tonight	**per stasera**
	payr sta-**say**-ra
for tomorrow night	**per domani sera**
	payr do-**ma**-nee **say**-ra
when does the performance end?	**a che ora finisce lo spettacolo?**
	a kay **o**-ra fee-**nee**-shay lo spet-**ta**-ko-lo?

Accommodation

Hotel

• Information on local hotels can be found at the tourist office.
• Hotels are star-rated. One star is generally quite basic with shared facilities. Two star might have ensuite facilities.
• Only the more modern hotels have air conditioning.
• A good option, if you want to stay in the countryside or if you have children, is to choose one of the numerous **agriturismi** (holiday farms). They are becoming increasingly popular: some of them offer really superb accommodation and good traditional food (although the rates can be not at all 'rustic').

have you a room for tonight?	**avete una camera per stanotte?**
	a-**vay**-tay **oo**-na **ka**-may-ra payr sta-**not**-tay?
a single room	**una camera singola**
	oo-na **ka**-may-ra **seen**-go-la
a double room	**una camera doppia**
	oo-na **ka**-may-ra **dop**-pa
a family room	**una camera per una famiglia**
	oo-na **ka**-may-ra payr **oo**-na fa-**meel**-ya
with bathroom	**con bagno**
	kon **ban**-yo
with shower	**con doccia**
	kon **dot**-cha
how much is it?	**quanto costa?**
	kwan-to **kos**-ta?
is breakfast included?	**comprende la colazione?**
	kom-**pren**-day la ko-lats-**yo**-nay?
I booked a room	**ho prenotato una camera**
	o pren-o-**ta**-to **oo**-na **ka**-may-ra

my name is...	**mi chiamo...**
	mee kee-**a**-mo...
I'd like to see	**vorrei vedere la camera**
the room	vor-**ray**-ee ved-**ay**-ray la **ka**-may-ra
is there anything	**c'è qualcosa di meno caro?**
cheaper?	che kwal-**ko**-za dee **may**-no **ka**-ro?
what time is...?	**a che ora c'è...?**
	a kay **o**-ra che...?
breakfast	**la colazione**
	la ko-lats-**yo**-nay
dinner	**la cena**
	la **chay**-na
we'll be back	**ritorniamo tardi stasera**
late tonight	ree-tor-nee-**a**-mo **tar**-dee sta-**say**-ra
the key, please	**la chiave, per favore**
	la kee-**a**-vay, payr fa-**vo**-ray
can you put these	**può mettere questi nella cassaforte?**
in the safe?	pwo met-**ter**-ray **kwes**-tee **nel**-la kas-sa-**for**-tay?
come in!	**avanti!**
	a-**van**-tee!
please come	**ritorni più tardi per favore**
back later	ree-**tor**-nee pee-**yoo tar**-dee payr fa-**vo**-ray
can we have	**possiamo fare la colazione in camera?**
breakfast in	pos-see-**a**-mo **fa**-ray la ko-lats-**yo**-nay een
our room?	**ka**-may-ra?
please bring...	**per favore mi porti...**
	payr fa-**vo**-ray mee **por**-tee...
ashtray	**un portacenere**
	oon por-ta-**chen**-ay-ray
soap	**il sapone**
	eel sa-**po**-nay
towels	**degli asciugamani**
	del-yee a-shoo-ga-**ma**-nee
a glass	**un bicchiere**
	oon beek-**yer**-ay
please clean...	**può pulire per favore...**
	pwo poo-**lee**-ray payr fa-**vo**-ray...

my room	la camera
	la **ka**-may-ra
the bathroom	il bagno
	eel **ban**-yo
I would like a wake-up call...	vorrei la sveglia...
	vor-**ray**-ee la **svel**-ya...
at 7 o'clock	alle sette
	al-lay **set**-tay
is there a laundry service?	c'è il servizio lavanderia?
	che eel ser-**veets**-yo la-van-day-**ree**-a?
I'm leaving tomorrow	parto domani
	par-to do-**ma**-nee
please prepare the bill	ci prepari il conto
	chee prep-**a**-ree eel **kon**-to

Self-catering

• Voltage in Italy is 220 with 2-pronged plugs.
• Take an adaptor for any electrical appliances you pack.
• Rubbish must be taken to the local collection point. These are mainly lidded skips which are widespread. There are recycling banks for glass, plastic and paper.
• The word for neighbours is **i vicini** (ee vee-**chee**-nee).

which is the key for this door?	qual è la chiave di questa porta?
	kwal e la kee-**a**-vay dee **kwes**-ta **por**-ta?
where are the fuses?	dove sono i fusibili?
	dov-ay so-no ee foo-**zee**-bee-lee?
can you show us how this works?	può farci vedere come funziona?
	pwo **far**-chee ved-**ay**-ray **ko**-may foonts-**yo**-na?
how does ... work?	come funziona...?
	ko-may foonts-**yo**-na...?
the dishwasher	la lavastoviglie
	la la-va-sto-**veel**-yay
the waterheater	lo scaldabagno
	lo **skal**-da-**ban**-yo

the washing machine	la lavatrice
	la la-va-**tree**-chay
the cooker	la cucina
	la koo-**chee**-na
who do we contact if there are any problems?	chi contattiamo se ci sono problemi?
	kee kon-tat-tee-**a**-mo say chee so-no prob-**lem**-ee?
where do we put the rubbish?	dove mettiamo la spazzatura?
	dov-ay met-tee-**a**-mo la spat-sa-**too**-ra?
the gas has run out	è finito il gas
	e fee-**nee**-to eel gaz
is there always hot water?	c'è sempre l'acqua calda?
	che **sem**-pray **lak**-wa **kal**-da?

Camping and caravanning

• •

• Campsites are not as widespread as one may think; in certain areas you won't find any at all.

• If you drive a camper, don't expect to be able to camp on the road; it is forbidden almost everywhere.

• Speed limits for cars towing caravans are lower than normal speed limits, i.e. 70kph on normal roads, 80kph on motorways.

we're looking for a campsite	cerchiamo un campeggio
	cher-kee-**a**-mo oon kam-**ped**-jo
have you a list of campsites?	avete una lista dei campeggi?
	a-**vay**-tay **oo**-na **lees**-ta **day**-ee kam-**ped**-jee?
have you any vacancies?	avete dei posti?
	a-**vay**-tee **day**-ee **pos**-tee?
how much is it per night?	quanto costa per notte?
	kwan-to **kos**-ta payr **not**-tay?
we'd like to stay for ... nights	vorremmo rimanere per ... notti
	vor-**rem**-mo ree-ma-**ner**-ay payr ... **not**-tee
is the campsite sheltered?	il campeggio è riparato?
	eel kam-**ped**-jo e ree-pa-**ra**-to?

can we have a more sheltered site?	**possiamo avere un posto più riparato?**
	pos-see-**a**-mo a-**vay**-ray oon **pos**-to pee-**yoo** ree-pa-**ra**-to?
this site is very muddy	**questo posto è molto fangoso**
	kwes-to **pos**-to e **mol**-to fan-**go**-zo
is there another site?	**c'è un altro posto?**
	che oon **al**-tro **pos**-to?
can we park our caravan here overnight?	**possiamo mettere la nostra roulotte qui per la notte?**
	pos-see-**a**-mo **met**-ter-ay la **nos**-tra roo-**lot** kwee payr la **not**-tay?
can we put our tent here?	**possiamo mettere la tenda qui?**
	pos-see-**a**-mo **met**-ter-ay la **ten**-da kwee?

Different travellers

Children

• •

• A small child is **bambino(a)**. An older child is **ragazzo(a)**.
• Children are welcome everywhere. Italian parents often take their children out with them in the evenings to restaurants, etc.
• On most public transport children under 5 travel free. Between 5 and 12 years of age they can get 50% discount.

a child's ticket	**un biglietto per bambini**
	oon beel-**yet**-to payr bam-**bee**-nee
he/she is ... years old	**ha ... anni**
	a ... **an**-nee
is there a reduction for children?	**c'è la riduzione per bambini?**
	che la ree-doots-**yo**-nay payr bam-**bee**-nee?
is there a children's menu?	**avete un menù per bambini?**
	a-**vay**-tay oon men-**oo** payr bam-**bee**-nee?
do you have...?	**avete...?**
	a-**vay**-tay...?
a high chair	**un seggiolone**
	oon sed-jo-**lo**-nay
a cot	**un lettino**
	oon let-**tee**-no
is it ok to bring children?	**si possono portare i bambini?**
	see **pos**-so-no por-**ta**-ray ee bam-**bee**-nee?
what is there for children to do?	**che cosa c'è da fare per i bambini?**
	kay **ko**-za che da **fa**-ray payr ee bam-**bee**-nee?
is it safe for children?	**va bene per bambini?**
	va **be**-nay payr bam-**bee**-nee?
is it dangerous?	**c'è pericolo?**
	che pe-**ree**-ko-lo?

I have two children	**ho due figli**
	o **doo**-ay **feel**-yee
do you have children?	**ha figli?**
	a **feel**-yee?

Special needs

• •

• Words for disabled are **disabili** and **handicappati** ('h' not pronounced). There are often discounts for entrance fees, etc.
• Most motorway services as well as many intercity trains have facilities for the disabled. They are marked with the disabled badge (orange or blue). Also trams and buses are being replaced with new low-platform ones, that offer easier access to wheelchairs. Not all metro stations are accessible for the disabled: check in advance by visiting the local public transport service website:
Milan **www.atm-mi.it** ; Rome **www.atac.roma.it**
• Disabled parking is usually available and indicated with an orange wheelchair badge.

is it possible to visit ... in a wheelchair?	**si può visitare ... nella la sedia a rotelle?**
	see pwo vee-zee-**ta**-ray ... **nel**-la la **sed**-ya a ro-**tel**-lay?
do you have toilets for the disabled?	**ci sono le toilette per i disabili?**
	chee so-no lay twa-**let** payr ee dee-**za**-bee-lee?
I need a bedroom on the ground floor	**ho bisogno di una camera al pian terreno**
	o bee-**zon**-yo dee **oo**-na ka-**may**-ra al **pee**-an ter-**ray**-no
is there a lift?	**c'è l'ascensore?**
	che la-shen-**so**-ray?
where is the lift?	**dov'è l'ascensore?**
	dov-**e** la-shen-**so**-ray?
are there many steps?	**ci sono tanti gradini?**
	chee so-no **tan**-tee gra-**dee**-nee?
is there an entrance for wheelchairs?	**c'è l'accesso per la sedia a rotelle?**
	che la-**ches**-so payr la **sed**-ya a ro-**tel**-lay?

is there a place on this train for a wheelchair?	**c'è un posto su questo treno per una sedia a rotelle?**
	che oon **pos**-to soo **kwes**-to **tray**-no payr **oo**-na **sed**-ya a ro-**tel**-lay?
is there a reduction for the disabled?	**c'è una riduzione per i disabili?**
	che **oo**-na ree-doots-**yo**-nay payr ee dee-**za**-bee-lee?

Exchange visitors

• These phrases are intended for families hosting Italian-speaking visitors. We've used the more familiar **tu** (rather than the more formal **lei**) form.
• Italians generally eat dinner at 7.30/8pm (later the further south you go) – Italian visitors might not be used to eating early.

did you sleep well?	**hai dormito bene?**
	a-ee dor-**mee**-to **be**-nay?
would you like to take a shower?	**vuoi fare la doccia?**
	vwoy-ee **fa**-ray la **dot**-cha?
what would you like for breakfast?	**che cosa prendi per colazione?**
	kay **ko**-za **pren**-dee payr ko-lats-**yo**-nay?
do you eat...?	**mangi...?**
	man-jee...?
what would you like to eat/drink?	**che cosa vuoi mangiare/bere?**
	kay **ko**-za **vwoy**-ee man-**ja**-ray/**be**-ray?
do you drink...?	**bevi...?**
	be-vee...?
what would you like to do today?	**che cosa vuoi fare oggi?**
	kay **ko**-za **vwoy**-ee **fa**-ray od-jee?
would you like to go shopping?	**vuoi andare a fare spese?**
	vwoy-ee an-**da**-ray a **fa**-ray spay-zay?
I will pick you up at...	**vengo a prenderti alle...**
	ven-go a **pren**-der-tee **al**-lay...
take care	**sta' attento(a)**
	sta at-**ten**-to(a)

did you enjoy yourself?	**ti sei divertito(a)?**
	tee **say**-ee dee-ver-**tee**-to(a)?
please be back by...	**devi essere a casa per le...**
	day-vee **es**-say-ray a **ka**-za payr lay...
we'll be in bed when you get back	**saremo a letto quando ritorni**
	sa-**ray**-mo a **let**-to **kwan**-do ree-**tor**-nee

• If you are invited to an Italian home for a meal, you wouldn't be expected to bring a bottle of wine or gift. However, it might be an idea to take some British specialities on holiday with you (shortbread, fudge, etc).
• When you enter someone's home, it is polite to say **permesso** (per-**mes**-so).

I like...	**mi piace...**
	me pee-**a**-chay...
I don't like...	**non mi piace...**
	non mee pee-**a**-chay...
that was delicious	**era buonissimo**
	ay-ra bwo-**nees**-see-mo
may I phone home?	**posso telefonare a casa?**
	pos-so te-le-fo-**na**-ray a **ka**-za?
may I make a local call?	**posso fare una telefonata?**
	pos-so **fa**-ray **oo**-na te-le-fo-**na**-ta?
can I have a key?	**posso avere la chiave di casa?**
	pos-so a-**vay**-ray la kee-**a**-vay dee **ka**-za?
can you take me by car?	**mi può portare in macchina?**
	mee pw**o** por-**ta**-ray een **ma**-kee-na?
can I borrow...?	**mi può prestare...?**
	mee pw**o** pres-**ta**-ray...?
an iron	**un ferro da stiro**
	oon **fer**-ro da **stee**-ro
a hairdryer	**un fon**
	oon fon
what time do I have to get up?	**a che ora devo alzarmi?**
	a kay **o**-ra **day**-vo alt-**sar**-mee?

please call me at...?	**per favore mi chiama alle...?**
	payr fa-**vo**-ray mee kee-**a**-ma **al**-lay...?
how long are you staying?	**quanto tempo resta?**
	kwan-to **tem**-po **res**-ta?
I'm leaving in a week	**parto tra una settimana**
	par-to tra **oo**-na set-tee-**ma**-na
thanks for everything	**grazie di tutto**
	grat-**see**-ay dee **toot**-to
I've had a great time	**mi sono proprio divertito(a)**
	mee **so**-no **pro**-pree-o dee-ver-**tee**-to(a)

Difficulties

Problems

....

• People are usually quite helpful and if you are lucky you'll also find someone who can speak English.
• Traffic wardens are an invaluable source of information and help, although their English might not be great.
• Try to stay calm. Not understanding each other can often aggravate the situation.

can you help me?	**può aiutarmi?**
	pwo a-yoo-**tar**-mee?
I don't speak Italian	**non parlo italiano**
	non **par**-lo ee-tal-lee-**a**-no
do you speak English?	**parla inglese?**
	par-la een-**glay**-zay?
does anyone speak English?	**c'è qualcuno che parla inglese?**
	che kwal-**koo**-no kay **par**-la een-**glay**-zay?
I'm lost	**mi sono smarrito(a)**
	mee **so**-no smar-**ree**-to(a)
I need to get to the station	**devo andare alla stazione**
	dev-o an-**da**-ray **al**-la stats-**yo**-nay
how do I get to...?	**come si fa per andare a...?**
	ko-may see fa payr an-**da**-ray a...?
I've missed...	**ho perso...**
	o **per**-so...
my plane	**l'aereo**
	la-**ay**-ray-o
my connection	**la coincidenza**
	la ko-een-chee-**dent**-sa

I've lost...	**ho perso...**
	o **per**-so...
my money	**i soldi**
	ee-**sol**-dee
my passport	**il passaporto**
	eel pas-sa-**por**-to
my suitcase	**non c'è la mia valigia**
isn't here	non che la **mee**-a va-**lee**-ja
I have no money	**non ho soldi**
	non o **sol**-dee
I've left my bag in...	**ho lasciato la mia borsa nel/nella...**
	o lash-**a**-to la **mee**-a **bor**-sa nel/**nel**-la...
on the coach	**sul pullman**
	sool **pool**-man
leave me alone!	**mi lasci in pace!**
	mee **la**-shee een **pa**-chay!
go away!	**se ne vada!**
	say nay **va**-da!

Complaints

● ●

● If you want to complain, it's always best to ask for the person in charge – **il responsabile** (eel res-pon-**sa**-bee-lay) or **il direttore** (eel dee-ret-**tor**-ay).
● You might be surprised at the way people queue in Italy – it's usually every man (or woman) for himself! Arm yourself with the phrase 'it's my turn!' **tocca a me** (**tok**-ka a me).

the light	**la luce**
	la **loo**-chay
the telephone	**il telefono**
	eel te-**le**-fo-no
...doesn't work	**...non funziona**
	...non foonts-**yo**-na
the toilet	**il water**
	eel **va**-ter

the heating	**il riscaldamento**
	eel ree-skal-da-**men**-to
the room is dirty	**la camera è sporca**
	la ka-**may**-ra e **spor**-ka
the bathroom is dirty	**il bagno è sporco**
	eel **ban**-yo e **spor**-ko
I don't like the room	**non mi piace la camera**
	non mee pee-**a**-chay la ka-**may**-ra
it's too noisy	**c'è troppo rumore**
	che **trop**-po roo-**mor**-ay
I didn't order this	**non ho ordinato questo**
	non o or-dee-**na**-to **kwes**-to
I would like to speak to whoever is in charge of...	**vorrei parlare con chi è incaricato di...**
	vor-**ray**-ee par-**la**-ray kon kee e in-kar-ee-**ka**-to dee...
I want a refund	**voglio un rimborso**
	vol-yo oon reem-**bor**-so
we're in a hurry	**abbiamo fretta**
	ab-bee-**a**-mo **fret**-ta
there is a mistake	**c'è un errore**
	che oon er-**ro**-ray
this is broken	**questo è rotto**
	kwes-to e **rot**-to
can you repair it?	**può ripararlo?**
	pwo ree-pa-**rar**-lo?

Emergencies

●●●

• All the emergency services can be called on 112 although each
has its own number: Carabinieri 112, Police 113, A&E 118,
Fire brigade 115.
• Police officers can be very helpful (especially on motorways).
• If you've been robbed or attacked, go to the police station to
report it and fill in a form. A copy is needed for insurance.

help!	**aiuto!**
	a-**yoo**-to!
can you help me?	**può aiutarmi?**
	pwo a-yoo-**tar**-mee?
there's been an accident	**c'è stato un incidente**
	che **sta**-to oon een-chee-**den**-tay
someone has been injured	**qualcuno si è fatto male**
	kwal-**koo**-no see e **fat**-to **ma**-lay
please call...	**per favore chiamate...**
	payr fa-**vo**-ray kee-a-**ma**-tay...
the police	**la polizia**
	la po-leet-**see**-a
an ambulance	**un'ambulanza**
	oon am-boo-**lant**-sa
he was going too fast	**andava troppo forte**
	an-**da**-va **trop**-po **for**-tay
that man keeps following me	**quell'uomo mi segue**
	kwel **wo**-mo mee **seg**-way
where's the police station?	**dov'è il comando dei Carabinieri?**
	dov-**e** eel ko-**mand**-o day ka-ra-been-**yer**-ee?
I want to report a theft	**vorrei denunciare un furto**
	vor-**ray**-ee den-oon-**cha**-ray oon **foor**-to
I've been robbed	**mi hanno derubato**
	mee **an**-no de-roo-**ba**-to
I've been attacked	**mi hanno assalito**
	mee **an**-no as-sa-**lee**-to

my car has been broken into	**hanno svaligiato la mia macchina** **an**-no sva-lee-**ja**-to la **mee**-a **ma**-kee-na
my car has been stolen	**mi hanno rubato la macchina** mee **an**-no roo-**ba**-to la **ma**-kee-na
I've been raped	**mi hanno violentata** mee **an**-no vee-o-len-**ta**-ta
I need a report for my insurance	**ho bisogno di un verbale per la mia assicurazione** o bee-**zon**-yo dee oon ver-**ba**-lay payr la **mee**-a as-see-koo-rats-**yo**-nay
how much is the fine?	**quant'è la multa?** kwan-**te** la **mool**-ta?
where do I pay it?	**dove devo pagarla?** **do**-vay **dev**-o pa-**gar**-la?
I have no money	**sono senza soldi** **so**-no **sent**-sa **sol**-dee
we're on our way	**arriviamo** ar-ree-vee-**a**-mo

Health

Health

• EU citizens are entitled to free emergency care in Italy.
You must have a European Health Insurance Card available from
www.dh.gov.uk/travellers
• If ill, ask the chemist where the nearest doctor is.
• You can go directly to the A&E of the nearest hospital. If you are
between 6 and 65 years of age, be prepared to pay 25 euros for the
visit. In case of serious emergencies it's always free.

have you something for...?	**può darmi qualcosa per...?** pwo **dar**-mee kwal-**ko**-za payr...?
car sickness/ diarrhoea	**il mal d'auto/la diarrea** eel mal **dow**-to/la dee-ar-**ray**-a
is it safe for children?	**va bene per i bambini?** va **be**-nay payr ee bam-**bee**-nee?
I feel ill	**mi sento male** mee **sen**-to **ma**-lay
I need a doctor	**ho bisogno di un medico** o bee-**zon**-yo dee oon **me**-dee-ko
my son/my daughter is ill	**mio figlio/mia figlia non sta bene** **mee**-o **feel**-yo/**mee**-a **feel**-ya non sta **ben**-ay
(s)he has a temperature	**ha la febbre** a la **feb**-bray
I'm on this medication	**sto prendendo queste medicine** sto pren-**den**-do **kwes**-tay med-ee-**chee**-nay
I have high blood pressure	**ho la pressione alta** o la pres-see-**o**-nay **al**-ta
I'm diabetic	**sono diabetico(a)** **so**-no dee-a-**bet**-ee-ko(a)

I'm pregnant	**sono incinta**
	so-no een-**cheen**-ta
I'm on the pill	**prendo la pillola**
	pren-do la **peel**-lo-la
I'm allergic to penicillin	**sono allergico(a) alla penicillina**
	so-no al-**ler**-jee-ko(a) **al**-la pe-nee-cheel-**lee**-na
my blood group is...	**il mio gruppo sanguigno è...**
	eel **mee**-o **groop**-po san-**gween**-yo e...
I'm breastfeeding	**sto allattando al seno**
	sto al-lat-**tan**-do al **say**-no
is it safe for me to take?	**posso prenderlo senza pericolo?**
	pos-so pren-**der**-lo **sent**-sa per-**ee**-ko-lo?
will he/she have to go to hospital?	**deve andare in opsedale?**
	dev-ay an-**da**-ray een o-spe-**da**-lay?
I need to go to casualty	**devo andare al pronto soccorso**
	dev-vo an-**da**-ray al **pron**-to sok-**kor**-so
where is the hospital?	**dov'è l'ospedale?**
	dov-**e** los-ped-**a**-lay?
when are visiting hours?	**qual è l'orario di visita?**
	kwal e lo-**rar**-yo dee **vee**-zee-ta?
which ward?	**quale reparto?**
	kwal-lay rep-**ar**-to?
I need a dentist	**ho bisogno di un dentista**
	o bee-**zon**-yo dee oon den-**tee**-sta
I have toothache	**ho mal di denti**
	o mal dee **den**-tee
the filling has come out	**è uscita l'otturazione**
	e oo-**shee**-ta lot-too-rats-**yo**-nay
I have an abscess	**ho un ascesso**
	o oon a-**shes**-so
it hurts	**fa male**
	fa **ma**-lay
can you repair my dentures?	**può riparare la mia dentiera?**
	pwo ree-pa-**ra**-ray la mee-a den-tee-**e**-ra?
do I have to pay straightaway?	**devo pagare subito?**
	dev-o pa-**ga**-ray **soo**-bee-to?

Health

75

Business

Business

• You will encounter bureaucracy for anything concerning the state (local government, etc). Things you think should take a short time may drag on.

I am...	sono... **so**-no...
here's my card	ecco il mio biglietto da visita **ek**-ko eel **mee**-o beel-**yet**-to da **vee**-zee-ta
I'm from the Smith Company	sono della ditta Smith **so**-no **del**-la **deet**-ta Smith
I'd like to arrange an appointment with Mr/Ms...	vorrei fissare un appuntamento vor-**ray**-ee fees-**sa**-ray oon ap-poon-ta-**men**-to con il Signor/la Signora... kon eel seen-**yor**/la seen-**yo**-ra...
for April 4th at 11 o'clock	per il quattro aprile alle undici payr eel **kwat**-tro a-**pree**-lay **al**-lay **oon**-dee-chee
can we meet at a restaurant?	possiamo incontrarci in un ristorante? pos-see-**a**-mo een-kon-**trar**-chee een oon rees-to-**ran**-tay?
I will send an email to confirm	manderó un'email di conferma man-der-**o** oon e-mail dee kon-**fer**-ma
I'm staying at Hotel...	sono all'Hotel... **so**-no al-lo-**tel**...
how do I get to your office?	come si arriva al suo ufficio? **ko**-may see ar-**ree**-va al **soo**-o oof-**fee**-cho?
here is some information about my company	ecco alcune informazioni sulla mia ditta **ek**-ko al-**koo**-nay een-for-mats-**yo**-nay **sool**-la **mee**-a **deet**-ta

I have an appointment with...	ho un appuntamento con...
	o oon ap-poon-ta-**men**-to kon...
at ... o'clock	alle...
	al-lay...
delighted to meet you!	molto piacere!
	mol-to pee-a-**chay**-ray!
my Italian isn't very good	parlo poco l'italiano
	par-lo **po**-ko lee-tal-ee-**a**-no
what is the name of the managing director?	come si chiama il direttore?
	ko-may see kee-**a**-ma eel dee-ret-**to**-ray?
I would like some information about your company	vorrei qualche informazione sulla sua ditta
	vor-**ray**-ee **del**-lay een-for-mats-**yo**-nee **sool**-la **soo**-a **deet**-ta
do you have a press office?	avete l'ufficio stampa?
	a-**vay**-tay loof-**fee**-cho **stam**-pa?
I need an interpreter	ho bisogno di un interprete
	o bee-**zon**-yo dee oon een-**ter**-pray-tay
can you photocopy this for me?	mi può fare una fotocopia?
	mee pwo **fa**-ray **oo**-na fo-to-**ko**-pee-a?
do you have an appointment?	ha un appuntamento?
	a oon ap-poon-ta-**men**-to?
at what time?	a che ora?
	a kay **o**-ra?

Phoning/texting

- International dialling codes: UK 0044; USA/Canada 001; Australia 0061. Take an adaptor for chargers.
- Freephone numbers (**numero verde**) begin with 800.
- You can buy phonecards at 5 or 10 euros.
- Italian phone numbers include the area code, even for local calls.
- A mobile is a **telefonino** or **cellulare**.

a phonecard	una scheda telefonica
	oo-na **skay**-da te-le-**fo**-nee-ka

I want to make a phone call	**vorrei fare una telefonata**
	vor-**ray**-ee **fa**-ray **oo**-na te-le-**fon**-na-ta
Mr Ponti, please	**il signor Ponti, per favore**
	eel seen-**yor** Ponti, payr fa-**vo**-ray
extension ..., please	**interno ..., per favore**
	een-**ter**-no ..., payr fa-**vo**-ray
can I speak to...?	**posso parlare con...?**
	pos-so par-**la**-ray kon...?
this is Jim Brown	**sono Jim Brown**
	so-no Jim Brown
I'll call back later	**richiamo più tardi**
	ree-kee-**a**-mo pee-**yoo tar**-dee
I'll call back tomorrow	**richiamo domani**
	ree-kee-**a**-mo do-**ma**-nee
can I have an outside line, please	**posso avere la linea, per favore**
	pos-so a-**vay**-ray la **lee**-nay-a, payr fa-**vo**-ray
hello	**pronto**
	pron-to
who is calling?	**chi parla?**
	kee **par**-la?
it's engaged	**la linea è occupata**
	la **lee**-nay-a e ok-koo-**pa**-ta
can you call back later?	**può richiamare più tardi?**
	pwo ree-kee-a-**ma**-ray pee-**yoo tar**-dee?
do you want to leave a message?	**vuole lasciare un messaggio?**
	vwo-lay la-**sha**-ray oon mes-**sad**-jo?
I'll text you	**ti mando un sms**
	tee **man**-do oon **es**-say **em**-may **es**-say
can you text me?	**può mandarmi un sms?**
	pwo man-**dar**-mee oon **es**-say **em**-may **es**-say?

E-mail/fax

• www. is **voo voo voo punto**. @ is **chiocciola** (kee-**och**-o-la), but 'at' is also understood.

I want to send an e-mail	**vorrei mandare un'e-mail**
	vor-**ray**-ee man-**da**-ray oon e-mail
I want to check my e-mail	**vorrei controllare le mie e-mail**
	vor-**ray**-ee kon-trol-**la**-ray lay **mee**-ay e-mail
what's your e-mail address?	**qual è il suo indirizzo e-mail?**
	kwal e eel **soo**-o een-dee-**reet**-so e-mail?
did you get my e-mail?	**ha ricevuto la mia e-mail?**
	a ree-**chay**-voo-to la **mee**-a e-mail?
my e-mail address is...	**il mio indirizzo e-mail è...**
	eel **mee**-o een-dee-**reet**-so e-mail e...
how do you spell it?	**come si scrive?**
	ko-may see **skree**-vay?
all one word	**tutto una parola**
	toot-to **oo**-na pa-**ro**-la
all lower case (smaller case)	**lettere minuscole**
	let-**te**-ray mee-**noos**-ko-lay
caro.smith@ anycompany.co.uk	**caro punto smith @ anycompany punto co punto uk**
	caro **poon**-to smith kee-**och**-o-la anycompany **poon**-to ko **poon**-to oo **kap**-pa
I want to send a fax	**vorrei mandare un fax**
	vor-**ray**-ee man-**da**-ray oon fax
do you have a fax?	**avete il fax?**
	a-**vay**-tay eel fax?
what's your fax number?	**qual è il suo numero di fax?**
	kwal e eel **soo**-o **noo**-may-ro dee fax?
did you get my fax?	**ha ricevuto il mio fax?**
	a ree-chay-**voo**-to eel **mee**-o fax?
I can't read it	**non riesco a leggerlo**
	non ree-**es**-ko a **led**-jer-lo

Internet/cybercafé

• You can find internet points in libraries, at tourist offices, larger post offices, stations and shopping centres. Make sure you have your passport with you as you will be required to show it: according to recent anti-terrorism laws all connections to the Net in public places have to be registered.
• Internet cafés in Italy can be found at **www.cybercafes.com**.
• The ending for Italian websites is **.it**

where can I plug in my laptop?	dove posso attaccare il mio portatile?
	dov-ay **pos**-so at-tak-**ka**-ray eel **mee**-o por-**ta**-tee-lay?
what is your website address?	qual è il suo indirizzo internet?
	kwal e eel **soo**-o een-dee-**reet**-so **een**-ter-net?
how much is it for 30 minutes/ for one hour?	quanto costa collegarsi per trenta minuti/ un'ora?
	kwan-to **kos**-ta kol-leg-**ar**-see payr **tren**-ta mee-**noo**-tee/oon **o**-ra?
how much is it to print something?	quanto costa stampare?
	kwan-to **kos**-ta stam-**pa**-ray?
I'd like to put these photos onto CD	vorrei mettere queste foto su un CD
	vor-**ray**-ee **met**-ter-ay **kwes**-tay **fo**-to soo oon chee-dee
can you print it out?	me lo può stampare?
	may lo pwo stam-**pa**-ray?
where can I buy a memory stick?	dove posso comprare una chiavetta di memoria?
	dov-ay **pos**-so kom-**pra**-ray **oo**-na kee-a-**vet**-ta dee mem-**or**-ya
can you help me, please?	mi può aiutare, per favore?
	mee pwo a-yoo-**ta**-ray payr fa-**vo**-ray?
it doesn't work	non funziona
	non foonts-**yo**-na
this computer has crashed	questo computer si è bloccato
	kwes-to kom-**pyoo**-ter see e blok-**ka**-to

Practical info

Numbers

0	zero	**tsay**-ro
1	uno	**oo**-no
2	due	**doo**-ay
3	tre	tray
4	quattro	**kwat**-tro
5	cinque	**cheen**-kway
6	sei	**say**-ee
7	sette	**set**-tay
8	otto	**ot**-to
9	nove	**no**-vay
10	dieci	dee-**ay**-chee
11	undici	**oon**-dee-chee
12	dodici	**do**-dee-chee
13	tredici	**tray**-dee-chee
14	quatt ordici	kwat-**tor**-dee-chee
15	quindici	**kween**-dee-chee
16	sedici	**say**-dee-chee
17	diciassette	dee-chas-**set**-tay
18	diciotto	dee-**chot**-to
19	diciannove	dee-chan-**no**-vay
20	venti	**ven**-tee
21	ventuno	ven-**too**-no
22	ventidue	ven-tee-**doo**-ay
30	trenta	**tren**-ta
40	quaranta	kwa-**ran**-ta
50	cinquanta	cheen-**kwan**-ta
60	sessanta	ses-**san**-ta
70	settanta	set-**tan**-ta

80	ottanta	ot-**tan**-ta
90	novanta	nov-**an**-ta
100	cento	**chen**-to
110	cento dieci	chent-to-dee-**ay**-chee
500	cinquecento	cheen-kway-**chen**-to
1,000	mille	**meel**-lay
2,000	duemila	doo-ay-**mee**-la
1,000,000	un millione	oon meel-**yo**-nay

1st/1°	primo	**pree**-mo
2nd/2°	secondo	sek-**on**-do
3rd/3°	terzo	**tert**-so
4th/4°	quarto	**kwar**-to
5th/5°	quinto	**kween**-to
6th/6°	sesto	**ses**-to
7th/7°	settimo	**set**-tee-mo
8th/8°	ottavo	ot-**ta**-vo
9th/9°	nono	**no**-no
10th/10°	decimo	**dech**-ee-mo

Days and months

Monday	lunedì	loo-ned-**ee**
Tuesday	martedì	mar-ted-**ee**
Wednesday	mercoledì	mayr-ko-led-**ee**
Thursday	giovedì	jov-ed-**ee**
Friday	venerdì	ven-er-**dee**
Saturday	sabato	**sa**-bat-o
Sunday	domenica	do-**men**-ee-ka

January	gennaio	jen-**na**-yo
February	febbraio	feb-**bra**-yo
March	marzo	**mar**-tso
April	aprile	a-**pree**-lay
May	maggio	**mad**-jo
June	giugno	**joon**-yo

July	luglio	**lool**-yo
August	agosto	a-**gos**-to
September	settembre	set-**tem**-bray
October	ottobre	ot-**tob**-ray
November	novembre	nov-**emb**-ray
December	dicembre	dee-**chemb**-ray
what's the date today?	quanti ne abbiamo oggi?	**kwan**-tee nay ab-bee-**a**-mo **od**-jee?
what day?	che giorno è?	kay **jor**-no e?
day	giorno	**jor**-no
week	settimana	set-tee-**ma**-na
month	mese	**me**-zay
year	anno	**an**-no
it's the 5th of October 2008	è il cinque ottobre duemilaotto	e eel **cheen**-kway ot-**tob**-ray doo-ay-**mee**-la-**ot**-to
on Saturday	sabato	**sa**-ba-to
on Saturdays	il sabato/di sabato	eel **sa**-ba-to/dee **sa**-ba-to
every Saturday	ogni sabato	**on**-yee **sa**-ba-to
this Saturday	questo sabato	**kwes**-to **sa**-ba-to
next Saturday	sabato prossimo	**sa**-ba-to **pros**-see-mo
last Saturday	sabato scorso	**sa**-ba-to **skor**-so

Time

excuse me, what time is it?	scusi, che ore sono?
	skoo-zee, kay **o**-ray so-no?
when does it open/close?	a che ora apre/chiude?
	a kay **o**ra **a**pray/kee-**oo**day?
when does it begin/finish?	a che ora comincia/finisce?
	a kay **o**ra ko-**meen**cha/fee-**nee**shay?
am	di mattina
	dee mat-**tee**-na
pm	di pomeriggio/sera
	dee po-mer-**eed**-jo/**say**-ra
at midday	a mezzogiorno
	a med-zo-**jor**-no
at midnight	a mezzanotte
	a med-za-**not**-tay
it's 1 o'clock	è l'una
	e **loo**-na
it's six o'clock	sono le sei
	so-no lay **say**-ee
it's half past 8	sono le otto e mezza
	so-no lay **ot**-to ay **med**-za
an hour	un'ora
	oon **o**-ra
half an hour	mezz'ora
	med-**zo**-ra
until 8 o'clock	fino alle otto
	fee-no **al**-lay **ot**-to

it is half past 10	sono le dieci e mezza
	so-no lay dee-**ay**-chee ay **med**-za
at 10 o'clock	alle dieci
	al-lay dee-**ay**-chee
at 22.00	alle (ore) ventidue
	al-lay (**o**-ray) ven-tee-**doo**-ay
at 22.30	alle (ore) ventidue e trenta
	al-lay (**o**-ray) ven-tee-**doo**-ay e **tren**-ta
soon	fra poco
	fra **po**-ko
later	più tardi
	pee-yoo **tar**-dee

Eating out

Italian cooking is among the best-loved in the world. It has travelled the globe along with the Italians who took their recipes with them. The emphasis has always been on good ingredients and what is available locally and in season, rather than quantity.

In the north of the country Italian cooking reveals the influences of its neighbours: France, Austria, Switzerland and Slovenia. The further south you go the lighter and more colourful the food becomes. In Milan and Lombardy you find veal and **risotto** dishes. The rice fields of the Po valley produce pudding-like rice which can be cooked with butter, parmesan and saffron. Liguria with its long coastline boasts numerous fish dishes as well as wonderful aromatic basil found in its **pesto**.

Another of Italy's great exports is Parma ham and Bolognese sauce. These come from the Emilia-Romagna with its cities of Parma and Bologna. As you reach Italy's calf and ankle, you find the mountainous areas of Puglia, Campania and Basilicata where lamb becomes one of the main ingredients of its dishes.

With the Mediterranean on all sides, its influences can be tasted everywhere: olives, fresh fish, pasta dishes, fresh fruit and vegetables. And Sicily, surrounded by sea, yields dishes of prehistoric-looking fish, with influences of neighbouring Africa such as couscous.

Breakfast (**prima colazione**) is light: coffee (**caffè** or **caffelatte** or **cappuccino**) with bread and jam, biscuits or croissant. Lunch (**pranzo**) for people who work can be a snack or canteen meal (usually between 12.30 and 2pm). The evening meal (**cena**) is normally the main meal of the day, usually eaten between 7.30 and 9pm. The further south, the later it can be, often after 9pm.

Ordering drinks

●●●

● It's cheaper to have a drink at the bar. If you're in a hurry and want a quick coffee, do as the locals do and stand.
● In city bars and caffè you pay first at the **cassa** and then present the receipt (**scontrino**) at the bar to whoever is serving you.
You need to be able to explain what you want at the **cassa** and again to the barman.

an espresso	**un caffè**
	oon kaf-**fe**
a cappuccino	**un cappuccino**
	oon kap-poo-**chee**-no
2 cappuccinos	**due cappuccini**
	doo-ay kap-poo-**chee**-nee
a tea	**un tè**
	oon te
with milk	**al latte**
	al **lat**-tay
with lemon	**al limone**
	al lee-**mo**-nay
a beer (lager)	**una birra**
	oo-na **beer**-ra
small	**piccola**
	peek-ol-la
medium	**media**
	med-ee-a
large	**grande**
	gran-day
a bottle of mineral water	**una bottiglia di acqua minerale**
	oo-na bot-**teel**-ya dee **ak**-wa mee-nay-**ra**-lay
sparkling	**gassata**
	gas-**za**-ta
still	**naturale**
	na-too-**ra**-lay

would you like a drink?	**prende qualcosa da bere?**
	pren-day kwal-**ko**-za da **ber**-ay?
what will you have?	**che cosa prende?**
	kay **ko**-za **pren**-day?
the wine list, please	**la lista dei vini, per favore**
	la **lee**-sta **day**-ee **vee**-nee, payr fa-**vo**-ray
a bottle of house wine	**una bottiglia di vino della casa**
	oo-na bot-**teel**-ya dee **vee**-no **del**-la **ka**-za
a glass of wine	**un bicchiere di vino**
	oon bee-kee-**e**-ray dee **vee**-no
a bottle of wine	**una bottiglia di vino**
	oo-na bot-**teel**-ya dee **vee**-no
red	**rosso**
	ros-so
white	**bianco**
	bee-**an**-ko

Ordering food

• •

• You don't have to have all the courses in a restaurant, pick and choose.
• 'Cheers' is **salute** or **cin cin** (sa-**loo**-tay, cheen cheen).
• It's polite to wish **buon appetito** (bwon ap-pay-**tee**-to). The reply is 'thanks and you, too', **grazie altrettanto** (**grat**-see-ay a al-tret-**tan**-to).

I'd like to book a table	**vorrei prenotare un tavolo**
	vor-**ray**-ee pren-o-**ta**-ray oon **ta**-vo-lo
for ... people	**per ... persone**
	payr ... per-**so**-nay
do you have a table?	**avete un tavolo?**
	a-**vay**-tay oon **ta**-vo-lo?
for tonight	**per stasera**
	payr sta-**say**-ra
at 8pm	**alle otto**
	al-lay **ot**-to

the menu, please	**il menù, per favore**
	eel men-**oo**, payr fa-**vo**-ray
is there a dish of the day?	**c'è un piatto del giorno?**
	che oon pee-**at**-to del **jor**-no?
have you a set-price menu?	**c'è un menù turistico?**
	che oon men-**oo** too-**rees**-tee-ko?
I'll have this	**prendo questo**
	pren-do **kwes**-to
I'll just have the first course	**prendo solo il primo**
	pren-do **so**-lo eel **pree**-mo
I'll just have the main course	**prendo solo il secondo**
	pren-do **so**-lo eel sek-**on**-do
what do you recommend?	**che cosa ci consiglia?**
	kay **ko**-za chee kon-**seel**-ya?
I don't eat meat	**non mangio carne**
	non **man**-jo **kar**-nay
do you have any vegetarian dishes?	**avete dei piatti per vegetariani?**
	a-**vay**-tay **day**-ee pee-**at**-tee payr ve-jay-ta-ree-**a**-nee?
excuse me!	**scusi!**
	skoo-zee!
please bring...	**ci porti...**
	chee **por**-tee...
more bread	**altro pane**
	al-tro **pa**-nay
another bottle	**un'altra bottiglia**
	oon **al**-tra bot-**teel**-ya
some butter	**del burro**
	del **boor**-ro
the bill, please	**il conto, per favore**
	eel **kon**-to, payr fa-**vo**-ray

Special requirements

• •

• Gluten-free is **senza glutine** (**sent**-sa **gloo**-tee-nay). These products are available in most supermarkets, but there are also special shops that sell only these products (**NaturaSì**).
• **Integrale** means wholemeal.
• **Biologico** or **bio** means 'organic'.
• On labels, **grassi** means 'fats'.

what's in this?	**cosa c'è dentro?**
	ko-za che **den**-tro?
I'm vegetarian	**sono vegetariano(a)**
	so-no ve-jay-ta-ree-**a**-no(a)
I don't eat meat/ pork	**non mangio carne/carne di maiale**
	non **man**-jo **kar**-nay/**kar**-nay dee ma-**ya**-lay
I don't eat fish/ shellfish	**non mangio pesce/i frutti di mare**
	non **man**-jo **pay**-shay/ee **froot**-tee dee **ma**-ray
I'm allergic to shellfish	**sono allergico(a) ai frutti di mare**
	so-no al-**ler**-jee-ko/a **a**-ee **froot**-tee dee **ma**-ray
I am allergic to peanuts	**sono allergico(a) alle arachidi**
	so-no al-**ler**-jee-ko(a) **al**-lay a-**ra**-kee-dee
is it raw?	**è crudo?**
	e **kroo**-do?
I have a gluten intolerance	**sono ciliaco(a)**
	so-no chee-lee-**a**-ko(a)
I can only eat gluten-free foods	**posso mangiare soltanto cibi senza glutine**
	pos-so man-**ja**-ray sol-**tan**-to **chee**-bee **sent**-sa **gloo**-tee-nay
I am on a diet	**sono a dieta**
	so-no a dee-**ay**-ta
I don't drink alcohol	**non bevo alcool**
	non **bev**-o **al**-kol

Eating photoguide

Eating places

Many bars and **caffè** serve food: mainly salads, sandwiches, pasta dishes and pizzas.

Market For lunch, buy produce in a morning market. There is a staggering array of bread, fruit, olives, cheese, etc. Be prepared to stand your ground in the queues at busy stalls. **Tocca a me!** = it's my turn!

Rosticceria sells spit-roasted chicken and food to be eaten there or to taken away. The food should be good and well-worth sampling.

Tabaccaio As well as a tobacconist, it is often a bar and may serve meals. There are no frills, but the food will be good.

Deli counter The types of cold meats you find in the starter, **antipasto misto**.
bresaola = cured beef, **p.** = **prosciutto** = ham
p. crudo = cured ham (Parma ham),
p. cotto = cooked ham

Restaurants are generally well sign-posted with the knife and fork symbol.

Crotto A rustic-style eating place where you can get cold meats (**salami**, **prosciutto**, etc) and dishes like **polenta**. They are gradually becoming more gentrified.

Closed Mondays
Bars and restaurants generally close one day a week. This one is shut **lunedì** (Mondays).

Local Cuisine

A **gelateria** is a bar selling ice cream where you can also get drinks.
gelati = ice creams

cono	1.40
cono grande	1.70
coppa piccola	1.40/
coppa media	2.00
coppa grande	2.90
supplemento panna	0.30
brioches con gelato	2.00
frappè	2.20
frullati	2.50

cono = cone
coppa = tub
grande = big
piccola = small
media = medium
frappè = milkshakes
frullati = smoothies

CIOCCOLATO
VANIGLIA
NOCCIOLA
LIMONE
FRAGOLA
BANANA
ALBICOCCA

gusti = flavours
cioccolato = chocolate
vaniglia = vanilla
nocciola = hazelnut
limone = lemon
fragola = strawberry
banana = banana
albicocca = apricot

PANINI MISTI

Sandwich Bar
Don't translate **panini** simply as sandwiches, they can be a feast in themselves.

Trattoria Traditionally, family-run and usually with less choice than a **ristorante**. However, it will have local dishes. Here the speciality is fish (**pesce**). It also has a terrace on the lake.

Pizza is served in **pizzerias** (rather than in normal restaurants), and these aren't as common as you might think.

Food To Go
riso freddo
= rice salad
pizza fredda
= cold pizza
focaccia di recco
= cheese focaccia
panini imbottiti
= filled sandwiches

Menù a prezzo fisso
(solo pranzo)
€ 9,50

Fixed-Price Menu
This is usually a 2-course meal, pasta and a meat dish.

MENU' TURISTICO
€ 13,00

Tourist Menu
Many restaurants offer tourist menus (sometimes including wine). Although generally good value, the food is aimed mainly at the tourist market.

PATATINE FRITTE

Chips

TOAST FARCITI

Toasted Sandwiches

Tavola Calda

Hot Meals

Reading the menu

MENU menu

ANTIPASTI starters

PRIMI first courses
pasta different types of pasta dishes
al pomodoro with a tomato sauce
al ragù with a Bolognese meat sauce
all'arrabbiata with a tomato and chilli pepper sauce
alla carbonara with a bacon and egg sauce
alla puttanesca with a tomato, chilli pepper and anchovy sauce
al pesto with a basil, pine nut and pecorino sauce
in brodo in broth (generally ravioli or other stuffed pasta)
risotto rice cooked in stock

SECONDI main dishes
carne meat
vitello veal
manzo beef
maiale pork
pollo chicken
agnello lamb
pesce fish
CONTORNI vegetables
FORMAGGI cheeses
DOLCI sweets
FRUTTA fruit

Restaurants must display their menu outside.

pane – coperto
Bread And Cover Charge In a restaurant they always charge for **pane** (bread) or **grissini** (breadsticks). If you eat it all you may ask for more.

bevande escluse
Drinks Not Included

bibite
Soft Drinks

da asporto
Take-Away

caldo freddo
Hot   Cold

Insalata verde	€ 2,50	*Insalata mista*	€ 4,00
Pomodori con cipolla	€ 3,00	*Insalatona + tonno e mozzarella*	€ 8,00
	Patate fritte	€ 2,50	

Salads

Insalata verde = green salad **Insalata mista** = mixed salad
Pomodori con cipolla = tomato and onion salad
Insalatona + tonno e mozzarella = large salad with tuna and mozzarella **Patate fritte** = chips

a scelta

Choice Of
There may be a couple of options to choose from.

nostrano

Local

cucina casalinga

Home Cooking

Cheese Board

Dish Of The Day with **polenta** – Beef stew or Rabbit or Veal stew. Watch out for the little words – **o** means 'or', **con** means 'with', **e** means 'and'.

stagione

In Season

Half Bottle Of Wine Included

Drinks and bills

Coffee If you ask for **un caffè** you'll get an **espresso**, very small, strong and black. For a white coffee, ask for **un caffelatte** or **un cappuccino**. You generally get a standard cup, not a choice of regular or large.

It is cheaper to have a drink standing at the bar. You pay high prices for sitting outside in top tourist areas like St Mark's Square in Venice.

Bill Your **ricevuta** (receipt) lists what you have consumed. It is advisable to check the prices. The word for the bill is **il conto**.

pagare alla cassa

When you enter a bar, check for the sign **pagare alla cassa** (pay at the cash desk). If there is a cashier, place your order with them, then go to the counter and give the barman your receipt, repeating your order.

Birra When you ask for **birra** in Italy, you'll be served lager. If you want ale or bitter, ask for **birra scura** or **birra rossa**. Draught beer (**alla spina**) will come either **piccola** (half pint approx.) or **media** (just under a pint). If you want to drink beer, look out for bars which call themselves pubs. However, they may be quite expensive.

Drinks

VENDEMMIA
1995

Tordi Falco

Murgia Rosso
VINO DA TAVOLA

IMBOTTIGLIATO
ALL'AZIENDA VINICOLA   PRODOTTO IN ITALIA
TORREVENTO s.r.l.   13% vol
CORADO - ITALIA   75d ml e
TORRE
VENTO   L. 600 F

Cantine del Borgo Reale

VERDICCHIO
DEI CASTELLI DI JESI
DENOMINAZIONE DI ORIGINE CONTROLLATA
CLASSICO
1997
75cl e   CANTINE DEL BORGO REALE - ITALIA   11,5% VOL
           IMBOTTIGLIATO DA F.G. S.p.A. - DIANO D'ALBA - ITALIA

Reading The Wine Label **Vino da tavola** (table wine) is the lowest class – rustic, usually rough-edged and rarely quaffable without food. Alcohol content 13% makes for quite a hefty wine. (11.5% is about average.)

DOC (Denominazione di Origine Controllata) operates like **AC** in France, with tight controls on wine production. The higher classification of **DOCG** does not necessarily promise a better wine, despite its adding of **Garantita** (guaranteed).

SANNIO BENEVENTANO
INDICAZIONE GEOGRAFICA TIPICA

Indicazione Geograficha Tipica is the equivalent of French **vin de pays**; it can either be rustic or superb.

Aperitivi

Happy Hour In cities, the 'happy hour' aperitif from 6.30–9pm is very common. Bars do fantastic things! When you order your cocktail or **crodino** (a non-alcoholic aperitif) you can have lots of nibbles: crisps, olives, slices of **focaccia**. You might even have to skip dinner afterwards.

Menu reader

abbacchio suckling or milk-fed lamb.

abbacchio alla cacciatora lamb cooked in olive oil, vinegar, anchovies, garlic and rosemary

acciughe anchovies: fresh, salted or in olive oil

acciughe ripiene fresh anchovies filled with salted anchovy fillets and cream cheese and fried in oil

aceto vinegar

aceto balsamico balsamic vinegar

acqua brillante tonic water

acqua cotta traditional Tuscan soup made from onions, peppers, celery and tomato. Beaten eggs and parmesan are added just before serving

acqua minerale mineral water; this can be still (**naturale**), with gas (**effervescente naturale**), or with added gas (**gassata** or **leggermente frizzante**)

affettato misto selection of cold meats: ham, salami, mortadella, etc

affogato poached

affogato al caffè vanilla ice cream with hot espresso coffee poured over it

affumicato smoked

aglio garlic

aglio, olio e peperoncino garlic, olive oil and hot chilli served on pasta

agnello lamb

agnello al forno roast lamb

agnello arrosto roast lamb

agnolotti pasta squares filled with white meat and cheese, usually served with bolognese sauce

agoni small fresh-water fish, usually marinated in vinegar and herbs

agrodolce sweet and sour sauce made from sugar, water, vinegar, wine, pine-nuts and sultanas; served with vegetables or meat such as rabbit or duck

ai ferri grilled

al, alla etc means with, or in the style of: e.g. **pasta al sugo** is pasta with tomato sauce, and **pollo alla cacciatora** is chicken hunter-style

albicocche apricots

albicocche ripiene stuffed apricots

alici fresh anchovies, often served dipped in flour and fried

alloro bayleaf

amarene sour cherries

amaretti macaroons, biscuits with a strong almond flavour

Amaretto di Saronno almond liqueur

amaro bitter liqueur drunk as a **digestivo** (to aid digestion)

amatriciana, ...all' bacon, tomato and onion sauce

analcolico non-alcoholic, bittersweet drink served as an aperitif

ananas pineapple

anatra duck

anatra in porchetta roast duck stuffed with ham and covered with slices of lard

anguilla eel

anguille alla comácchio stewed eels with tomato and vinegar

anguille carpionate fried eels in a vinegar sauce

anguille in umido stewed eels

anguria watermelon

anice aniseed

anisetta powerful aniseed liqueur

antipasto starter/appetizer

antipasto misto selection of cold starters such as ham, salami and pickles

aperitivo aperitif

Aperol type of slightly alcoholic aperitif

aragosta lobster

arance oranges

aranciata orangeade

arancini di riso rice croquettes filled with cheese, minced veal and peas

arrabbiata, ...all' tomato sauce with bacon, onion, tomatoes and hot chillies

arrosto roast meat, usually cooked in casserole with wine and herbs

arrosto di maiale roast pork

arrosto di manzo roast beef

arrosto di vitello roast veal

asparagi asparagus

asparagi alla parmigiana lightly boiled asparagus with melted butter and sprinkled with parmesan

astice crayfish

baccalà salt cod

baccalà alla livornese salt cod cooked in a tomato sauce

baccalà alla vicentina salt cod cooked in milk with anchovies, garlic and parsley

baccalà fiorentina salt cod cooked in tomato sauce

bagna cauda hot garlic and anchovy dip

banana banana

basilico basil

Bel Paese soft mild cheese

ben cotto well done

besciamella béchamel sauce

bianco, in literally it means white, pasta or rice served with butter or olive oil and parmesan cheese

bietola beetroot

birra lager-type beer; draught beer is **birra alla spina**

biscotti biscuits

bistecca steak

bistecca fiorentina thickly cut, charcoal-grilled T-bone steak

bistecchini di cinghiale wild boar steaks

bitter non-alcoholic, bitter drink served as an aperitif

bocconcini di vitello pieces of veal cooked in wine and butter

bollito boiled

bollito misto different kinds of meat and vegetables boiled together

bolognese, ...alla tomato and minced meat sauce, served with parmesan

bomba doughnut with custard filling

bonet alla Piemontese chocolate pudding made with biscuits, macaroons and rum

budino chocolate or vanilla pudding

borlotti dried red haricot beans

boscaiola, ...alla with mushroom and ham sauce

bottarga preserved mullet roes, grated and sprinkled on pasta dishes, or served in thin slices as a starter (Sardinian speciality)

brace, ...alla grilled

braciola rib steak/chop

brasato beef stew

bresaola dried cured beef, finely sliced and served with black pepper, lemon and olive oil

broccoli broccoli

brodetto di pesce fish soup made with different kinds of fish

brodo bouillon or broth often served with meat-stuffed pasta such as ravioli (**in brodo**)

bruschetta thickly-sliced grilled bread rubbed with garlic and olive oil, often served topped with tomato

bucatini thick spaghetti-like pasta with hole running through it

budino a blancmange-type pudding, usually chocolate or vanilla

burro butter

burro, ...al fried in butter, usually wih garlic and sage

burro e salvia butter and sage sauce

busecca rich tripe and cheese soup

cacciatora, ...alla meat or game, hunter-style – cooked with tomato, herbs, garlic and wine

cachi persimmons

caciocavallo cow's cheese, quite strong when mature

caffè coffee – if you ask for **un caffè** you'll be served **un espresso** (small, strong and black)

caffè americano black filter coffee

caffè corretto coffee laced with **grappa** or any strong spirit

caffè doppio a large coffee (twice normal size)

caffèllatte or **caffè macchiato** milky coffee

calamaretti imbottiti baby squid stuffed with breadcrumbs and anchovies

calamari squid

calamari fritti squid rings dipped in batter and fried

calzone folded over pizza with filling. There are lots of local variations

camomilla camomile tea

Campari bitter-tasting aperitif made with herbs and fruit

canederli tirolesi Tyrolean dumplings made with smoked cured ham and bread

cannella cinnamon

cannellini small white beans

cannelloni meat-filled pasta tubes covered with béchamel sauce and baked. Vegetarian options are filled with spinach and ricotta

cannoli fried pastries stuffed with ricotta, candied fruit and bitter chocolate from Sicily

cantucci nutty biscuits

caponata Sicilian dish of aubergines, potatoes and peppers, cooked in a sweet and sour sauce

cappelletti literally 'little hats' filled with cheese or meat filling, can be served with bolognese meat sauce or in broth

capperi capers

cappon magro an elaborate salad of cold seafood, fish and cooked vegetables

cappuccino frothy white coffee

caprese tomato and mozzarella salad with basil

capretto baby goat (kid)

capretto arrosto oven-roasted kid with vegetables and wine

caprino soft goat's cheese, usually eaten with a sprinkling of olive oil and freshly ground black pepper

caramelle sweets

carbonara, ...alla smoked bacon, egg, cream and parmesan

carciofi artichokes

carciofi alla Giudia young artichokes, flattened and deep-fried

carciofi alla romana, carciofi ripieni artichokes stuffed with breadcrumbs, parsley and anchovies

cardi cardoons (similar to fennel)

carne meat

carote carrots

carpa carp

carpaccio raw sliced lean beef eaten with lemon juice, olive oil and thickly grated parmesan cheese

carpione, in pickled in vinegar, wine and lemon juice. Fried fish is often served this way

casalinga, ...alla home-made

cassata layers of ice cream with candied fruits

cassata alla siciliana sponge dessert with ricotta and candied fruits

cassola pork, cabbage and vegetable casserole

castagnaccio chestnut cake

castagne chestnuts

cavolfiore cauliflower

cavolo cabbage

ceci chickpeas

céfalo grey mullet

cena dinner

Centerbe herbal liqueur

cervella calves' brains, usually fried

cetriolo cucumber

China bittersweet liqueur

chinotto fizzy, bitter-orange soft drink

cialzons alla carnia pasta squares filled with spinach, chocolate and cinnamon

ciambella ring-shaped fruit cake

ciambellini ring-shaped aniseed biscuits

cicoria chicory

ciliege cherries

cime di rapa leafy, green vegetable similar to turnip tops, often served with **orecchiette**

cinghiale wild boar

Cinzano popular aperitif

cioccolata calda rich hot chocolate, often served with whipped cream

cioccolatini chocolates

cioccolato chocolate

cipolle onions

cocco coconut

cocomero watermelon

coda di bue oxtail

coda alla vaccinara famous Roman dish of oxtail stewed with tomatoes and herbs

Colomba bird-shaped cake with orange peel, topped with sugared almonds, eaten at Easter

conchiglie shell-shaped pasta

confetti sugared almonds

congelato frozen

coniglio rabbit

coniglio in umido rabbit stew

contorni vegetable side dishes

cornetto ice-cream cone; a croissant filled with jam, custard or chocolate

cosciotto d'agnello all'abruzzese braised leg of lamb with garlic, tomatoes, rosemary and wine

cotechino spicy pork sausage boiled and served with lentils

cotoletta cutlet/chop

cotoletta al prosciutto veal cutlet with a slice of Parma ham

cotoletta alla bolognese veal cutlet topped with ham and cheese

cotoletta alla milanese veal cutlet dipped in egg and breadcrumbs then fried

cotoletta alla valdostana breaded veal chop topped with Fontina cheese and ham

cotoletta di vitello veal cutlet

cotolette di abbacchio lamb chops

cotolette di agnello alla brace marinated, grilled lamb chops

cotto cooked

cozze mussels

crema di... cream soup or sauce/custard

crêpe pancake

crespella stuffed pancake

crocchette di patate potato croquettes

crodino bittersweet, non-alcoholic aperitif

crostata tart, usually filled with jam

crostata di frutta tart filled with fruit and glazed

crostini di fegatini chicken liver pâté on toast

crudo raw

cuori di carciofo artichoke hearts

Cynar bitter aperitif (made from artichokes)

dente, ...al pasta cooked so it is still quite firm

dèntice sea bream

digestivo bitter, herb-flavoured liqueur to aid digestion

dolce dessert

dolcelatte soft, creamy blue cheese

dragoncello tarragon

entrecote steak

fagiano pheasant

fagiano con funghi pheasant with porcini mushrooms

fagiano in salmì pheasant stewed in wine

fagioli beans

fagioli al tonno haricot beans with tuna fish in olive oil

fagioli con cotiche bean stew with pork rinds

fagioli nel fiasco haricot beans cooked in a flask

fagiolini runner beans

faraona guinea fowl

farcito stuffed

farfalle butterfly-shaped pasta

farsu magru veal stuffed and rolled up, cooked in wine (Sicilian speciality)

fave broad beans

fave al guanciale broad beans cooked with bacon and onion

fegatini di pollo chicken livers

fegato liver (mainly calves')

fegato alla veneziana calves' liver fried in butter and onion

ferri, ...ai grilled without oil

fettuccine fresh ribbon pasta

fichi figs

fichi d'India prickly pears

filetto fillet steak

filetto di tacchino alla bolognese turkey breast served with a slice of ham and cheese

Filu Ferru very strong **grappa** from Sardinia

finanziera, ...alla mince of chicken livers, mushrooms and wine sauce

finocchio fennel

fiori di zucchini courgette flowers, often served fried in batter

focaccia flat bread brushed with salt and olive oil, sprinkled with herbs or onions

fonduta cheese fondue made with Fontina cheese, eggs, butter and truffles. Eaten with crusty bread

Fontina mild to strong cow's milk cheese (from the Val d'Aosta)

formaggio cheese

forno, ...al cooked in the oven

fragole strawberries

frittata omelette, usually with different ingredients

fritto fried

fritto misto selection of fried seafood

frullato di frutta fruit smoothie

frutta fruit

frutti di mare shellfish/seafood

funghi mushrooms – very popular and varied in Italy. In autumn many Italians take to the woods in search of the prized **porcini**

funghi trifolati sliced mushrooms fried with garlic and parsley

Fuoco dell'Etna very strong liqueur from Sicily

fusilli spiral-shaped pasta

gamberi prawns

gamberoni giant prawns

gazzosa fizzy bottled lemonade

gelato ice cream

gelato misto a selection of different flavoured ice creams

girasole sunflower

gnocchi small dumplings generally made from potato and flour. Boiled and served with tomato sauce or ragù

gnocchi alla romana disk-shaped dumplings made from semolina, butter and parmesan, oven-baked

gnocchi verdi spinach and potato dumplings, usually cooked in butter, garlic and sage

Gorgonzola a blue cows' milk soft cheese: it can be **dolce** (mild) or **piccante** (strong)

grana hard cows' milk cheese; generic name given to Parmesan cheese

granchio crab

granita slush puppy, crushed ice drink

granita al caffè cold coffee with crushed ice

granita al limone lemon drink with crushed ice sorbet

granseola large crab

grappa strong spirit from grape pressings, often added to coffee

grattugiato grated

griglia, ...alla grilled

grigliata di cervo grilled venison steaks

grigliata mista mixed grill consisting of various barbecued meats

grissini breadsticks

guanciale streaky bacon made from pig's cheek

gulasch spicy beef stew

impepata di cozze peppery mussels stew

insalata salad

insalata caprese tomato, basil and mozzarella salad

insalata di mare mixed seafood salad

insalata di pomodori tomato salad

insalata di riso rice salad

insalata mista mixed salad

insalata russa cold diced vegetables seved with mayonnaise

insalata verde green salad
involtini rolls of veal or pork stuffed in various ways
lamponi raspberries
lasagne layers of pasta with bolognese and béchamel sauces, baked
lasagne verdi layers of green pasta with bolognese (or ricotta) and béchamel sauces
latte milk
lattuga lettuce
lemonsoda fizzy lemon drink
lenticchie lentils
lepre hare
lepre in salmì hare stewed in wine
lesso boiled
limonata bottled lemon drink
limoncello lemon liqueur
limone lemon
lingua tongue
linguine flat spaghetti
lombata di maiale pork chop
lonza type of pork fillet
luccio pike
lumache snails
maccheroni macaroni
maccheroni ai quattro formaggi pasta with four cheeses
macedonia (con gelato) fresh fruit salad (with ice cream)
macinata mince
magro, di a meatless dish (often a fish alternative)
maiale pork
maionese mayonnaise
mandorle almonds

manzo beef
marmellata jam
Marsala dark dessert wine from Sicily
Martini famous Italian aperitif
mascarpone rich cream cheese used in desserts such as **tiramisù**
mela apple
melagrana pomegranate
melanzane aubergines
melanzane alla Parmigiana layers of fried aubergine baked with tomato sauce, parmesan and mozzarella
melanzane ripiene stuffed aubergines
melone melon
menta mint
meringata meringue and ice cream dessert
merluzzo cod
miele honey
milanese, ...alla normally applied to veal cutlets dipped in egg and breadcrumbs before frying
minestra soup
minestrone vegetable soup (with either pasta or rice)
missultin grilled dried fish, often eaten with **polenta**
misto di funghi mushroom stew
more blackberries
mortadella type of salami
mostarda pickled fruit. Served with **bollito** (boiled meats)
mozzarella fresh cheese preserved in whey, used in pizzas

mozzarella di bufala mozzarella made with buffalo milk

mozzarella in carrozza mozzarella sandwiched in bread, dipped in egg and fried

mugnaia, ...alla usually fish dusted in flour then fried in butter

nocciole hazelnuts

noci walnuts

norma, ...alla tomato and fried aubergine Sicilian sauce

olio oil

olio d'oliva olive oil

olive olives

orecchiette ear-shaped pasta, served with either tomoato sauce or **cime di rapa** (type of broccoli)

orecchiette ai broccoli pasta with broccoli

origano oregano

orzata cool, milky drink made from barley

ossobuco marrow-bone veal steak cooked in tomato and wine sauce

ostriche oysters

paglia e fieno green and plain ribbon pasta

pan pepato sweet loaf with mixed nuts and spices

pancetta streaky bacon

pandoro soft cork-shaped yeast cake sprinkled with icing-sugar, traditionally eaten at Christmas

pane bread

pane e coperto cover charge

pane integrale wholemeal bread

panettone cork-shaped yeast cake with orange peel and raisins, traditionally eaten at Christmas

panforte a hard, dried-fruit and nut cake

panino bread roll or sandwich

panna cream

pansotti pasta squares filled with herbs and cheese and served in a walnut and parmesan sauce

panzerotti folded pizza dough stuffed with mozzarella, salami and ham, usually fried

pappardelle wide ribbon-shaped pasta

pappardelle al sugo di lepre wide ribbon pasta with hare, wine and tomato sauce

parmigiana di melanzane aubergine layers, oven-baked with tomato sauce, mozzarella and parmesan cheese

parmigiano parmesan cheese. A hard cow's milk cheese used extensively in Italian cooking

pasta the dry variety takes 10–15 minutes to cook, the fresh just 3 or 4

pasta al forno oven-baked pasta with a variety of different ingredients

pasta all'uovo fresh pasta made from flour and eggs

pasta asciutta pasta served with a sauce, such as **spaghetti al sugo**, and not in a soup form, such as **ravioli in brodo** (ravioli in bouillon)

pasta e fagioli pasta with beans

pasta fresca fresh pasta

pasticcio pie

pastina in brodo pasta pieces in clear broth

patate potatoes

patate fritte chips

patatine crisps

patatine fritte french fries

pecorino hard tangy cheese made from sheep's milk

penne quill-shaped pasta

penne rigate ribbed quill-shaped pasta

pepe pepper

peperonata sweet peppers cooked with tomatoes and olive oil

peperoncino hot chilli pepper

peperoni peppers

peperoni ripieni stuffed peppers

pere pears

pesca peach

pesca noce nectarine

pesce fish

pesce arrosto baked fish

pesce persico perch

pesce spada swordfish, often grilled or served in a tomato sauce

pesto sauce of pounded basil, garlic, pine-nuts, olive oil and Parmesan cheese

petto di pollo chicken breast

piada or **piadina** similar to tortilla wrap (but originally from Emilia-Romagna) filled with ham, cheese, etc. A tasty alternative to a **panino**

piatto del giorno dish of the day

piatti tipici regional dishes

piccante hot (as in chilli) or strong (as in **gorgonzola**)

piccata al limone tender thinly sliced veal in butter and lemon

pietanze main courses

pinoli pine nuts

piselli peas

pistacchio pistachio

pizza originally from Naples, cooked in wood-burning ovens

pizza ai frutti di mare pizza with seafood

pizza ai funghi mushroom pizza

pizza alla Siciliana pizza with tomato, anchovy, black olives and capers

pizza capricciosa pizza with baby artichoke, ham and egg

pizza margherita named after the first queen of a united Italy, symbolising the colours of the Italian flag: red (tomatoes), green (basil) and white (mozzarella)

pizza marinara tomato and garlic pizza

pizza Napoli/Napoletana pizza with tomato, cheese, anchovy, olive oil and oregano

pizza quattro formaggi a pizza divided into four sections, each with a different cheese topping

pizza quattro stagioni pizza divided into four sections with a selection of toppings on each one

pizzaiola, ...alla cooked with tomatoes, garlic and herbs

pizzetta small cheese and tomato pizza

pizzoccheri buckwheat pasta noodles, cooked with cabbage, potatoes and cheese and dressed with fried butter and garlic

polenta coarse corn or maize meal solidified porridge. A perfect accompaniment to stews. Can also be fried

polenta uncia polenta baked with butter, garlic and cheese

pollame poultry/fowl

pollo chicken

pollo alla diavola chicken grilled with herbs and chilli pepper

pollo alla romana chicken with tomatoes and peppers

pollo arrosto roast chicken

polpette fried meatballs

polpo octopus, served in salad (cold) or tomato sauce

polpo affogato octopus cooked in tomato sauce

pomodoro tomato

pomodoro, ...al tomato sauce (same as **sugo**)

pomodori da sugo plum tomatoes

pomodori ripieni stuffed tomatoes

pompelmo grapefruit

porceddu roast suckling pig (Sardinian style)

porchetta roast suckling pig thinly sliced

porcini prized cep mushrooms, often dried

porri leeks

pranzo lunch

prezzemolo parsley

prima colazione breakfast

primo first course

prosciutto ham

prosciutto cotto boiled ham

prosciutto crudo cured Parma ham which is sliced off the bone

prosciutto di cinghiale cured ham made from wild boar

prosciutto e melone Parma ham and melon slices

Prosecco sparkling dry white wine

provolone cow's milk cheese, mild to strong

prugne plums

puttanesca, ...alla tomato, garlic, hot chilli, anchovies and capers

quaglie quails

radicchio red-leaf lettuce

ragù, ...al minced meat, tomato and garlic (same as **bolognese**)

rana pescatrice monkfish

rane frogs (only the legs are eaten)

ravioli pasta cushions filled with meat or cheese and vegetables

ribes blackcurrants

riccio di mare sea urchin

ricotta soft white cheese often used as filling for pasta as well as in desserts

rigatoni ribbed tubes of pasta

ripieno stuffed

risi e bisi thick rice and pea soup (almost liquid risotto) cooked with bacon

riso rice

risotto rice cooked in broth with parmesan and butter; it can be flavoured with countless different ingredients

risotto ai funghi with porcini mushrooms

risotto al nero di seppia with squid ink

risotto alla milanese with saffron

risotto alla pescatora with seafood

robiola creamy cheese with a mild taste

rognone kidney

rosmarino rosemary

rucola rocket (in Rome: **rughetta**)

salame salami (there are many types)

sale salt

salmone salmon

salsa sauce

salsa verde sauce made of olive oil, anchovies, hard boiled egg and parsley, usually served with boiled meat or fish

salsicce sausages: there are many regional variations but they are mainly thick pork sausages which can be boiled or grilled

saltimbocca alla romana veal cooked in white wine with parma ham

salvia sage

Sambuca aniseed liqueur, served with coffee beans and set alight

sampietro John Dory (type of fish)

sangue, ...al rare

sarde sardines

sarde al beccafico sardines marinated and stuffed with breadcrumbs, Pecorino cheese, garlic and parsley, then fried

sarde in saor fried sardines marinated in vinegar, onions, sultanas and pine nuts

sartù di riso rice and meat timbale (rather like a pie)

scaloppine veal escalopes

scaloppine al limone veal escalopes cooked in lemon juice

scaloppine al marsala veal escalopes cooked in marsala

scaloppine alla milanese veal escalopes dipped in egg, breadcrumbs and fried in butter, served with wedges of lemon

scaloppine alla pizzaiola thinly sliced steak fried in a tomato and herb sauce

scamorza a soft cow's milk cheese (type of dried mozzarella)

scamorza affumicata smoked scamorza

scampi scampi

secondo second course, usually meat or fish

sedano celery

semifreddo chilled dessert

senape mustard

seppia cuttlefish

servizio compreso service included

sfogliatelle puff pastry cakes

sgombro mackerel

soffritto sliced onion and/or garlic

fried in olive oil, generally used to prepare sauces or meat dishes

sogliola sole

soppressata type of salami, with pistachio

sott'olio in olive oil

spaghetti spaghetti

spaghetti aglio, olio e peperoncino spaghetti with garlic, chilli pepper and olive oil

spaghetti alla chitarra square-shaped pasta

spaghetti all'amatriciana spaghetti with bacon, onion and tomato sauce

spaghetti alle vongole spaghetti with clams

speck type of smoked cured ham from mountain regions

spezzatino stew

spiedini meat kebabs

spiedo, ...allo spit-roasted, or on skewer

spinaci spinach

spremuta freshly squeezed fruit juice

spremuta di pompelmo fresh grapefruit juice

spumante sparkling wine

stoccafisso dried stockfish which requires lots of soaking before cooking

stracciatella consommé with egg stirred in and grated parmesan; or ice-cream with chocolate chips

stracotto braised beef slow-cooked with vegetables. Often served with polenta

Strega strong herb-flavoured liqueur

succo di frutta fruit juice

sugo sauce, often refers to the basic tomato, basil and garlic sauce (same as **al pomodoro**)

surgelato frozen

tacchino turkey

tagliata thinly-sliced meat, briefly cooked on a griddle and served with herbs or parmesan chips

tagliata di pesce spada thinly-sliced swordfish, served raw with lemon juice and olive oil

tagliatelle ribbon-like pasta often served in cream sauce

Taleggio soft, creamy cheese similar to Camembert

tartine canapés

tartufo truffles: black (nero) and white (bianco) are used extensively in risotto and game dishes

tartufo di cioccolato rich chocolate ice cream shaped like a truffle

tè tea. Normally served with lemon (**al limone**). If you want it with milk you must ask for **tè al latte**

timballo a baked pie

timo thyme

tinca tench

tiramisù dessert made with mascarpone, sponge, coffee and marsala

tónica tonic water

tonno tuna fish

tonno, ...al tuna sauce

tonno e fagioli tuna and bean salad

torrone nougat, traditionally eaten at Christmas

torta cake/flan/tart

tortellini meat-filled pasta cushions

tortellini panna e prosciutto tortellini served with cream and ham

tramezzini sliced white bread with mixed fillings

trenette long thin strips of pasta, traditionally served with pesto sauce

triglie red mullet

triglie alla livornese red mullet fried with chillies in tomato sauce

trippa tripe, often cooked with tomatoes and onions

trota trout

uccelli scappati pork kebabs

umido, in stewed

uova eggs

uova alla fiorentina poached eggs on spinach tarts

uva grapes

uva passa raisins

vaniglia vanilla

Vecchia Romagna Italian cognac

verdure vegetables

vermicelli very thin pasta

Vermut very popular aperitif made from herbs and wine

verza Savoy (green) cabbage

vin brûlé mulled wine

vino wine

vino bianco white wine

vino dolce sweet wine

vino frizzante sparkling wine

vino rosato rosé wine

vino rosso red wine

vino secco dry wine

vitello veal

vongole clams

vongole, ...alle clam, parsley, garlic and olive oil

wurstel Frankfurter sausages

yogurt yoghurt

zabaglione frothy dessert made with egg yolks and sugar beaten with marsala over heat

zafferano saffron, used in **risotto alla milanese**

zampone pig's trotter filled with spicy sausage, sliced and served hot

zucca marrow, pumpkin

zucchero sugar

zucchini courgettes

zuccotto rich cream, coffee and nut pudding

zuppa soup

zuppa di cozze mussel soup

zuppa di fagioli bean soup

zuppa di pesce seafood soup with many delicious regional variations

zuppa inglese dessert similar to trifle

zuppa pavese a bread soup with broth and poached eggs, topped with grated cheese

Grammar

Nouns

In Italian all nouns are either masculine or feminine. Where in English we say 'the apple' and 'the book', in Italian it is la mela and il libro because mela is feminine and libro is masculine. The gender of nouns is shown in the article (il, la, un, una, etc.).

the:	masculine singular	feminine singular
	il	la
	l' (+vowel)	l' (+vowel)
	lo (+z, gn, pn, ps, x, s+consonant)	
	masculine plural	feminine plural
	i	le
	gli (+vowel, +z, gn, pn, s+consonant)	
a, an:	masculine	feminine
	un	una
	uno (+z, gn, pn, s+consonant)	un' (+vowel)

Note: Definite articles (il, la, i, le, etc.) used after the prepositions a (to, at), da (by, from), su (on), di (of, some) and in (in, into) contract as follows:

a + il = al	da + il = dal	su + il = sul
a + lo = allo	da + lo = dallo	su + lo = sullo
a + l' = all'	da + l' = dall'	su + l' = sull'
a + la = alla	da + la = dalla	su + la = sulla
a + i = ai	da + i = dai	su + i = sui
a + gli = agli	da + gli = dagli	su + gli = sugli
a + le = alle	da + le = dalle	su + le = sulle

di + il = del	in + il = nel
di + lo = dello	in + lo = nello
di + l' = dell'	in + l' = nell'
di + la = della	in + la = nella
di + i = dei	in + i = nei
di + gli = degli	in + gli = negli
di + le = delle	in + le = nelle
alla casa (<u>to the</u> house)	sul tavolo (<u>on the</u> table)

Formation of plurals

For most nouns, the singular ending changes as follows:

masculine singular	masculine plural	example
o	i	libro → libri
e	i	padre → padri
a	i	artista → artisti

Note: Nouns ending in e can be either masculine or feminine. In the plural they all end in i.

la televisione	le televisioni
il mare	i mari

Note: Most nouns ending in co and go become chi and ghi in the plural to keep the c and g hard sounding. Some exceptions occur in the masculine, e.g. amico – amici.

feminine singular	feminine plural	example
a	e	mela → mele
e	i	madre → madri

Note: Nouns ending in ca and ga become che and ghe in the plural to keep the c and g hard sounding. Nouns ending in cia and gia often become ce and ge to keep the c and g soft sounding.

la barca   le barche
la boccia   le bocce

Adjectives

Adjectives normally follow the noun they describe in Italian,
e.g. la mela rossa (the <u>red</u> apple).

Some common exceptions which go before the noun are:

bello beautiful, breve short, brutto ugly, buono good,
cattivo bad, giovane young, grande big, lungo long, nuovo new,
piccolo small, vecchio old e.g. una bella giornata (a beautiful day)

Italian adjectives have to reflect the gender of the noun they
describe. To make an adjective feminine, an a replaces the o of the
masculine, e.g. rosso – rossa. Adjectives ending in e, e.g. giovane,
can be either masculine or feminine. The plural forms of the
adjective change in the way described for nouns (above).

My, your, his, her, our, their

These words also depend on the gender and number of the noun
they accompany, and not on the sex of the 'owner'.

	with masc. sing. noun	with fem. sing. noun	with masc. plur. noun	with fem. plur. noun
my	il mio	la mia	i miei	le mie
your (polite)	il suo	la sua	i suoi	le sue
your (familiar)	il tuo	la tua	i tuoi	le tue
your (plural)	il vostro	la vostra	i vostri	le vostre
his/her	il suo	la sua	i suoi	le sue
our	il nostro	la nostra	i nostri	le nostre
their	il loro	la loro	i loro	le loro

Pronouns

A **pronoun** is a word that you use to refer to someone or something when you do not need to use a noun, often because the person or thing has been mentioned earlier e.g. **it**, **she**, **something** and **myself**.

subject		object	
I	io	me	mi
you	lei	you	la
he	lui/egli	him	lo/l' (+vowel)
she	lei/ella	her	la/l' (+vowel)
it (masc.)	esso	it (masc.)	lo/l' (+vowel)
it (fem.)	essa	it (fem.)	la/l' (+vowel)
we	noi	us	ci
you	voi	you	vi
they	loro	them (masc.)	li
(things:masc.)	essi	them (fem.)	le
(things:fem.)	esse		

The object pronouns shown above are also used to mean **to me**, **to us**, etc., except:

to him/to it	= gli
to her/to it/to you	= le
to them	= loro

Object pronouns (other than loro) usually go before the verb:

lo vedo	but	scriverò loro
I see him		I will write to them

When used with an infinitive (the verb form given in the dictionary), the pronoun follows and is attached to the infinitive less its final e:

voglio comprarlo	I want to buy it

Subject pronouns (io, tu, egli, etc.) are often omitted in Italian, since the verb ending generally distinguishes the person:

parlo	I speak
parliamo	we speak
parlano	they speak

In Italian there are two forms for **you** – lei (singular) and voi (plural). Tu, the familiar form for **you**, should only be used with people you know well, or children.

Verbs

A **verb** is a word such as **sing**, **walk** or **cry** which is used with a subject to say what someone or something does or what happens to them. **Regular verbs** follow the same pattern of endings. **Irregular verbs** do not follow a regular pattern so you need to learn the different endings. There are three main patterns of endings for verbs in Italian – those ending -are, -ere and -ire in the dictionary. Two examples of the -ire verbs are shown, since two distinct groups of endings exist. Subject pronouns are shown in brackets because these are often not used:

	parlare	**to speak**	vendere	**to sell**
(io)	parlo	I speak	vendo	I sell
(tu)	parli	you speak	vendi	you sell
(lui/lei)	parla	(s)he speaks	vende	(s)he sells
(noi)	parliamo	we speak	vendiamo	we sell
(voi)	parlate	you speak	vendete	you sell
(loro)	parlano	they speak	vendono	they sell
past participle:	parlato (with avere)		venduto (with avere)	

	dormire	**to sleep**	finire	**to finish**
(io)	dormo	I sleep	finisco	I finish
(tu)	dormi	you sleep	finisci	you finish
(lui/lei)	dorme	(s)he sleeps	finisce	(s)he finishes
(noi)	dormiamo	we sleep	finiamo	we finish
(voi)	dormite	you sleep	finite	you finish
(loro)	dormono	they sleep	finiscono	they finish

past participle: dormito (with avere)   finito (with avere)

Irregular verbs

Among the most important irregular verbs are the following:

	essere	**to be**	avere	**to have**
(io)	sono	I am	ho	I have
(tu)	sei	you are	hai	you have
(lui/lei)	è	(s)he is	ha	(s)he has
(noi)	siamo	we are	abbiamo	we have
(voi)	siete	you are	avete	you have
(loro)	sono	they are	hanno	they have

past participle: stato (with essere)   avuto (with avere)

	andare	**to go**	fare	**to do**
(io)	vado	I go	faccio	I do
(tu)	vai	you go	fai	you do
(lui/lei)	va	(s)he goes	fa	(s)he does
(noi)	andiamo	we go	facciamo	we do
(voi)	andate	you go	fate	you do
(loro)	vanno	they go	fanno	they do

past participle: andato (with essere)   fatto (with avere)

	potere	**to be able**	volere	**to want**
(io)	posso	I can	voglio	I want
(tu)	puoi	you can	vuoi	you want
(lui/lei)	può	(s)he can	vuole	(s)he wants
(noi)	possiamo	we can	vogliamo	we want
(voi)	potete	you can	volete	you want
(loro)	possono	they can	vogliono	they want

past participle: potuto (with avere)   voluto (with avere)

	dovere	**to have to (must)**
(io)	devo	I must
(tu)	devi	you must
(lui/lei)	deve	he/she must
(noi)	dobbiamo	we must
(voi)	dovete	you must
(loro)	devono	they must

past participle: dovuto (with avere)

Past tense

To make a simple past tense you need an **auxiliary verb** with the past participle of the main verb, e.g. **I have** (auxiliary) **been** (past participle), **I have** (auxiliary) **eaten** (past participle). In Italian the basic auxiliary verbs are avere (to have) and essere (to be).

To form the simple past tense, I spoke/I have spoken, I sold/I have sold, etc. combine the present tense of the verb avere – **to have** with the past participle of the verb, e.g.

ho parlato   I spoke/I have spoken
ho venduto   I sold/I have sold

parlare (past)		vendere (past)	
ho parlato	I spoke	ho venduto	I sold
hai parlato	you spoke	hai venduto	you sold
ha parlato	(s)he spoke	ha venduto	(s)he sold
abbiamo parlato	we spoke	abbiamo venduto	we sold
avete parlato	you spoke	avete venduto	you sold
hanno parlato	they spoke	hanno venduto	they sold

dormire (past)		finire (past)	
ho dormito	I slept	ho finito	I finished
hai dormito	you slept	hai finito	you finished
ha dormito	(s)he slept	ha finito	(s)he finished
abbiamo dormito	we slept	abbiamo finito	we finished
avete dormito	you slept	avete finito	you finished
hanno dormito	they slept	hanno finito	they finished

Note: Not all verbs take avere (ho, hai, etc.) as their auxiliary verb, some take essere (sono, sei, etc.). These are mainly verbs of motion or staying, e.g. andare – **to go**, stare – **to be** (located at):

sono andato	I went
sono stato a Roma	I was in Rome

When the auxiliary verb essere is used, the past particple (andato, stato) becomes an adjective and should agree with the subject of the verb.

sono andata	I went (fem. sing.)
siamo stati	we went (masc. plural)

To make a sentence negative e.g. I am not eating, you use non before the verb.

non mangio	I am not eating
non sono andato	I did not go

Dictionary

A

a(n) un/una/uno
abbey l'abbazia f
able: *to be able (to)* essere capace (di)
abortion l'aborto m
about su; circa
a book about... un libro su...
about ten o'clock circa le dieci
above sopra
abroad all'estero m
to go abroad andare all'estero
abscess l'ascesso m
accelerator l'acceleratore m
accent l'accento m
to accept accettare
access l'accesso m
wheelchair access accesso per disabili
accident l'incidente m
**accident & emergency
 department** il pronto soccorso
accommodation l'alloggio m
to accompany accompagnare
account (bill) il conto
(in bank) il conto in banca
account number il numero di conto
to ache fare male
it aches fa male
acid l'acido m
actor m/f l'attore/l'attrice
adaptor (electrical appliance) il riduttore
address l'indirizzo m
what is the address? qual è l'indirizzo?
address book la rubrica
admission charge/fee il biglietto
 d'ingresso
to admit (to hospital) ricoverare
adult l'adulto(a)
for adults per adulti
advance: *in advance* in anticipo
advertisement la pubblicità
(in newspaper) l'annuncio m
to advise consigliare
A&E il pronto soccorso

aerial l'antenna f
aeroplane l'aeroplano m
aerosol l'aerosol m
afraid: *to be afraid* avere paura
after dopo
afternoon il pomeriggio
in the afternoon di pomeriggio
this afternoon oggi pomeriggio
tomorrow afternoon domani
 pomeriggio
aftershave il dopobarba
again ancora; di nuovo
against contro
age l'età f
agency l'agenzia f
ago fa
a week ago una settimana fa
to agree essere d'accordo
agreement l'accordo m
AIDS l'AIDS m
air ambulance l'elisoccorso m
airbag l'airbag m
airbed il materassino gonfiabile
air-conditioning l'aria condizionata f
air freshener il deodorante per
 l'ambiente
airline la linea aerea
air mail: *by air mail* per via aerea
airplane l'aeroplano m
airport l'aeroporto m
airport bus l'autobus per l'aeroporto m
air ticket il biglietto d'aereo
aisle il corridoio
alarm l'allarme m
alarm clock la sveglia
alcohol l'alcool m
alcohol-free analcolico(a)
alcoholic alcolico(a)
all tutto(a)
allergic to allergico(a) a
I'm allergic to... sono allergico(a) a...
allergy l'allergia f
to allow permettere

all right (agreed) va bene
are you all right? sta bene?
almost quasi
alone solo(a)
Alps le Alpi
already già
also anche
altar l'altare *m*
aluminium foil la carta stagnola
always sempre
a.m. del mattino
am: *I am* sono
amber (light) il giallo
ambulance l'ambulanza *f*
America l'America *f*
American americano(a)
anaesthetic l'anestetico *m*
general anaesthetic l'anestesia
  generale
local anaesthetic l'anestetico locale
anchor l'ancora *f*
ancient antico(a)
and e
angina l'angina pectoris *f*
angry arrabbiato(a)
animal l'animale *m*
ankle la caviglia
anniversary l'anniversario *m*
to announce annunciare
announcement l'annuncio *m*
annual annuale
another un altro/un'altra
another beer un'altra birra
another coffee un altro caffè
answer la risposta
to answer rispondere
answerphone la segreteria telefonica
antacid l'antiacido *m*
antenna l'antenna *f*
antibiotic l'antibiotico *m*
antifreeze l'antigelo *m*
antihistamine l'antistaminico
antiques i pezzi d'antiquariato
antique shop il negozio d'antiquariato
antiseptic l'antisettico *m*
any dei/delle/degli (di)
have you any apples? ha delle mele?

I haven't any money non ho soldi
anyone qualcuno; chiunque
anything qualcosa; qualsiasi cosa
apartment l'appartamento *m*
appendicitis l'appendicite *f*
apple la mela
application form il modulo di domanda
appointment l'appuntamento *m*
I have an appointment ho un
  appuntamento
approximately circa
apricots le albicocche
April aprile
architect *m/f* l'architetto
architecture l'architettura *f*
arm il braccio
armbands (swimming) i braccioli
armchair la poltrona
to arrange sistemare
to arrest arrestare
arrivals (plane, train) gli arrivi
to arrive arrivare
art l'arte *f*
art gallery la galleria d'arte; la pinacoteca
arthritis l'artrite *f*
artificial finto(a); artificiale
artist *m/f* l'artista
ashtray il portacenere
to ask (question) domandare
(for something) chiedere
asleep: *he/she is asleep* dorme
asparagus gli asparagi
aspirin l'aspirina *f*
asthma l'asma *f*
I have asthma ho l'asma
at a; (@) chiocciola; at
at home a casa
at once subito
at night di notte
at 8 o'clock alle otto
ATM il Bancomat®
to attack aggredire
attractive attraente
aubergine la melanzana
auction l'asta *f*
audience il pubblico
August agosto

aunt la zia
au pair la ragazza alla pari
Australia l'Australia *f*
Australian australiano(a)
author *m/f* l'autore/l'autrice
automatic automatico(a)
automatic car la macchina con cambio automatico
auto-teller il Bancomat®
autumn l'autunno *m*
available disponibile
avalanche la valanga
avenue il viale
average medio(a)
to avoid evitare
awake: to be awake essere sveglio(a)
away via
awful terribile
awning (for caravan etc) il tendalino
axle (car) l'asse *m*

B

baby il/la bambino(a)
baby food gli alimenti per bambini
baby milk il latte per bambini
baby wipes le salviettine per bambini
baby's bottle il biberon
babyseat (in car) il seggiolino per bambini
babysitter il/la babysitter
back (of body) la schiena
backpack lo zaino
bacon la pancetta
bad (weather, news) brutto(a)
(food) andato(a) a male
badminton il badminton .
bag la borsa
baggage i bagagli
baggage allowance il peso consentito di bagaglio
baggage reclaim il ritiro bagagli
bait (for fishing) l'esca *m*
baked al forno
baker's la panetteria; il panificio
balcony il balcone
bald (person) calvo(a)
(tyre) liscio(a)

ball (large) il pallone
(small) la pallina
ballet il balletto
balloon il palloncino
banana la banana
band (musical) la banda
(rock, pop) il gruppo
bandage la benda
bank la banca
(river) la riva
bank account il conto in banca
banknote la banconota
bankrupt fallito(a)
bar il bar
bar of chocolate la tavoletta di cioccolato
barbecue la grigliata
to have a barbecue fare una grigliata
barber il barbiere
to bark abbaiare
barn il granaio
barrel (wine/beer) il barile
basement il seminterrato
basil il basilico
basket il cestino
basketball la pallacanestro
bat (baseball, etc) la mazza
bath il bagno
to have a bath fare il bagno
bathing cap la cuffia
bathroom il bagno
with bathroom con bagno
battery (radio, etc) la pila
(car) la batteria
(rechargeable) la batteria ricaricabile
bay (along coast) la baia
B&B il bed & breakfast
to be essere
beach la spiaggia
naturist beach la spiaggia per nudisti
private beach la spiaggia privata
sandy beach la spiaggia di sabbia
beach hut la cabina
bean il fagiolo
beard la barba
beautiful bello(a)
beauty salon l'istituto di bellezza *m*

because perché
to become diventare
bed il letto
double bed il letto matrimoniale
single bed il letto singolo
sofa bed il divano letto
twin beds a due letti
bed and breakfast il bed & breakfast
bed clothes le coperte e le lenzuola
bedroom la camera da letto
bee l'ape *f*
beef il manzo
beer la birra
draught beer la birra alla spina
before prima di
before breakfast prima di colazione
to begin cominciare
behind dietro
beige beige
to believe credere
bell (church) la campana
(doorbell) il campanello
to belong to appartenere a
it belongs to... appartiene a...
below sotto
belt la cintura
bend (in road) la curva
berth (train, ship) la cuccetta
beside (next to) accanto a
beside the bank accanto alla banca
best: *the best* il/la migliore
bet la scommessa
to bet scommettere
better (than) meglio (di)
between fra
to beware of stare attento(a) a
beyond oltre
bib (baby's) il bavaglino
bicycle la bicicletta; la bici
by bicycle in bicicletta
bicycle pump la pompa da bicicletta
bicycle repair kit il kit per riparare la bici
bidet il bidet
big grande
bigger (than) più grande (di)
bike (pushbike) la bici
(motorbike) la moto

bike lock il lucchetto della bici
bikini il bikini
bill (hotel, restaurant) il conto
(for work done) la fattura
(gas, telephone) la bolletta
bin (dustbin) il bidone
bin liner il sacco per la pattumiera
binoculars il binocolo
bird l'uccello *m*
biro la biro
birth la nascita
birth certificate il certificato di nascita
birthday il compleanno
happy birthday! auguri! buon compleanno
my birthday is on... il mio compleanno è il...
birthday card il biglietto d'auguri di compleanno
birthday present il regalo di compleanno
biscuits i biscotti
bit il pezzo
a bit un po'
bite (of insect) la puntura
(of dog) la morsicatura
a bite to eat qualcosa da mangiare
to bite (animal) mordere
(insect) pungere
bitten morso(a)
(by insect) punto(a)
bitter (taste) amaro(a)
black nero(a)
black ice il ghiaccio sulla strada
blank (disk, tape) *adj* vuoto(a); vergine
blanket la coperta
bleach la candeggina
to bleed sanguinare
blender il frullatore
blind (person) cieco(a)
(window) la veneziana; la tapparella
blister la vescica
block of flats il palazzo; il condominio
blocked (pipe, sink) tappato(a)
(road) bloccato(a)
blond (person) biondo(a)

blood il sangue
blood group il gruppo sanguigno
blood pressure la pressione sanguigna
blood test l'analisi del sangue *f*
blouse la camicetta
blowout (of tyre) *n* lo scoppio (di pneumatico)
to blow-dry asciugare con il fon
blue (light) azzurro(a)
dark blue blu scuro
light blue azzurro(a)
blunt (knife, blade) non taglia
BMX la bici da cross
boar il cinghiale
to board (plain, train, etc) salire su
boarding card/pass la carta d'imbarco
boarding house la pensione
boat la barca; il battello
(rowing) la barca a remi
boat trip la gita in battello
body il corpo
(dead) il cadavere
to boil bollire
boiler la caldaia
boiled bollito(a)
bomb la bomba
bone l'osso *m*
fish bone la spina di pesce
bonfire il falò
bonnet (car) il cofano
book il libro
book of tickets il blocchetto di biglietti
to book prenotare
booking la prenotazione
booking office (train) la biglietteria
bookshop la libreria
booster seat (car) il seggiolino per bambini
boot (of car) il bagagliaio
boots (long) gli stivali
(ankle) gli stivaletti
border (of country) la frontiera
boring noioso(a)
born: *to be born* essere nato(a)
to borrow prendere in prestito

boss il capo
both tutti e due
bottle la bottiglia
a bottle of wine una bottiglia di vino
a half-bottle una mezza bottiglia
bottle opener l'apribottiglie
bowl (cereal, soup) la scodella
bow tie la cravatta a farfalla
box la scatola
box office il botteghino
boxer shorts i boxer
boy (young child) il bambino
(teenage) il ragazzo
boyfriend il ragazzo
bra il reggiseno
bracelet il braccialetto
brain il cervello
to brake frenare
brake cable il cavo del freno
brake fluid il liquido dei freni
brake light il fanalino dello stop
brake pads le pastiglie dei freni
brakes i freni
branch (of tree) il ramo
(of bank, etc) la succursale
brand (make) la marca
brass l'ottone *m*
brave coraggioso(a)
bread il pane
brown bread il pane integrale
French bread il filoncino
sliced bread il pancarré
bread roll il panino
to break rompere
breakable fragile
breakdown (car) il guasto
(nervous) l'esaurimento nervoso *m*
breakdown van il carro attrezzi
breakfast la (prima) colazione
breast il seno
to breast-feed allattare
to breathe respirare
brick il mattone
bride la sposa
bridegroom lo sposo
bridge il ponte
briefcase la cartella

Brillo-pad la paglietta
to bring portare
Britain la Gran Bretagna
British britannico(a)
broadband n la banda larga
broccoli i broccoli
brochure l'opuscolo m
broken rotto(a)
broken down (car, etc) guasto(a)
bronchitis la bronchite
bronze il bronzo
brooch la spilla
broom (brush) la scopa
brother il fratello
brother-in-law il cognato
brown marrone
bruise il livido
brush la spazzola
bubble bath il bagnoschiuma
bucket il secchiello
buffet car il vagone ristorante
to build costruire
building l'edificio m
bulb (lightbulb) la lampadina
bumbag il marsupio
bumper (on car) il paraurti
bunch (of flowers) il mazzo di fiori
(of grapes) il grappolo d'uva
bungee jumping il bungee jumping
bureau de change l'agenzia di cambio f
burger l'hamburger m
burglar il/la ladro(a)
burglar alarm l'antifurto m
to burn bruciare
(CD) masterizzare
bus l'autobus m
bus pass la tessera dell'autobus
bus station la stazione delle autolinee
bus stop la fermata (dell'autobus)
bus ticket il biglietto d'autobus
business gli affari
on business per affari
business card il biglietto da visita
business centre il centro affari
business class la business class
businessman/woman l'uomo/
la donna d'affari

business trip il viaggio d'affari
busy occupato(a); impegnato(a)
but ma; però
butcher's il macellaio
butter il burro
button il bottone
to buy comprare
by (next to) accanto a
by bus in autobus
by car in macchina
by ship in nave
by train in treno
bypass (road) la circonvallazione

C

cab (taxi) il taxi
cabaret il cabaret
cabin (on boat) la cabina
cabin crew l'equipaggio di bordo m
cablecar la funivia
café il bar
internet café l'internet café m;
  l'internet point m
cafetière la caffettiera
cake (big) la torta
(small) il pasticcino
cake shop la pasticceria
calculator la calcolatrice
calendar il calendario
call (phone call) la chiamata
to call chiamare
(phone) telefonare
calm calmo(a)
camcorder la videocamera
camera la macchina fotografica
digital camera la fotocamera digitale
camera case la custodia della
  macchina fotografica
camera phone il videofonino
to camp campeggiare
camping gas il gas da campeggio
camping stove il fornellino da
  campeggio
campsite il campeggio
can il barattolo; la scatola
can (to be able) potere
can I...? posso...?

can we...? possiamo...?
I can posso
we can possiamo
I cannot non posso
we cannot non possiamo
Canada il Canada
Canadian canadese
canal il canale
to cancel cancellare; annullare
cancellation la cancellazione
cancer il cancro
candle la candela
canoe la canoa
to canoe andare in canoa
can opener l'apriscatole *m*
cap (hat) il berretto
(diaphragm) il diaframma
capital (city) la capitale
cappuccino il cappuccino *m*
car la macchina; l'auto *m*
car alarm l'antifurto *m*
car ferry il traghetto
car hire l'autonoleggio *m*
car insurance l'assicurazione della
   macchina *f*
car keys le chiavi della macchina
car park il parcheggio
car parts i pezzi di ricambio
car port il ricovero per auto
car radio l'autoradio *f*
car seat (for children) il seggiolino per
   bambini
carrots le carote
carwash l'autolavaggio *m*
carafe la caraffa
caravan la roulotte
card (greetings) il biglietto d'auguri
(business) il biglietto da visita
(playing cards) le carte da gioco
cardboard il cartone
cardigan il cardigan
careful attento(a)
to be careful fare attenzione
carpet (fitted) la moquette
(rug) il tappeto
carriage (railway) il vagone
carrots le carote

to carry portare
carton il cartone
case (suitcase) la valigia
cash i contanti
to cash (cheque) incassare
cash desk la cassa
cash machine il Bancomat®
cashier il/la cassiere(a)
cashpoint il Bancomat®
casino il casinò
casserole dish la pirofila
cassette la cassetta VHS
cassette player il registratore VHS
castle il castello
casualty department il pronto
   soccorso
cat il gatto
cat food il cibo per gatti
CAT scan la TAC
catacombs le catacombe
catalogue il catalogo
catalytic converter il catalizzatore
to catch (train, etc) prendere
cathedral il duomo
Catholic cattolico(a)
cauliflower il cavolfiore
cave la grotta
cavity (in tooth) la carie
CD il CD
(blank) il CD vuoto
CD player il lettore CD
ceiling il soffitto
celery il sedano
cellar la cantina
cellphone il cellulare
cemetery il cimitero
cent (euro) il centesimo
centimetre il centimetro
central centrale
central heating il riscaldamento
central locking (car) la chiusura
   centralizzata
centre il centro
century il secolo
ceramics la ceramica
cereal (for breakfast) i cereali
certificate il certificato

chain la catena
chair la sedia
chairlift la seggiovia
chalet lo chalet
challenge la sfida
chambermaid la cameriera
Champagne lo Champagne
change il cambio
(small coins) gli spiccioli
(money returned) il resto
to change: to change money cambiare soldi
to change clothes cambiarsi
to change train cambiare treno
changing room lo spogliatoio
Channel (English) la Manica
chapel la cappella
charcoal il carbone
charge (fee) la tariffa
(for mobile, etc) la carica
I've run out of charge mi si è scaricata la batteria
to charge (mobile, etc) (ri)caricare
I need to charge my phone devo ricaricare il telefonino
to charge addebitare
charge it to my account lo metta sul mio conto
charge card carta di credito (del supermercato)
charger (for battery) il caricabatterie
charter flight il volo charter
chatroom (internet) la chatroom
cheap economico(a)
cheaper più economico(a)
cheap rate (phone) la tariffa economica
to check controllare
to check in (airport) fare il check-in
(at hotel) firmare il registro
check-in il check-in
cheek la guancia
cheers! salute!; cin-cin!
cheese il formaggio
chef il cuoco
chemist's la farmacia
cheque l'assegno m
cheque book il libretto degli assegni

cheque card la carta assegni
cherries le ciliegie
chess gli scacchi
chest (of body) il petto
chewing gum la gomma da masticare
chicken il pollo
chicken breast il petto di pollo
chickenpox la varicella
chilli il peperoncino
child il/la bambino(a)
children (small) i bambini
(older children) i ragazzi
for children per bambini
child safety seat (car) il seggiolino di sicurezza per bambini
chimney il camino
chin il mento
china la porcellana
chips (french fries) le patatine fritte
chiropodist il podologo
chocolate il cioccolato
chocolates i cioccolatini
choir il coro
choice la scelta
to choose scegliere
chop (meat) la costoletta
chopping board il tagliere
christening il battesimo
Christian name il nome di battesimo
Christmas il Natale
Merry Christmas! Buon Natale!
Christmas card il biglietto d'auguri natalizi
Christmas Eve la vigilia di Natale
church la chiesa
cigar il sigaro
cigarette la sigaretta
cigarette lighter l'accendino
cigarette papers le cartine
cinema il cinema
circle (theatre) la galleria
circuit breaker il salvavita
circus il circo
cistern la cisterna
(of toilet) la cassetta dell'acqua
city la città
city centre il centro città

class: *first class* prima classe
second class seconda classe
clean pulito(a)
to clean pulire
cleaner (person) l'addetto(a) alle pulizie
cleanser il detergente
clear chiaro(a)
client il/la cliente
cliff (on coast) la scogliera
(mountain) la rupe
to climb scalare
climbing l'alpinismo *m*
climbing boots gli scarponi da montagna
Clingfilm® la pellicola per alimenti
clinic la clinica
cloakroom il guardaroba
clock l'orologio *m*
to close chiudere
closed (shop, etc) chiuso(a)
cloth il panno
clothes i vestiti
clothes peg la molletta
clothes shop il negozio d'abbigliamento
cloudy nuvoloso(a)
club il club
clutch (car) la frizione
clutch fluid il liquido della frizione
coach il pullman
coach station la stazione dei pullman
coach trip la gita in pullman
coal il carbone
coast la costa
coastguard il guardacoste
coat il cappotto
coat hanger la gruccia
cockroach lo scarafaggio
cocktail il cocktail
cocktail bar il cocktail bar
cocoa il cacao
code il codice
coffee (espresso) il caffè
black coffee il caffè americano
cappuccino il cappuccino
coffee shop la caffetteria
instant coffee il caffè solubile
white coffee il caffellatte; il caffè
macchiato

coil (IUD) la spirale
coin la moneta
Coke® la Coca®
colander lo scolapasta
cold freddo(a)
I'm cold ho freddo
it's cold fa freddo
cold (illness) il raffreddore
I have a cold ho il raffreddore
cold sore l'herpes *m*
Coliseum il Colosseo
collar il colletto
collar bone la clavicola
colleague il/la collega
to collect raccogliere
(to collect someone) andare a prendere
qualcuno
collection (of stamps) la collezione
(of letters) la levata
(of rubbish) la rimozione
colour il colore
colour-blind daltonico(a)
colour film (for camera) la pellicola
a colori
comb il pettine
to come venire
(to arrive) arrivare
to come back tornare
to come in entrare
come in! avanti!
comedy la commedia
comfortable comodo(a)
company (firm) la ditta
compartment lo scompartimento
compass la bussola
to complain fare un reclamo
complaint il reclamo
complete completo(a)
to complete (finish) finire
(form) riempire
compulsory obbligatorio(a)
computer il computer
computer disk il dischetto
computer game il videogioco
computer program il programma di
computer
concert il concerto

concert hall la sala da concerti
concession la riduzione
concussion la commozione cerebrale
condensed milk il latte condensato
conditioner il balsamo
condoms i preservativi
conductor (on bus) il bigliettaio
cone il cono
conference il congresso
to confirm confermare
confirmation (of flight, etc) la conferma
confused confuso(a)
congratulations le congratulazioni
connection (train, etc) la coincidenza
constipated stitico(a)
consulate il consolato
to consult consultare
to contact mettersi in contatto con
contact details gli estremi
contact lens cleaner il liquido per lenti a contatto
contact lenses le lenti a contatto
to continue continuare
contraceptive l'anticoncezionale
contract il contratto
convenient: is it convenient? conviene?
convulsions le convulsioni
to cook cucinare
cooked cotto(a)
cooker la cucina
cookies i biscotti
cool fresco(a)
cool-box (picnic) la borsa termica
copper il rame
copy la copia
to copy copiare
cordless phone il cordless
cork il tappo
corkscrew il cavatappi
corner l'angolo m
cornflakes i cornflakes
corridor il corridoio
cosmetics i cosmetici
to cost costare
how much does it cost? quanto costa?

costume (swimming) il costume da bagno
cot il lettino
cottage il cottage
cotton il cotone
cotton bud il cotton fioc®
cotton wool il cotone idrofilo
couchette la cuccetta
cough la tosse
to cough tossire
cough mixture lo sciroppo per la tosse
cough sweets le pasticche per la tosse
counter (in shop, etc) il banco
country (not town) la campagna
(nation) il paese
countryside la campagna
couple (two people) la coppia
a couple of... un paio di...
courgettes gli zucchini
courier service il corriere
course (of meal) il piatto
(of study) il corso
cousin il/la cugino(a)
cover charge il coperto
cow la mucca
crafts l'artigianato m
craft fair la fiera dell'artigianato
craftsperson l'artigiano(a)
cramps i crampi
crash (car) lo scontro
to crash (car) avere un incidente
crash helmet il casco
cream (lotion) la crema
(dairy) la panna
soured cream la panna acida
whipped cream la panna montata
creche il presepe
credit (on mobile phone) n credito
credit card la carta di credito
crime il reato
crisps le patatine
croissant la brioche
to cross (road) attraversare
cross la croce
cross-country skiing lo sci di fondo
crossing (sea, lake) la traversata
crossroads l'incrocio m

crossword puzzle il cruciverba
crowd la folla
crowded affollato(a)
crown la corona
cruise la crociera
crutches le grucce
to cry (weep) piangere
crystal (made of) di cristallo
cucumber il cetriolo
cufflinks i gemelli
cul-de-sac il vicolo cieco
cup la tazza
cupboard l'armadio *m*
curlers i bigodini
currant l'uva sultanina
current la corrente
curtain la tenda
cushion il cuscino
custom (tradition) l'abitudine; l'usanza
customer il/la cliente
customs (duty) la dogana
cut il taglio
to cut tagliare
cutlery le posate
to cycle andare in bicicletta
cycle track la pista ciclabile
cycling il ciclismo
cyst la cisti
cystitis la cistite

D

daily (each day) ogni giorno; quotidiano(a)
dairy produce i latticini
dam la diga
damage il danno
damp umido(a)
dance il ballo
to dance ballare
danger il pericolo
dangerous pericoloso(a)
dark (colour) scuro(a)
(night) buio(a)
after dark a notte fatta
date la data
date of birth la data di nascita
daughter la figlia

daughter-in-law la nuora
dawn l'alba *f*
day il giorno
(span of time) la giornata
every day ogni giorno
per day al giorno
dead morto(a)
deaf sordo(a)
dear caro(a)
debts i debiti
debit card la carta di addebito
decaffeinated decaffeinato(a)
have you decaff coffee? ha del decaffeinato?
December dicembre
deckchair la sedia a sdraio
to declare dichiarare
nothing to declare niente da dichiarare
deep profondo(a)
deep freeze il surgelatore
deer il cervo
to defrost scongelare
to de-ice sbrinare
delay il ritardo
how long is the delay? di quant'è il ritardo?
delayed: to be delayed (flight) subire un ritardo
delicatessen il negozio di specialità gastronomiche
delicious delizioso(a)
demonstration la manifestazione
dental floss il filo interdentale
dentist il/la dentista
dentures la dentiera
deodorant il deodorante
to depart partire
department il reparto
department store il grande magazzino
departure la partenza
departure lounge la sala partenze
deposit il deposito
to describe descrivere
description la descrizione
desk la scrivania
(information, etc) il banco
dessert il dolce

details i dettagli
detergent il detersivo
detour la deviazione
to develop (photos) sviluppare
diabetes il diabete
diabetic diabetico(a)
I'm diabetic sono diabetico(a)
to dial fare il numero
dialect il dialetto
dialling code il prefisso telefonico
dialling tone il segnale di libero
diamond il diamante
diapers i pannolini
diaphragm il diaframma
diarrhoea la diarrea
diary l'agenda f
dice il dado
dictionary il dizionario; il vocabolario
to die morire
diesel il gasolio
diet la dieta
I'm on a diet sono a dieta
special diet una dieta specifica
different diverso(a)
difficult difficile
digital camera la fotocamera digitale
to dilute diluire
dinghy (rubber) il canotto
dining room la sala da pranzo
dinner (evening meal) la cena
to have dinner cenare
dinner jacket lo smoking
direct (train, etc) diretto(a)
directions le indicazioni
to ask for directions chiedere la strada
directory (telephone) l'elenco
  telefonico
directory enquiries il servizio
  informazioni
dirty sporco(a)
disability l'handicap m
disabled (person) disabile;
  handicappato(a)
to disagree non essere d'accordo
to disappear scomparire
disaster il disastro
disco la discoteca

discount lo sconto
to discover scoprire
disease la malattia
dishtowel lo strofinaccio dei piatti
dishwasher la lavastoviglie
disinfectant il disinfettante
disk il disco
to dislocate (joint) lussarsi
disposable (camera) usa e getta
distance la distanza
distilled water l'acqua distillata f
district (of town) il quartiere
to disturb disturbare
to dive tuffarsi
diversion la deviazione
diving i tuffi
divorced divorziato(a)
DIY shop il negozio di bricolage
dizzy: *to be dizzy* avere capogiri
to do fare
doctor il medico/la dottoressa
documents i documenti
dog il cane
dog food il cibo per cani
dog lead il guinzaglio
doll la bambola
dollars i dollari
domestic (flight) nazionale
donor card la tessera dell'A.I.D.O.
door la porta
doorbell il campanello
double doppio(a)
double bed il letto matrimoniale
double room la camera doppia
down: *to go down* scendere
Down's syndrome la sindrome
  di Down
he/she has Down's syndrome è Down
downstairs giù; dabbasso
drain lo scarico
draught (of air) la corrente (d'aria)
there's a draught c'è corrente
draught lager la birra alla spina
drawer il cassetto
drawing il disegno
dress il vestito
to dress (oneself) vestirsi

dressing (for food) il condimento
(for wound) la fasciatura
dressing gown la vestaglia
drill (tool) il trapano
drink (soft) la bibita
to drink bere
drinking water l'acqua potabile *f*
to drive guidare
driver (of car) il guidatore
(race) il pilota
driving licence la patente
drought la siccità
to drown affogare
drug (medicine) il farmaco
(narcotics) la droga
drunk ubriaco(a)
dry secco(a); asciutto(a)
to dry asciugare
dry-cleaner's la tintoria; il lavasecco
dummy (for baby) la tettarella; il ciuccio
during durante
dust la polvere
duster lo straccio

dustpan and brush la paletta e
lo scopino
duty-free esente da dogana
duvet il piumino
duvet cover il copripiumone
DVD il DVD
DVD player il lettore DVD
dye la tinta
dynamo la dinamo

E

each ogni
ear l'orecchio *m*
earache il mal d'orecchi
earlier più presto
early presto
to earn guadagnare
earphones le cuffie
earplugs i tappi per le orecchie
earrings gli orecchini
earth la terra
earthquake il terremoto
east l'est *m*
Easter la Pasqua

Happy Easter! Buona Pasqua!
easy facile
to eat mangiare
ecological ecologico(a)
economy (class) la classe turistica
eco-tourism l'ecoturismo *m*
egg l'uovo *m*
eggs le uova
fried egg l'uovo fritto
hard-boiled egg l'uovo sodo
scrambled eggs le uova strapazzate
soft-boiled egg l'uovo alla coque
either ... or o ... o
elastic band l'elastico *m*
Elastoplast il cerotto
elbow il gomito
electric elettrico(a)
electric blanket la coperta elettrica
electrician l'elettricista *m/f*
electricity l'elettricità *f*
electricity meter il contatore
dell'elettricità
electric razor il rasoio elettrico
electric shock la scossa
electric toothbrush lo spazzolino da
denti elettrico
electronic elettronico(a)
electronic organizer l'agenda
elettronica *f*
elevator l'ascensore *m*
e-mail la posta elettronica; l'e-mail *f*
to e-mail s.o. mandare un'e-mail a
qualcuno
e-mail address l'indirizzo; l'indirizzo
e-mail
embassy l'ambasciata *f*
emergency l'emergenza *f*
emergency exit l'uscita d'emergenza *f*
emery board la limetta per le unghie
empty vuoto(a)
end la fine
engaged (to be married) fidanzato(a)
(phone, toilet, etc) occupato(a)
engine il motore
England l'Inghilterra *f*
English inglese
(language) l'inglese *m*

to enjoy divertirsi
(to like) piacere
enjoy your meal! buon appetito!
I enjoy swimming mi piace nuotare
I enjoyed the trip la gita mi è piaciuta
enough abbastanza
that's enough basta così
enquiry desk il banco informazioni
to enter entrare
entertainment il divertimento
entrance l'entrata *f*; l'ingresso *m*
entrance fee il biglietto d'ingresso
envelope la busta
epileptic epilettico(a)
epileptic fit la crisi epilettica
equal uguale; pari
equipment l'attrezzatura *f*
eraser la gomma per cancellare
error l'errore *m*
eruption l'eruzione *f*
escalator la scala mobile
to escape fuggire
essential essenziale
estate agent's l'agenzia immobiliare *f*
estate car la station wagon *f*
euro l'euro *m*
euro cent il centesimo
Europe l'Europa *f*
European europeo(a)
European Union l'Unione Europea *f*
eve la vigilia
evening la sera
in the evening la sera
this evening stasera
tomorrow evening domani sera
evening dress l'abito da sera *m*
evening meal la cena
every ogni; ciascuno; tutti
everyone tutti
everything tutto
everywhere dappertutto
examination l'esame *m*
example: *for example* per esempio
excellent ottimo(a)
except salvo
excess baggage il bagaglio in eccedenza
to exchange cambiare

exchange rate il cambio
exciting emozionante
excursion l'escursione *f*
to excuse scusare
excuse me! (sorry) mi scusi!
(when passing) permesso!
exercise l'esercizio *m*
exhaust pipe il tubo di scappamento
exhibition la mostra
exit l'uscita *f*
expenses le spese
expensive costoso(a); caro(a)
expert l'esperto(a)
to expire (ticket, etc) scadere
to explain spiegare
explosion l'esplosione *f*
to export esportare
express (train) l'espresso *m*
express (parcel, etc) espresso(a)
extension (phone) l'interno *m*
(electrical) la prolunga
extra (spare) in più
(more) supplementare
an extra bed un letto in più
eye l'occhio *m*
eyebrows le sopracciglia
eye drops il collirio
eyelashes le ciglia
eye shadow l'ombretto *m*

F

fabric la stoffa
face la faccia
face cloth il guanto di spugna
facial la pulizia del viso
facilities (leisure facilities) le attrezzature
factor (sunblock) fattore di protezione
factory la fabbrica
to fail fallire
to faint svenire
fainted svenuto(a)
fair (just) giusto(a)
(blond) biondo(a)
fair (trade) la fiera
(funfair) il luna park
fake falso(a)

fall (autumn) l'autunno m
to fall cadere
he/she has fallen è caduto(a)
false teeth la dentiera
family la famiglia
famous famoso(a)
fan (hand-held) il ventaglio
(electric) il ventilatore
(football) il/la tifoso(a)
fan belt la cinghia della ventola
fancy dress il costume; la maschera
far lontano(a)
is it far? è lontano?
fare la tariffa
farm la fattoria
farmer l'agricoltore m
farmhouse la fattoria
fashionable alla moda
fast veloce
too fast troppo veloce
to fasten (seatbelt, etc) allacciare
fat grasso(a)
(noun) il grasso

134

saturated fats i grassi saturi
unsaturated fats i grassi insaturi
father il padre
father-in-law il suocero
fault (defect) il difetto
it's not my fault non è colpa mia
favour il favore
favourite preferito(a)
fax il fax
by fax per fax
to fax mandare un fax
February febbraio
to feed dare da mangiare
to feel sentire; sentirsi
I don't feel well non mi sento bene
I feel sick ho la nausea
feet i piedi
felt-tip pen il pennarello
female femmina; femminile
ferry il traghetto
festival la festa
to fetch (bring) portare
(to go and get) andare a prendere
fever la febbre

few pochi
a few alcuni
fiancé(e) il/la fidanzato(a)
field il campo
to fight combattere; lottare
file (folder) il raccoglitore
(computer) il file m
to fill riempire
to fill in (form) compilare
fill it up! (petrol) il pieno!
fillet il filetto
filling (dental) l'otturazione f
film (at cinema) il film
(for camera) la pellicola
Filofax® l'agenda f
filter il filtro
to find trovare
fine (to be paid) la multa
finger il dito
to finish finire
finished finito(a)
fire il fuoco; l'incendio m
fire! al fuoco!
fire alarm l'allarme antincendio m
fire brigade i vigili del fuoco
fire engine l'autopompa f
fire escape la scala antincendio
fire extinguisher l'estintore
fireplace il caminetto
fireworks i fuochi d'artificio
firm (company) l'azienda f; la ditta
first primo(a)
first aid il pronto soccorso
first aid kit la cassetta di pronto
 soccorso
first class la prima classe
first name il nome di battesimo
fish il pesce
to fish pescare
fisherman il pescatore
fishing permit la licenza di pesca
fishing rod la canna da pesca
fishmonger's la pescheria
to fit (clothes) andare bene
it doesn't fit non va bene
fit (seizure) l'attacco m
to fix riparare; sistemare

can you fix it? può ripararlo?
fizzy gassato(a)
flag la bandiera
flame la fiamma
flash (for camera) il flash
flashlight la pila; la torcia elettrica
flask (thermos) il thermos
flat l'appartamento *m*
flat piatto(a)
flat battery la batteria scarica
flat tyre la gomma a terra
flavour il gusto
what flavour? che gusto?
flaw il difetto
fleas le pulci
fleece il pail *m*
flesh la carne
flex il filo flessibile
flight il volo
flip flops le infradito
flippers le pinne
flood l'alluvione *f*
flash flood l'inondazione *f*
floor (of building) il piano
(of room) il pavimento
on the ground floor al pianterreno
on the first floor al primo piano
on the second floor al secondo piano
what floor? a che piano?
floorcloth lo straccio per pavimenti
Florence Firenze
florist's shop il fioraio
flour la farina
flowers i fiori
flu l'influenza *f*
fly la mosca
to fly volare
flysheet (tent) la tenda da campo
fog la nebbia
foggy nebbioso(a)
foil (silver paper) la carta stagnola
to fold ripiegare
to follow seguire
food il cibo
food poisoning l'intossicazione
  alimentare *f*
foot il piede

on foot a piedi
football il calcio; il pallone
football match la partita di calcio
football pitch il campo di calcio
football player il calciatore
footpath il sentiero
for per
for me/us per me/noi
for him/her per lui/lei
for you per te/lei/voi
forbidden proibito(a)
forehead la fronte
foreign straniero(a)
foreigner lo/la straniero(a)
forest la foresta
forever per sempre
to forget dimenticare
fork (for eating) la forchetta
(in road) il bivio
form (document) il modulo
fortnight quindici giorni
forward avanti
foul (football) il fallo
fountain la fontana
four-wheel drive a quattro ruote
  motrici
fox la volpe
fracture la frattura
fragile fragile
fragrance la fragranza
frame (picture) la cornice
France la Francia
free (not occupied) libero(a)
(costing nothing) gratis
free-range eggs le uova di polli
  ruspanti *fpl*
freezer il congelatore
French francese
(language) il francese
French fries le patatine fritte
frequent frequente
fresh fresco(a)
fresh water l'acqua dolce *f*
Friday il venerdì
fridge il frigorifero
fried fritto(a)
friend l'amico(a)

friendly amichevole
frog la rana
from da
from England dall'Inghilterra
from Scotland dalla Scozia
front davanti
in front of... di fronte a...
front door la porta d'ingresso
frost la brina
frozen (food) surgelato(a)
fruit la frutta
dried fruit la frutta secca
fruit juice il succo di frutta
fruit salad la macedonia
to fry friggere
frying-pan la padella
fuel (petrol) la benzina
fuel gauge la spia della benzina
fuel pump la pompa
fuel tank il serbatoio della benzina
full pieno(a)
(occupied) completo(a)
full board la pensione completa
fumes (of car) i gas di scarico
fun il divertimento
funeral il funerale
funfair il luna park
funny (amusing) divertente
fur il pelo
furnished ammobiliato(a)
furniture i mobili
fuse il fusibile
fuse box la scatola dei fusibili
future il futuro

G

gallery la galleria
game il gioco (meat) la selvaggina
garage (private) il garage
(for repairs) l'autofficina f
(for petrol) la stazione di servizio
garden il giardino
garlic l'aglio m
gas il gas
gas cooker la cucina a gas
gas cylinder la bombola del gas
gastritis la gastrite

gate il cancello
(airport) l'uscita f
gay (person) gay
gear (car) la marcia
first gear la prima
second gear la seconda
third gear la terza
fourth gear la quarta
neutral folle
reverse la retromarcia
gearbox il cambio
gear lever la leva del cambio
generous generoso(a)
gents' (toilet) la toilette (per uomini)
genuine (leather, silver) vero(a)
(antique, etc) autentico(a)
German tedesco(a)
(language) il tedesco
German measles la rosolia
Germany la Germania
to get (obtain) ottenere
(to receive) ricevere
(to fetch) prendere
to get in/on (vehicle) salire in/su
to get off (bus, etc) scendere da
gift il regalo
gift shop il negozio di souvenir
gigabyte il gigabyte m
gigahertz il gigahertz m
girl (young child) la bambina
(teenage) la ragazza
girlfriend la ragazza
to give dare
to give back restituire
glacier il ghiacciaio
glass (substance) il vetro
(for drinking) il bicchiere
a glass of water un bicchiere d'acqua
a glass of wine un bicchiere di vino
glasses (specs) gli occhiali
glasses case la custodia degli occhiali
gloves i guanti
glue la colla
gluten il glutine m
GM-free privo(a) di organismi
geneticamente modificati (OGM)
to go andare

I'm going to... vado a...
we're going to... andiamo a...
to go back ritornare
to go in entrare in
to go out (leave) uscire
goat la capra
God Dio
goggles gli occhialini
(for skiing) gli occhiali da sci
gold l'oro *m*
golf il golf
golf ball la pallina da golf
golf clubs le mazze da golf
golf course il campo da golf
good buono(a)
(pleasant) bello(a)
very good ottimo(a)
good afternoon buon giorno
(after 5pm) buona sera
goodbye arrivederci
good day buon giorno
good evening buona sera
good morning buon giorno
good night buona notte
goose l'oca *f*
GPS (global positioning system) il Gps
gram il grammo
grandchild il/la nipote
granddaughter la nipote
grandfather il nonno
grandmother la nonna
grandparents i nonni
grandson il nipote
grapefruit il pampelmo
grapes l'uva *f*
grass l'erba *f*
grated grattugiato(a)
grater la grattugia
greasy grasso(a)
great (big) grande
(wonderful) fantastico(a)
Great Britain la Gran Bretagna
green verde
green card (car insurance) la carta verde
greengrocer's il fruttivendolo
greetings card il biglietto d'auguri
grey grigio(a)

grill la griglia
to grill cuocere alla griglia
grilled alla griglia
grocer's il negozio di alimentari
ground la terra
ground floor il pianterreno
on the ground floor a pianterreno
groundsheet il telone impermeabile
group il gruppo
guarantee la garanzia
guard (on train) il capotreno
guest (house guest) l'ospite *m/f*
(in hotel) il/la cliente
guesthouse la pensione
guide (tourist) la guida
guidebook la guida
guided tour la visita guidata
guitar la chitarra
gun (pistol) la pistola
(rifle) il fucile
gym (place) la palestra
gym shoes le scarpe da ginnastica
gynaecologist il/la ginecologo/a

H

haemorrhoids le emorroidi
hail la grandine
hair i capelli
hairbrush la spazzola per capelli
haircut il taglio di capelli
hairdresser il parrucchiere/
  la parrucchiera
hair dryer il fon
hair dye la tintura per capelli
hair gel il gel per capelli
hairgrip la molletta per capelli
hair mousse la spuma
hair spray la lacca per capelli
half la metà
a half bottle of... una mezza bottiglia
  di...
half an hour mezz'ora
half board mezza pensione
half fare il ridotto
half-price metà prezzo
ham (cooked) il prosciutto cotto
(cured) il prosciutto crudo

hamburger l'hamburger *m*
hammer il martello
hand la mano
handbag la borsa
handbrake il freno a mano
handicapped disabile;
  handicappato(a)
handkerchief il fazzoletto
handle il manico
handlebars il manubrio
hand luggage il bagaglio a mano
hand-made fatto a mano
hands-free kit (for phone) il vivavoce
handsome bello(a)
hanger (coat hanger) la gruccia per abiti
hang gliding il volo con deltaplano
hangover i postumi della sbornia
to happen succedere
what happened? cos'è successo?
happy felice
happy birthday! buon compleanno!
harbour il porto
hard duro(a)
(difficult) difficile
hardware shop il negozio di ferramenta
to harm nuocere
harvest il raccolto; la vendemmia
hat il cappello
to have avere
do you have...? ha/hai/avete...?
I have... ho...
I don't have... non ho...
we have... abbiamo...
we don't have... non abbiamo...
to have to dovere
hay fever il raffreddore da fieno
he egli; lui
head la testa
headache il mal di testa
I have a headache ho mal di testa
headlights i fari
headphones le cuffie
health la salute
health-food shop l'erboristeria *f*
healthy sano(a)
to hear sentire
hearing aid l'apparecchio acustico *m*

heart il cuore
heart attack l'infarto *m*
heartburn il bruciore di stomaco
to heat up (food) riscaldare
heater il termosifone
heating il riscaldamento
heavy pesante
heel il tallone
heel bar il banco del calzolaio
height l'altezza *f*
helicopter l'elicottero *m*
hello! salve!; ciao!
(on telephone) pronto
helmet il casco
help! aiuto!
to help aiutare
can you help me? può aiutarmi?
hem l'orlo *m*
hepatitis l'epatite *f*
her il/la suo(a)
her passport il suo passaporto
her room la sua camera
herb l'erba aromatica *f*
herbal tea la tisana
here qui/qua
here is... ecco...
here is my passport ecco il mio
  passaporto
hernia l'ernia *f*
hi! ciao!
to hide nascondere
high alto(a)
(speed) forte
high blood pressure la pressione alta
high chair il seggiolone
hill la collina
hill-walking il trekking
him lui; lo; gli
hip l'anca *f*
hip replacement la protesi dell'anca
hire il noleggio
bike hire il noleggio bici
boat hire il noleggio barche
car hire il noleggio auto
ski hire il noleggio sci
to hire noleggiare
hired car la macchina a noleggio

138

his il/la suo(a)
his passport il suo passaporto
his room la sua camera
historic storico(a)
history la storia
to hit colpire
to hitchhike fare l'autostop
hobby il passatempo
to hold tenere
(to contain) contenere
hold-up (traffic) l'ingorgo *m*
hole il buco
holiday la festa
on holiday in vacanza
holiday rep il/la rappresentante dell'agenzia di viaggio
home la casa
at home a casa
homeopathic (remedy etc) omeopatico(a)
homeopathy l'omeopatia *f*
homesick: to be homesick avere nostalgia di casa
I'm homesick ho nostalgia di casa
homosexual omosessuale
honest onesto(a)
honey il miele
honeymoon la luna di miele
hood (on jacket) il cappuccio
hook (for fishing) l'amo *m*
to hope sperare
I hope so/not spero di sì/no
hors d'œuvre l'antipasto *m*
horse il cavallo
horse racing le corse dei cavalli *fpl*
to horse-ride andare a cavallo
hosepipe la canna dell'acqua
hospital l'ospedale *m*
hostel l'ostello *m*
hot caldo(a)
I'm hot ho caldo
it's hot (weather) fa caldo
hot-water bottle la borsa dell'acqua calda
hotel l'albergo *m*; l'hotel *m*
hour l'ora *f*
half an hour mezz'ora

1 hour un'ora
2 hours due ore
house la casa
housewife la casalinga
house wine il vino della casa
housework i lavori di casa
how? (in what way) come?
how are you? come sta?
how many? quanti(e)?
how much? quanto(a)?
hungry: to be hungry avere fame
hunt la caccia
to hunt andare a caccia
hunting permit la licenza di caccia
hurry: I'm in a hurry ho fretta
to hurt fare male
that hurts fa male
husband il marito
hut (bathing/beach) la cabina
(mountain) la baita
hydrofoil l'aliscafo *m*
hypodermic needle l'ago ipodermico *m*

I

I io
ice il ghiaccio
with ice con ghiaccio
without ice senza ghiaccio
ice box il freezer
ice cream il gelato
iced coffee il caffè freddo
iced tea il tè freddo
ice lolly il ghiacciolo
ice rink la pista di pattinaggio su ghiaccio
to ice skate pattinare sul ghiaccio
ice skates i pattini da ghiaccio
idea l'idea *f*
identity card la carta d'identità
if se
ignition l'accensione *f*
ignition key la chiave dell'accensione
ill malato(a)
I'm ill sto male
illness la malattia
immediately subito
immersion heater lo scaldabagno elettrico

immigration l'immigrazione *f*
immobilizer (on car)
  l'immobilizzatore *m*
immunisation l'immunizzazione *f*
to import importare
important importante
impossible impossibile
to improve migliorare
in in
in 2 hours in due ore
in London a Londra
in front of davanti a
included compreso(a); incluso(a)
inconvenient scomodo(a)
to increase aumentare
to increase volume alzare il volume
indicator (in car) la freccia
indigestion l'indigestione *f*
indigestion tablets le compresse
  per digerire
indoors dentro; al chiuso
infection l'infezione *f*
infectious contagioso(a)
informal (clothes) sportivo(a)
information le informazioni
ingredients gli ingredienti
inhaler l'inalatore *m*
injection l'iniezione *f*; la puntura
to injure ferire
injured ferito(a)
injury la lesione
ink l'inchiostro *m*
inn la locanda
inner tube la camera d'aria
inquiries le informazioni
insect l'insetto *m*
insect bite la puntura d'insetto
insect repellent l'insettifugo;
  il repellente per insetti
inside dentro
instant coffee il caffè solubile
instead of invece di
instructor l'istruttore/l'istruttrice
insulin l'insulina *f*
insurance l'assicurazione *f*
insurance certificate il certificato
  di assicurazione

to insure assicurare
insured: *to be insured* essere
  assicurato(a)
to intend to avere intenzione di
interesting interessante
international internazionale
internet l'internet *f*
internet access: *do you have
  internet access?* sei collegato a
  internet?
internet café l'internet café *m*;
  l'internet point *m*
interpreter l'interprete *m/f*
interval l'intervallo *m*
interview l'intervista *f*
into in
into the centre in centro
into town in città
to introduce someone to
  presentare qualcuno a
invitation l'invito *m*
to invite invitare
invoice la fattura
iPod® l'iPod *m*
Ireland l'Irlanda *f*
Irish irlandese
iron (for clothes) il ferro da stiro
(metal) il ferro
to iron stirare
ironing board l'asse da stiro
ironmonger's il negozio di ferramenta
is è
island l'isola *f*
it esse/essa; lo/la
Italian italiano(a)
(language) l'italiano *m*
Italy l'Italia *f*
to itch prudere
my eyes itch mi prudono gli occhi
my leg itches mi prude la gamba
item (on bill) la voce
itemised bill il conto dettagliato
IUD la spirale

J

jack (for car) il cric
jacket la giacca

140

waterproof jacket il giaccone impermeabile
jam (food) la marmellata
jammed bloccato(a)
January gennaio
jar (honey, jam, etc) il vaso
jaundice l'itterizia f
jaw la mascella
jealous geloso(a); invidioso(a)
jeans i blue jeans
jelly (dessert) la gelatina
jellyfish la medusa
jet ski l'acqua scooter m
jetty il molo
jeweller's la gioielleria
jewellery i gioielli
Jewish ebreo(a)
job il lavoro
to jog fare jogging
to join (club) iscriversi a
to join in (game) partecipare a
joint (hip, etc) l'articolazione f
joke la barzelletta
(practical) lo scherzo m
to joke scherzare
journalist il/la giornalista
journey il viaggio
judge il giudice m
jug la brocca
juice il succo
a carton of juice un cartone di succo di frutta
orange juice il succo d'arancia
July luglio
to jump saltare
jumper il maglione
jump leads (for car) i cavi per far partire la macchina
junction (road) l'incrocio m
June giugno
just: *just two* solamente due
I've just arrived sono appena arrivato(a)

K

to keep (retain) tenere
keep the change! tenga il resto

kennel il canile
kettle il bollitore
key la chiave
keyboard la tastiera
keycard la chiave elettronica
keyring il portachiavi
to kick dare calci a
kid (child) il bambino
kidneys (in body) i reni
to kill uccidere
kilo il chilo
a kilo of apples un chilo di mele
2 kilos due chili
kilogram il chilogrammo
kilometre il chilometro
kind (sort) il tipo
kind (person) gentile
king il re
kiosk l'edicola f; il chiosco
kiss il bacio
to kiss baciare
kitchen la cucina
kitchen paper la carta assorbente da cucina
kite l'aquilone m
kiwi fruit il kiwi
knee il ginocchio
knee highs i gambaletti
knickers le mutandine
knife il coltello
to knit lavorare a maglia
to knock (on door) bussare
to knock down (car) investire
to knock over (glass, vase) rovesciare
knot il nodo
to know (facts) sapere
(to be acquainted with) conoscere
I don't know non lo so
to know how to sapere
to know how to swim saper nuotare
kosher kasher

L

label l'etichetta f
lace il pizzo
laces (shoe) i lacci
ladder la scala

141

ladies' (toilet) la toilette (per signore)
lady la signora
lager la birra (bionda)
lake il lago
lamb l'agnello *m*
lame zoppo(a)
lamp la lampada
lamppost il lampione
lampshade il paralume
land la terra
to land (plane) atterrare
landlady la padrona di casa
landlord il padrone di casa
landline phone il telefono fisso
landslide la frana
lane la stradina
(of motorway) la corsia
language la lingua
language school la scuola di lingue
laptop il laptop; il portatile
laptop bag la borsa per il computer
  portatile
large grande

last ultimo(a); scorso(a)
last night ieri notte
last time l'ultima volta
last week la settimana scorsa
last year l'anno scorso
the last bus l'ultimo autobus
the last train l'ultimo treno
late tardi
sorry we're late scusi il ritardo
the train's late il treno è in ritardo
later più tardi
to laugh ridere
launderette la lavanderia automatica
laundry il bucato
lavatory la toilette
lavender la lavanda
law la legge
lawn il prato all'inglese
lawyer *m/f* l'avvocato
laxative il lassativo
layby la piazzola di sosta
lazy pigro(a)
lead (electric) il filo
lead (metal) il piombo

lead-free senza piombo
leaf la foglia
leak (of gas, liquid) la perdita
(in roof) il buco
to leak: *it's leaking* perde
to learn imparare
learning disability: *he/she has
  a learning disability* ha difficoltà
  di apprendimento
lease (rental) l'affitto *m*
leather il cuoio; la pelle
to leave (leave behind) lasciare
(train, bus, etc) partire
when does the bus leave? quando
  parte l'autobus?
when does the train leave? quando
  parte il treno?
leeks i porri
left la sinistra
on/to the left a sinistra
left-handed mancino(a)
left-luggage il deposito bagagli
left-luggage locker l'armadietto per
  despositare i bagagli *m*
leg la gamba
lemon il limone
lemonade la limonata
to lend prestare
length la lunghezza
lens (camera) l'obiettivo *m*
(contact lens) la lente a contatto
lenses le lenti
lesbian lesbica
less meno
less than meno di
lesson la lezione
to let (allow) permettere
(to hire out) affittare
letter la lettera
letterbox la cassetta delle lettere
lettuce la lattuga
level crossing il passaggio a livello
library la biblioteca
licence il permesso
(driving) la patente
lid il coperchio
to lie mentire

lie (untruth) la bugia
to lie down sdraiarsi
life belt il salvagente
lifeboat la scialuppa di salvataggio
lifeguard il bagnino
life insurance l'assicurazione sulla vita *f*
life jacket il giubbotto salvagente
life raft la zattera di salvataggio
lift (elevator) l'ascensore *m*
(in car) il passaggio
light (not heavy) leggero(a)
(colour) chiaro(a)
light la luce
have you a light? ha da accendere?
light bulb la lampadina
lighter l'accendino *m*
lighthouse il faro
lightning il fulmine
like come
to like piacere
I'd/we'd like... vorrei/vorremmo...
I don't like... non mi piace...
I like coffee mi piace il caffè
lilo il materassino
lime (fruit) il lime
line (row, queue) la fila
(telephone) la linea
linen il lino; la biancheria
lingerie la biancheria intima da donna
lip reading la lettura delle labbra
lips le labbra
lip salve il burro di cacao
lipstick il rossetto
liqueur il liquore
list l'elenco *m*; la lista
to listen (to) ascoltare
litre il litro
a litre of milk un litro di latte
litter (rubbish) i rifiuti
little (small) piccolo(a)
a little... un po' di...
to live vivere; abitare
he lives in a flat abita in un appartamento
I live in London vivo a Londra
liver il fegato
living room il salotto

loaf of bread la pagnotta
local locale
to lock chiudere a chiave
lock la serratura
the lock is broken la serratura è rotta
locker l'armadietto *m*
locksmith il fabbro
log book (car) la carta di circolazione; il libretto
logs i ceppi
lollipop il lecca lecca
London Londra
in/to London a Londra
long lungo(a)
for a long time molto tempo
long-sighted presbite
to look after prendersi cura di
to look at guardare
to look for cercare
loose (not fastened) slegato(a)
it's come loose (knot) si è allentato(a)
lorry il camion
to lose perdere
lost (object) perso(a)
I've lost my... ho perso il/la...
I'm lost mi sono smarrito(a)
we're lost ci siamo smarriti(e)
lost property office l'ufficio oggetti smarriti *m*
lot: *a lot* molto
lottery la lotteria
loud forte
loudspeaker l'altoparlante *m*
lounge (in hotel) il salone
(in house) la sala
(in airport) la sala d'attesa
love l'amore *m*
to love (person) amare
I love swimming mi piace nuotare
I love you ti amo
lovely bellissimo(a)
low basso(a)
(standard, quality) scadente
low-alcohol a basso contenuto alcolico
to lower volume abbassare il volume
low-fat magro(a)

luck la fortuna
lucky fortunato(a)
luggage i bagagli
luggage rack il portabagagli
luggage tag l'etichetta *f*
luggage trolley il carrello
lump (swelling) il gonfiore
lunch il pranzo
lunch break l'intervallo del pranzo *m*
lung il polmone
luxury di lusso

M

machine la macchina
mad (insane) matto(a)
(angry) arrabbiato(a)
magazine la rivista
maggot il verme
magnet la calamita
magnifying glass la lente
  d'ingrandimento
maid (in hotel) la cameriera
maiden name il nome da ragazza
mail la posta
main principale
main course (meal) il secondo
main road la strada principale
to make (generally) fare
(meal) preparare
make-up il trucco
male maschio; maschile
mall (shopping) centro commerciale
mallet la mazza
man l'uomo *m*
to manage (be in charge of) dirigere
manager il direttore; il responsabile
mango il mango
manicure il manicure
manual (gear change) cambio
  manuale
many molti(e)
map (of country) la carta geografica
(city) la piantina
marble il marmo
March marzo
margarine la margarina
marina il porticciolo

mark (stain) la macchia; il segno
(brand) la marca
market il mercato
where is the market? dov'è il
  mercato?
when is the market? quando c'è il
  mercato?
marmalade la marmellata d'arance
married sposato(a)
are you married? è sposato(a)?
I'm married sono sposato(a)
marry: to get married sposarsi
marsh la palude
mascara il mascara
mass (in church) la messa
massage il massaggio
mast l'albero della nave *m*
masterpiece il capolavoro
match (game) la partita
matches i fiammiferi
material il materiale
(cloth) il tessuto
to matter importare
it doesn't matter non importa
what's the matter? cosa c'è?
mattress il materasso
May maggio
mayonnaise la maionese
mayor *m* il sindaco
maximum il massimo
Mb (megabyte) il megabyte
128 megabytes 128 megabyte
me me; mi
meal il pasto
to mean (signify) voler dire
what does it mean? cosa vuol dire?
measles il morbillo
to measure misurare
meat la carne
mechanic il meccanico
medical insurance l'assicurazione
  medica *f*
medical treatment le cure mediche
medicine la medicina
Mediterranean il Mediterraneo
medium rare (steak) poco cotto(a)
to meet incontrare

pleased to meet you! piacere!
meeting la riunione
(by chance) l'incontro *m*
meeting point il punto d'incontro;
il ritrovo
megahertz il megahertz *m*
melon il melone
to melt sciogliere
member (of club, etc) il/la socio(a)
membership card la tessera
memory la memoria
(memories) i ricordi
memory card (for camera) la memory
card
memory stick (for camera, etc) la
chiavetta di memoria
men gli uomini
to mend riparare
meningitis la meningite
menu il menù
à la carte menu il menù alla carta
set menu il menù a prezzo fisso; il
menù turistico
message il messaggio
metal il metallo
meter il contatore
metre il metro
metro (underground) la metropolitana
metro station la stazione del metrò
microwave oven il forno a microonde
microphone il microfono
midday il mezzogiorno
at midday a mezzogiorno
middle il mezzo
middle-aged di mezz'età
midge il moscerino
midnight la mezzanotte
at midnight a mezzanotte
migraine l'emicrania *f*
I have a migraine ho l'emicrania
Milan Milano
mild dolce; mite
milk il latte
fresh milk il latte fresco
hot milk il latte caldo
long-life milk il latte a lunga
conservazione

powdered milk il latte in polvere
semi-skimmed milk il latte
parzialmente scremato
soya milk il latte di soia
whole milk il latte intero
with/without milk con/senza latte
milkshake il frappé; il frullato
millimetre il millimetro
mince (meat) la carne macinata
mind: *do you mind?* le dà fastidio?
I don't mind non mi dà fastidio
mineral water l'acqua minerale *f*
minibar il minibar
minidisk il minidisk
minimum il minimo
minister (church) il sacerdote
(political) il ministro
minor road la strada secondaria
mint (herb) la menta
mint tea il tè alla menta
minute il minuto
mirror lo specchio
to misbehave comportarsi male
miscarriage l'aborto spontaneo *m*
to miss (train, etc) perdere
Miss Signorina
missing (thing) smarrito(a)
(person) scomparso(a)
mistake l'errore *m*
misty nebbioso(a)
misunderstanding il malinteso
to mix mescolare
mobile phone il cellulare
mobile phone charger il carica
telefono
mobile number il numero di cellulare
modem il modem
modern moderno(a)
moisturizer l'idratante *m*
mole (on skin) il neo
moment: *just a moment* un
momento
monastery il monastero
Monday il lunedì
money i soldi
I have no money non ho soldi
money belt il marsupio

money order il vaglia
month il mese
this month questo mese
last month il mese scorso
next month il mese prossimo
monthly mensilmente
monument il monumento
moon la luna
mooring l'ormeggio *m*
mop lo straccio per lavare i pavimenti
moped il motorino
more (than) più (di)
more than 3 più di tre
more wine ancora un po' di vino
morning la mattina
in the morning di mattina
this morning stamattina
tomorrow morning domani mattina
morning-after pill la pillola del giorno dopo
mosquito la zanzara
mosquito net la zanzariera
mosquito repellent l'antizanzare

most il/la più
moth (clothes) la tarma
mother la madre
mother-in-law la suocera
motor il motore
motorbike la moto
motorboat il motoscafo
motorway l'autostrada *f*
mould la muffa
mountain la montagna
mountain bike la mountain bike
mountain biking andare in mountain bike
mountain rescue il soccorso alpino
mountaineering l'alpinismo *m*
mouse il topo
(computer) il mouse
moustache i baffi
mouth la bocca
mouthwash il collutorio
move muoversi
it isn't moving non si muove
movie il film
MP3 player il lettore di MP3

Mr Signor
Mrs Signora
Ms Signora
much molto
too much troppo
muddy (ground) fangoso(a)
mugging lo scippo
mumps gli orecchioni
muscle il muscolo
museum il museo
mushrooms i funghi
music la musica
musical il musical
mussels le cozze
must (to have to) dovere
I must devo
we must dobbiamo
I mustn't non devo
we mustn't non dobbiamo
mustard la senape
my il/la mio(a)
my passport il mio passaporto
my room la mia camera

N

nail (metal) il chiodo
(fingernail) l'unghia *f*
nailbrush lo spazzolino per unghie
nail clipper il tagliaunghie
nail file la limetta per le unghie
nail polish/varnish lo smalto per le unghie
nail polish remover l'acetone *m*
nail scissors le forbicine
name il nome
my name is... mi chiamo...
what is your name? come si chiama?
nanny la bambinaia
napkin il tovagliolo
Naples Napoli
nappies i pannolini
narrow stretto(a)
national nazionale
national park il parco nazionale
nationality la nazionalità
natural naturale
nature la natura

nature reserve la riserva naturale
navy blue blu
near to vicino(a) a
is it near? è vicino?
near the bank vicino alla banca
necessary necessario(a)
neck il collo
necklace la collana
nectarine la pescanoce
to need avere bisogno di...
I need... ho bisogno di...
we need... abbiamo bisogno di...
needle l'ago *m*
a needle and thread un ago e filo
negative (photo) il negativo
neighbour il/la vicino(a)
nephew il nipote
net la rete
the Net la Rete *m*
neutral (car) in folle
never mai
I never drink wine non bevo mai il
  vino
new nuovo(a)
news le notizie
(on television) il telegiornale
newsagent's il giornalaio
newspaper il giornale
newsstand l'edicola *f*
New Year il Capodanno
happy New Year! buon Anno!
New Year's Eve la notte di San
  Silvestro; l'ultimo dell'anno *m*
New Zealand la Nuova Zelanda
next prossimo(a)
next to accanto(a) a
next week la settimana prossima
the next bus il prossimo autobus
the next stop la prossima fermata
the next train il prossimo treno
nice piacevole
(person) simpatico(a)
niece la nipote
night la notte
at night di notte
last night ieri sera
per night a notte

tomorrow night domani sera
tonight stasera
nightclub il nightclub
nightdress la camicia da notte
night porter il portiere notturno
no no
(without) senza
no entry vietato l'ingresso
no ice senza ghiaccio
no problem non c'è problema
no smoking vietato fumare
no sugar senza zucchero
no thanks no, grazie
nobody nessuno
noise il rumore
noisy rumoroso(a)
it's very noisy è molto rumoroso(a)
non-alcoholic analcolico(a)
none nessuno(a)
non-smoker non-fumatore
non-smoking per non-fumatori
north il nord
Northern Ireland l'Irlanda del Nord *f*
nose il naso
not non
I do not know non lo so
note (bank note) la banconota
(letter) il biglietto
note pad il bloc-notes
nothing niente
nothing else nient'altro
notice l'avviso *m*
notice board la bacheca
novel il romanzo
November novembre
now adesso
nowhere da nessuna parte
nuclear nucleare
nudist beach la spiaggia nudista
number il numero
number plate (car) la targa
nurse l'infermiera/l'infermiere *f/m*
nursery (children's) l'asilo *m*
(for plants) il vivaio
nursery slope la pista per principianti
nut (to eat) la noce
(for bolt) il dado

O

oars i remi
oats l'avena f
to obtain ottenere
occupation (work) il lavoro
ocean l'oceano m
October ottobre
octopus il polpo
odd (strange) strano(a)
(number) dispari
of di
a bottle of wine una bottiglia di vino
a glass of water un bicchiere d'acqua
made of... fatto di...
off (machine, etc) spento(a)
(milk, food) andato(a) a male
this meat is off questa carne è andata
   a male
office l'ufficio m
often spesso
how often? ogni quanto?
oil l'olio m
oil filter il filtro dell'olio
oil gauge l'indicatore del livello
   dell'olio m
ointment la pomata
OK! va bene!
old vecchio(a)
how old are you? quanti anni ha?
I'm ... years old ho ... anni
old age pensioner il/la pensionato(a)
olive oil l'olio d'oliva m
olives le olive
on (light, engine) acceso(a)
(tap) aperto(a)
on the table sulla tavola
on time in orario
once una volta
at once subito
one-way (street) a senso unico
onions le cipolle
only solo(a)
open aperto(a)
to open aprire
opera l'opera f
operation l'operazione f
operator (telephone) il/la centralinista

opposite di fronte a
opposite the hotel di fronte all'albergo
quite the opposite al contrario
optician's l'ottico m
or o
orange (colour) arancione
(fruit) l'arancia f
orange juice il succo d'arancia
orchestra l'orchestra f
order l'ordine f
out of order fuori servizio
to order (food, etc) ordinare
oregano l'origano m
organic biologico(a)
to organize organizzare
ornament il soprammobile
other l'altro(a)
the other one l'altro
have you any others? ne ha degli
   altri?
our il/la nostro(a)
our car la nostra macchina
our hotel il nostro albergo
out (light) spento(a)
he/she's out è fuori
he's gone out è uscito
outdoor (pool, etc) all'aperto
outside: *it's outside* è fuori
oven il forno
ovenproof dish la pirofila
over (on top of) sopra
to overbook accettare troppe
   prenotazioni
to overcharge far pagare troppo
overdone (food) troppo cotto(a)
overdose l'overdose f
to overheat surriscaldare
to overload sovraccaricare
to oversleep non svegliarsi in tempo
to overtake sorpassare
to owe dover
I owe you... le devo...
you owe me... mi deve...
owner il/la proprietario(a)
oxygen l'ossigeno m

P

pace il passo
pacemaker il pacemaker
to pack (suitcase) fare la valigia
package il pacco
package tour il viaggio organizzato
packet il pacchetto
padded envelope la busta imbottita
paddling pool la piscina per bambini
padlock il lucchetto
Padua Padova
page la pagina
paid pagato(a)
I've paid ho pagato
pain il dolore
painful doloroso(a)
painkiller l'analgesico *m*
to paint (wall, etc) verniciare
(picture) dipingere
painting (picture) il quadro
pair il paio
palace il palazzo
pale pallido(a)
palmtop il computer palmare
pan (saucepan) la pentola
(frying pan) la padella
pancake la crêpe
panties le mutandine
pants le mutande
panty liner il proteggislip
paper la carta
paper hankies i fazzolettini di carta
paper napkins i tovaglioli di carta
paragliding il parapendio
paralysed paralizzato(a)
paramedic il paramedico
parcel il pacco
pardon? scusi?
I beg your pardon mi scusi
parents i genitori
park il parco
to park parcheggiare
parking disk il disco orario
parking meter il parchimetro
parking ticket (fine) la multa per
  sosta vietata
parmesan il parmigiano

grated parmesan il parmigiano
  grattugiato
part la parte
partner (business) il/la socio(a)
(boy/girlfriend) il/la compagno(a)
party (celebration) la festa
(political) il partito
pass (mountain) il passo; il valico
(bus, train) la tessera
passenger il/la passeggero(a)
passport il passaporto
passport control il controllo
  passaporti
password la password; la parola
  d'ordine
pasta la pasta
pastry la pasta
(fancy cake) il pasticcino
path il sentiero
patient (in hospital) il/la paziente
pavement il marciapiede
to pay pagare
I want to pay vorrei pagare
where do I pay? dove pago?
payment il pagamento
payphone il telefono pubblico
PDA l'agenda elettronica *f*
peace la pace
peaches le pesche
peak rate la tariffa nelle ore di punta
peanut allergy l'allergia alle arachidi *f*
pearls le perle
pears le pere
peas i piselli
pedal il pedale
pedalo il pedalò
pedestrian il pedone
pedestrian crossing il passaggio
  pedonale
to pee fare la pipì
to peel (fruit) sbucciare
peg (for clothes) la molletta
(for tent) il picchetto
pen la penna
pencil la matita
penfriend l'amico(a) di penna
penicillin la penicillina

penis il pene
penknife il temperino
pension la pensione
pensioner il/la pensionato(a)
people la gente
people carrier il pulmino
pepper (spice) il pepe
(vegetable) il peperone
per per
per day al giorno
per hour all'ora
per week alla settimana
per person a persona
100 km per hour 100 km all'ora
perfect perfetto(a)
performance la rappresentazione
perfume il profumo
perhaps forse
period (time) il periodo
(menstrual) le mestruazioni
perm la permanente
permit il permesso
person la persona
personal organizer l'agenda
   elettronica *f*
pet l'animale domestico *m*
pet food il cibo per gli animali domestici
pet shop il negozio di animali
   domestici
petrol la benzina
unleaded petrol la benzina verde
petrol cap il tappo del serbatoio
petrol tank il serbatoio della benzina
petrol pump la pompa della benzina
petrol station la stazione di servizio
pharmacy la farmacia
pharmacist il farmacista
phone il telefono
by phone per telefono
to phone telefonare
phonebook l'elenco telefonico *m*
phonebox la cabina telefonica
phonecard la scheda telefonica
photocopier la fotocopiatrice
photocopy la fotocopia
I need a photocopy mi serve una
   fotocopia

to photocopy fotocopiare
photograph la foto
to take a photo fare una foto
phrase book il manuale di
   conversazione
piano il pianoforte
to pick (fruit, flowers) cogliere
(to choose) scegliere
pickpocket il borseggiatore
pickle i sottaceti
picnic il picnic
to have a picnic fare un picnic
picnic hamper il cestino per il picnic
picnic rug il plaid
picnic table il tavolo da picnic
picture (painting) il quadro
(photo) la foto
pie (sweet) la torta
(savoury) il pasticcio
piece il pezzo
pier il pontile
pig il maiale
pill la pillola
to be on the pill prendere la pillola
pillow il guanciale; il cuscino
pillowcase la federa
pilot il pilota
pin lo spillo
PIN number il numero di PIN
pink rosa
pipe (water, etc) il tubo
(smoker's) la pipa
pitch (place for tent/caravan) il posto
   tenda/il posto per il caravan
pity: *what a pity!* che peccato!
pizza la pizza
place il luogo
place of birth il luogo di nascita
plain (obvious) chiaro(a)
(unflavoured) naturale
plait la treccia
plan il piano
to plan progettare
plane l'aereo *m*
plant la pianta
plaster (sticking) il cerotto
(for broken limb) l'ingessatura

plastic (made of) di plastica
plastic bag il sacchetto di plastica
plate il piatto
platform (railway) il binario
from which platform? da quale binario?
play (theatre) la commedia
to play (games) giocare
play area l'area giochi *f*
playground il parco giochi
play park il parco giochi
playroom la stanza dei giochi
pleasant piacevole
please per favore; prego
pleased: *pleased to meet you* piacere
plenty l'abbondanza *f*
pliers le pinze
plug (electrical) la spina
(for sink) il tappo
to plug in attaccare
plum la prugna; la susina
plumber l'idraulico *m*
plumbing l'impianto idraulico *m*
plunger lo sturalavandini
p.m. del pomeriggio
poached (egg) in camicia
(fish) bollito(a)
pocket la tasca
point il punto
poison il veleno
poisonous velenoso(a)
police la polizia
policeman/woman il poliziotto/ la donna poliziotto
police station il commissariato; la questura
polish (for shoes) il lucido
(for furniture) la cera
pollen il polline
polluted inquinato(a)
pony il pony
pony trekking le escursioni a cavallo
pool (swimming) la piscina
pool attendant il bagnino
poor povero(a)
pope il papa

pop socks i gambaletti
pork la carne di maiale
port (seaport, wine) il porto
porter il portiere
(for luggage) il facchino
portion la porzione
Portugal il Portogallo
Portuguese portoghese
possible possibile
post: *by post* per posta
to post (letters, etc) imbucare
postbox la buca delle lettere
postcard la cartolina
postcode il codice postale
poster il poster
postman/woman il/la postino(a)
post office la posta; l'ufficio postale *m*
to postpone rimandare
pot (cooking) la pentola
potato la patata
baked potato la patata al forno
boiled potatoes le patate lesse
fried potatoes le patate fritte
mashed potatoes il purè di patate
roast potatoes le patate arrosto
potato masher lo schiacciapatate
potato peeler il pelapatate
potato salad l'insalata di patate *f*
pothole la buca
pottery la terracotta
pound (money) la sterlina
to pour versare
powder: *in powder form* in polvere
powdered milk il latte in polvere
power (electricity) l'elettricità
power cut l'interruzione di corrente *f*
pram la carrozzina
to pray pregare
to prefer preferire
pregnant incinta
I'm pregnant sono incinta
to prepare preparare
to prescribe ordinare
prescription la ricetta
present (gift) il regalo
preservative il conservante
president il presidente

pressure: *tyre pressure* la pressione dei pneumatici
blood pressure la pressione del sangue
pretty carino(a)
price il prezzo
price list il listino prezzi
priest il prete
print (photo) la foto
printer la stampante
printout la stampata
prison il carcere; la prigione
private privato(a)
prize il premio
probably probabilmente
problem il problema
professor il professore/la professoressa
programme il programma
prohibited proibito(a)
promise la promessa
to promise promettere
to pronounce pronunciare
how's it pronounced? come si pronuncia?

protein la proteina
Protestant protestante
to provide fornire
public pubblico(a)
public holiday la festa nazionale
pudding il dessert
to pull tirare
to pull over (car) accostare
pullover il pullover; il maglione
pump la pompa
puncture la gomma a terra
puncture repair kit il kit per riparare le gomme
puppet il burattino
puppet show lo spettacolo di burattini
purple viola
purse il borsellino
to push spingere
pushchair il passeggino
to put (to place) mettere
to put back rimettere
pyjamas il pigiama

Q

quality la qualità
quantity la quantità
quarantine la quarantena
to quarrel litigare
quarter: *a quarter* un quarto
quay il molo
queen la regina
question la domanda
queue la coda
to queue fare la coda
quick veloce
quickly velocemente
quiet (place) tranquillo(a)
a quiet room una stanza tranquilla
quilt la trapunta
quite (rather) piuttosto
it's quite expensive è piuttosto caro(a)
quite the opposite al contrario
quiz show il gioco a quiz

R

rabbit il coniglio
rabies la rabbia
race (sport) la gara
race course l'ippodromo *m*
racket (tennis, etc) la racchetta
radiator (car) il radiatore
(heater) il termosifone
radio la radio
raft la zattera
railcard la tessera di riduzione ferroviaria
railway station la stazione ferroviaria
rain la pioggia
to rain piovere
it's raining piove
raincoat l'impermeabile *m*
rake il rastrello
rape lo stupro
raped violentata
I've been raped sono stata violentata
rare (unique) raro(a)
(steak) al sangue
rash (skin) l'orticaria *f*
raspberries i lamponi
rate (cost) la tariffa

rate of exchange il cambio
raw crudo(a)
razor il rasoio
razor blades le lamette
to read leggere
ready pronto(a)
to get ready prepararsi
real vero(a)
to realize rendersi conto di
rearview mirror lo specchietto
 retrovisore
receipt la ricevuta
receiver (phone) il ricevitore
reception (desk) la reception
receptionist l'addetto(a)
to recharge ricaricare
recharger (mobile) il caricatelefono
(battery) il caricabatterie
recipe la ricetta
to recognize riconoscere
to recommend raccomandare
to record (programme) registrare
to recover (from illness) rimettersi
to recycle riciclare
red rosso(a)
to reduce ridurre
reduction la riduzione
to refer to (for information) rivolgersi a
refill (pen) il ricambio
(lighter) la bomboletta di gas
refund il rimborso
to refuse rifiutare
regarding riguardo a
region la regione
register il registro
to register (letter) assicurare
(car) immatricolare
(for class) iscriversi
registered letter la lettera
 raccomandata
registration form il modulo
 d'iscrizione
to reimburse rimborsare
relation (family) il/la parente
relationship il rapporto
to remain restare; rimanere
to remember ricordare

I don't remember non mi ricordo
remote control il telecomando
removal firm la ditta di traslochi
to remove togliere
rent l'affitto *m*
to rent (house) affittare
(car) noleggiare
rental (house) l'affitto *m*
(car) il nolo
repair la riparazione
to repair riparare
to repeat ripetere
to reply rispondere
report il resoconto
to report (crime) denunciare
request la richiesta
to request richiedere
to rescue salvare
reservation la prenotazione
to reserve prenotare
reserved prenotato(a)
resident residente
resort la località di vacanza
rest (repose) il riposo
(remainder) il resto
to rest riposarsi
restaurant il ristorante
restaurant car il vagone ristorante
retired: *I'm retired* sono in pensione
to return (go back) ritornare
(to give back) restituire
return ticket il biglietto di andata e
 ritorno
to reverse fare marcia indietro
to reverse the charges fare una
 telefonata a carico del destinatario
reverse charge call la chiamata a
 carico del destinatario
reverse gear la retromarcia
rheumatism il reumatismo
rib la costola
rice il riso
rich ricco(a)
ride (in a car) il giro in macchina
to ride a horse andare a cavallo
right (correct) giusto(a)
right la destra

at/to the right a destra
on the right sulla destra
right of way la precedenza
to ring (bell) suonare
(phone) squillare
it's ringing suona
ring l'anello *m*
ring road la circonvallazione
ripe maturo(a)
river il fiume
road la strada
road map la carta stradale
road sign il cartello stradale
roadworks i lavori stradali
roast arrosto(a)
roll (bread) il panino
rollerblades i rollerblades
romantic romantico(a)
roof il tetto
roof-rack il portabagagli
room (hotel) la camera
(space) lo spazio
double room la camera doppia
family room la camera per famiglia
single room la camera singola
room number il numero di camera
room service il servizio in camera
root la radice
rope la corda
rose la rosa
rosé wine il vino rosato
rotten (food) marcio(a)
rough (sea) mosso(a)
round rotondo(a)
roundabout la rotatoria
row (in theatre, etc) la fila
to row (boat) remare
rowing boat la barca a remi
rubber (eraser) la gomma per
cancellare
(material) la gomma
rubber band l'elastico *m*
rubber gloves i guanti di gomma
rubbish la spazzatura
rubella la rosolia
rucksack lo zaino
rug (carpet) il tappeto

ruins le rovine
ruler (to measure) il righello
to run correre
runner beans i fagiolini
rush hour l'ora di punta *f*
rusty arrugginito(a)

S

sad triste
saddle la sella
safe (for valuables) la cassaforte
safe (medicine, etc) senza pericolo;
sicuro(a)
is it safe? è senza pericolo?
safety la sicurezza
safetybelt la cintura di sicurezza
safety pin la spilla di sicurezza
to sail andare in barca a vela
sailboard la tavola da windsurf
sailing la vela
sailing boat la barca a vela
saint il/la santo(a)
salad l'insalata *f*
green salad l'insalata verde
mixed salad l'insalata mista
potato salad l'insalata di patate
tomato salad l'insalata di pomodori
salad dressing il condimento per
l'insalata
salami il salame
salary lo stipendio
sales (reductions) i saldi
salesman/woman il/la commesso(a)
sales rep il/la rappresentante
salt il sale
salt water l'acqua salata *f*
salty salato(a)
same stesso(a)
sample il campione
sand la sabbia
sandals i sandali
sandwich il panino; il tramezzino
toasted sandwich il toast
sanitary towels gli assorbenti
Sardinia la Sardegna
satellite dish l'antenna parabolica *f*
satellite TV la televisione via satellite

satnav (satellite navigation system, for car) il navigatore satellitare
Saturday il sabato
sauce la salsa
tomato sauce la salsa di pomodoro
saucepan la pentola
saucer il piattino
sauna la sauna
sausage la salsiccia
to save (life) salvare
(money) risparmiare
savoury (not sweet) salato(a)
to say dire
scales (weighing) la bilancia
to scan scannerizzare
scanner lo scanner
scarf la sciarpa
(headscarf) il foulard
scenery il paesaggio
schedule il programma
(timetable) l'orario *m*
school la scuola
primary school la scuola elementare
secondary school il liceo
scissors le forbici
score il punteggio
to score (goal) segnare
Scot lo/la scozzese
Scotland la Scozia
Scottish scozzese
scouring pad la paglietta
screen lo schermo
screen wash il liquido lavavetri
screw la vite
screwdriver il cacciavite
phillips screwdriver il cacciavite a stella
scuba diving le immersioni subacquee
sculpture la scultura
sea il mare
seacat il catamarano
seafood i frutti di mare
seam (of dress) la cucitura
to search cercare
sea sickness il mal di mare
seaside: *at the seaside* al mare
season (of year) la stagione

(holiday) il periodo delle vacanze
in season di stagione
seasonal stagionale
seasoning il condimento
season ticket l'abbonamento
seat (chair) la sedia
(theatre, plane, etc) il posto
seatbelt la cintura di sicurezza
seaweed le alghe
second secondo(a)
(time) il secondo
second class la seconda classe
second-hand di seconda mano
secretary la segretaria
security la sicurezza
security check il controllo di sicurezza
security guard la guardia giurata
sedative il sedativo
to see vedere
to seize afferrare
self-catering con uso di cucina
self-employed autonomo(a)
self-service il self-service
to sell vendere
do you sell...? vende...?
sell-by date la data di scadenza
Sellotape® il nastro adesivo
to send mandare; spedire; inviare
senior citizen l'anziano(a)
sensible pratico(a)
separated separato(a)
separately: *to pay separately* pagare separatamente
September settembre
septic tank la fossa biologica
serious grave
(not funny) serio(a)
to serve servire
service (in church) la funzione
(in restaurant) il servizio
is service included? il servizio è incluso?
service charge il servizio
service station la stazione di servizio
set menu il menù turistico/fisso
settee il divano
several alcuni(e)

to sew cucire
sewerage la fognatura
sex (gender) il sesso
(intercourse) i rapporti sessuali
shade l'ombra *f*
in the shade all'ombra
to shake (bottle) agitare
shallow basso(a)
shampoo lo shampoo
shampoo and set lo shampoo e messa in piega
to share dividere
sharp (razor, blade) affilato(a)
to shave farsi la barba
shaver il rasoio
shaving cream la crema da barba
shawl lo scialle
she ella; lei
sheep la pecora
sheet (bed) il lenzuolo
shelf la mensola
shell (seashell) la conchiglia
shellfish i frutti di mare

sheltered riparato(a)
to shine brillare
shingles (illness) il fuoco di sant'Antonio
ship la nave
shirt la camicia
shock (mental) lo shock
(electric) la scossa
shock absorber l'ammortizzatore *m*
shoe la scarpa
shoelaces i lacci delle scarpe
shoe polish il lucido per scarpe
shoe repairer il calzolaio
shoe shop il negozio di calzature
shop il negozio
to shop fare la spesa; fare acquisti
to shop online fare acquisti su internet
shop assistant il/la commesso(a)
shop window la vetrina
shopping: *to go shopping* fare acquisti; fare la spesa
shopping centre il centro commerciale
shore la riva

short corto(a)
(person) basso(a)
short circuit il corto circuito
short cut la scorciatoia
shortage la carenza
shorts i calzoncini corti
short-sighted miope
shoulder la spalla
to shout gridare
show (theatre) lo spettacolo
to show mostrare
shower la doccia
(rain) il rovescio
to take a shower fare la doccia
shower cap la cuffia da doccia
shower gel il docciaschiuma
to shrink restringersi
shrub l'arbusto *m*
shut (closed) chiuso(a)
shutter l'imposta *f*
shuttle service la navetta
Sicily la Sicilia
sick (ill) malato(a)
I feel sick mi sento male
I feel sick (nauseous) ho la nausea
side il lato
side dish il contorno
sidelight la luce di posizione
sidewalk il marciapiede
sieve il setaccio
sightseeing tour il giro turistico
sign il segno
(on road) il segnale
to sign firmare
signal: *there's no signal* non c'è campo
signature la firma
signpost il segnale
silk la seta
silver l'argento *m*
SIM card la (carta) SIM
similar to simile a
since (time) da
to sing cantare
single (unmarried) non sposato(a)
(not double) singolo(a)
(ticket) di (sola) andata

single bed il letto a una piazza
single room la camera singola
sink il lavandino
sir Signore
sister la sorella
sister-in-law la cognata
to sit sedersi
please, sit down prego, si accomodi
site (website) sito
size (of clothes) la taglia
(of shoes) il numero
to skate (on ice) pattinare sul ghiaccio
skateboard lo skateboard
skates (ice) i pattini da ghiaccio
(roller) i pattini a rotelle
to ski sciare
to skid slittare; sbandare
skis gli sci
ski boots gli scarponi da sci
ski instructor il/la maestro(a) di sci
ski jump il trampolino
ski lift lo ski-lift
ski pass lo skipass
ski pole/stick la racchetta da sci
ski run la pista
ski suit la tuta da sci
skid *n* la slittata; la sbandata
skin la pelle
skirt la gonna
sky il cielo
sledge la slitta
to sleep dormire
to sleep in dormire fino a tardi
sleeper (on train) la cuccetta
sleeping bag il sacco a pelo
sleeping car il vagone letto
sleeping mat il materassino
sleeping pill il sonnifero
slice (piece of) la fetta
sliced bread il pancarrè
slide (photo) la diapositiva
to slip scivolare
slippers le pantofole
slow lento(a)
to slow down rallentare
slowly lentamente
small piccolo(a)

smaller (than) più piccolo (di)
smell l'odore (m)
bad smell la puzza
nice smell il profumo
to smell (bad) puzzare
to smell of avere odore di
smile il sorriso
to smile sorridere
smoke il fumo
to smoke fumare
can I smoke? posso fumare?
I don't smoke non fumo
smoke alarm l'allarme antincendio *m*
smoked (food) affumicato(a)
smokers (sign) fumatori
smooth liscio(a)
SMS message il messaggio SMS
snack lo spuntino
to have a snack fare uno spuntino
snake il serpente
(grass) la biscia
snake bite il morso di vipera
to sneeze starnutire
snorkel il boccaglio
snorkelling lo snorkelling
snow la neve
to snow: *it's snowing* nevica
snowboard lo snowboard
snowboarding: *to go
 snowboarding* andare a fare
 lo snowboard
snow chains le catene da neve
snow tyres i pneumatici da neve
snow plough lo spazzaneve
snowed up isolato(a) a causa della
 neve
soap il sapone
soap powder il detersivo in polvere
sober sobrio(a)
socket (electric) la presa
socks i calzini
soda water l'acqua di selz *f*
sofa il divano
sofa bed il divano letto
soft soffice; morbido(a)
soft drink la bibita
software il software

soldier il soldato
sole (of foot, shoe) la suola
soluble solubile
some di (del/della)
(a few) alcuni/alcune
someone qualcuno
something qualcosa
sometimes qualche volta
son il figlio
son-in-law il genero
song la canzone
soon presto
as soon as possible il più presto
  possibile
sore throat il mal di gola
sorry: *I'm sorry!* mi scusi!
sort il tipo
what sort? che tipo?
soup la minestra
sour aspro(a); agro(a)
soured cream la panna acida
south il sud
souvenir il souvenir
spa la stazione termale
space lo spazio
(parking) il posteggio
spade il badile
Spain la Spagna
spam (email) messaggi indesiderati,
  email spazzatura (but also spam)
Spanish spagnolo(a)
spanner la chiave inglese
spare parts i pezzi di ricambio
spare room la stanza degli ospiti
spare tyre la gomma di scorta
spare wheel la ruota di scorta
sparkling frizzante
sparkling water l'acqua gassata
sparkling wine il vino frizzante
spark plugs le candele
to speak parlare
do you speak English? parla inglese?
speaker l'altoparlante *m*
special speciale
specialist lo/la specialista
speciality la specialità
special needs: *people with special*

needs le persone con esigenze
  particolari *fpl*
speech il discorso
speed la velocità
speedboat il motoscafo
speed limit il limite di velocità
to exceed the speed limit superare
  il limite di velocità
speeding l'eccesso di velocità *m*
speeding ticket la multa per eccesso
  di velocità
speedometer il tachimetro
to spell scrivere
how's it spelt? come si scrive?
to spend spendere
spice le spezie
spicy piccante
spider il ragno
to spill rovesciare
spinach gli spinaci
spin-dryer la centrifuga
spine la spina dorsale
spirits (alcohol) i liquori
splinter la scheggia
spoke (of wheel) il raggio
sponge la spugna
spoon il cucchiaio
sport lo sport
sports centre il centro sportivo
sports shop il negozio di articoli
  sportivi
spot (stain) la macchia
(place) il posto
sprain la slogatura
spring (season) la primavera
(metal) la molla
square (in town) la piazza
squash (game) lo squash
(drink) il centrifugato di frutta/verdura
to squeeze spremere; stringere
squid il calamaro
stadium lo stadio
staff il personale
stage (theatre) il palcoscenico
stain la macchia
stained glass il vetro colorato
stain remover lo smacchiatore

158

stairs le scale
stale (bread) raffermo(a)
stalls (in theatre) la platea
stamp il francobollo
to stand stare in piedi
star la stella
starfish la stella marina
start l'inizio *m*
to start cominciare
starter (food) l'antipasto *m*
(in car) il motorino d'avviamento
station la stazione
stationer's la cartoleria
statue la statua
stay il soggiorno
enjoy your stay! buona permanenza!
to stay (remain) rimanere
I'm staying at the Grand Hotel
  sono al Grand Hotel
steak la bistecca
to steal rubare
steamed al vapore
to steam cuocere a vapore
steel l'acciaio *m*
steep: *is it steep?* è in salita?
steeple il campanile
steering wheel il volante
step (stair) il gradino
stepdaughter la figliastra
stepfather il patrigno
stepmother la matrigna
stepson il figliastro
stereo lo stereo
sterling la sterlina
steward lo steward
stewardess la hostess
to stick (with glue) incollare
(door) incepparsi
sticking plaster il cerotto
still (motionless) fermo(a)
(water) naturale
(yet) ancora
sting la puntura
to sting pungere
stitches i punti
stock cubes i dadi
stockings le calze

stolen rubato(a)
stomach lo stomaco; la pancia
stomachache il mal di stomaco
stone la pietra
to stop (come to a halt) fermarsi
(stop doing something) smettere
stop sign lo stop
store (shop) il negozio
storey il piano
storm la tempesta; il temporale
story il racconto
straightaway subito
straight on diritto
strange strano(a)
straw (drinking) la cannuccia
strawberries le fragole
stream il ruscello
street la strada
street map la piantina
strength (of person) la forza
(of wine) la gradazione alcolica
stress lo stress
strike (of workers) lo sciopero
string lo spago
striped a strisce
stroke (medical) l'ictus *m*
to have a stroke avere un ictus
strong forte
strong coffee il caffè ristretto
strong tea il tè forte
stuck bloccato(a)
student lo studente/la studentessa
student discount lo sconto per studenti
stuffed farcito(a); ripieno(a)
stung punto(a)
stupid stupido(a)
subscription l'abbonamento *m*
subtitles i sottotitoli
subway (train) la metropolitana
(passage) il sottopassaggio
suddenly all'improvviso
suede la pelle scamosciata
sugar lo zucchero
sugar-free senza zucchero
to suggest proporre
suit (man's) l'abito *m*
(woman's) il tailleur

suitcase la valigia
sum (of money) la somma
summer l'estate f
summer holidays le vacanze estive
summit il vertice
sun il sole
to sunbathe prendere il sole
sunblock la protezione solare totale
sunburn la scottatura solare
suncream la crema solare
Sunday la domenica
sunglasses gli occhiali da sole
sunny: it's sunny c'è il sole
sunrise l'alba f
sunroof (car) il tettuccio apribile
sunscreen la crema solare protettiva
sunset il tramonto
sunshade l'ombrellone m
sunstroke l'insolazione f
suntan l'abbronzatura f
suntan lotion la crema abbronzante
supermarket il supermercato
supper (dinner) la cena

supplement il supplemento
to supply fornire
sure sicuro(a); certo(a)
I'm sure sono sicuro(a)
to surf fare il surf
to surf the net navigare in internet
surfboard la tavola da surf
surgery (surgical treatment) la
  chirurgia
surname il cognome
my surname is... di cognome mi
  chiamo...
surprise la sorpresa
suspension (in car) la sospensione
to survive sopravvivere
to swallow inghiottire
to swear (bad language) dire le
  parolacce
to sweat sudare
sweater il maglione
sweatshirt la felpa
sweet (not savoury) dolce
sweetener il dolcificante
sweets le caramelle

to swell gonfiare
to swim nuotare
swimming pool la piscina
swimsuit il costume da bagno
swing l'altalena f
Swiss svizzero(a)
switch l'interruttore m
to switch off spegnere
to switch on accendere
Switzerland la Svizzera
swollen gonfio(a)
synagogue la sinagoga
syringe la siringa

T

table la tavola
tablecloth la tovaglia
tablet (pill) la pastiglia
table tennis il ping pong
table wine il vino da tavola
tailor il sarto
to take (carry) portare
(to grab, seize) prendere
how long does it take? quanto
  tempo ci vuole?
takeaway (food) da asporto
to take off decollare
to take out (of bag) tirar fuori
talc il borotalco
to talk parlare
tall alto(a)
tampons gli assorbenti interni
tangerine il mandarino
tank la cisterna
(car) il serbatoio
(fish) l'acquario m
tap il rubinetto
tap water l'acqua del rubinetto f
tape il nastro
tape measure il metro a nastro
tape recorder il registratore
target lo scopo
tart la crostata
taste il sapore
to taste assaggiare; provare
can I taste some? ne posso assaggiare
  un po'?

tax la tassa; l'imposta *f*
taxi il taxi
taxi driver il/la tassista
taxi rank il posteggio dei taxi
tea il tè
fruit tea il tè alla frutta
herbal tea la tisana
lemon tea il tè al limone
tea with milk il tè al latte
tea bag la bustina di tè
tea pot la teiera
to teach insegnare
teacher l'insegnante *m/f*
team la squadra
tear (in material) lo strappo
teaspoon il cucchiaino
teat (on bottle) la tettarella
tea towel lo strofinaccio per i piatti
teenager l'adolescente
teeth i denti
telegram il telegramma
telephone il telefono
to telephone telefonare
telephone box la cabina telefonica
telephone call la telefonata
telephone card la scheda telefonica
telephone directory l'elenco
  telefonico *m*
telephone number il numero
  di telefono
television la televisione
to tell dire
temperature la temperatura
to have a temperature avere
  la febbre
temporary provvisorio(a)
tenant l'inquilino(a)
tendon il tendine
tennis il tennis
tennis ball la pallina da tennis
tennis court il campo da tennis
tennis racket la racchetta da tennis
tent la tenda
tent peg il picchetto
terminal (airport) il terminal
terrace la terrazza
terracotta la terracotta

to test (try out) provare
testicles i testicoli
tetanus jab l'antitetanica *f*
text message l'sms *m*
to text mandare un sms
I'll text you ti manderó un sms
than di
to thank ringraziare
thank you grazie
thanks very much molte grazie
that quel/quella/quello
that one quello là
the (sing) il/lo/la
(plural) i/gli/le
theatre il teatro
theft il furto
their il/la loro
them loro; li; le
there (over there) lì/là
there is/there are c'è/ci sono
thermometer il termometro
these questi/queste
these ones questi qui
they loro; essi/esse
thick spesso(a)
thief il/la ladro(a)
thigh la coscia
thin sottile
(person) magro(a)
thing la cosa
my things la mia roba
to think pensare
thirsty: *to be thirsty* avere sete
this questo/questa
this one questo(a)
those quei/quelle/quegli
those ones quelli(e)
thread il filo
throat la gola
throat lozenges le pastiglie per la gola
through attraverso
to throw away buttare via
thumb il pollice
thunder il tuono
thunderstorm il temporale
Thursday il giovedì
thyme il timo

ticket (bus, train, etc) il biglietto
(entry fee) il biglietto d'ingresso
a return ticket un biglietto di andata e ritorno
a single ticket un biglietto di (sola) andata
book of tickets il carnet di biglietti
tourist ticket il biglietto turistico
ticket inspector il controllore
ticket office la biglietteria
tidy ordinato(a)
to tidy up fare ordine
tie la cravatta
tight stretto(a)
tights i collant; la calzamaglia
tile (floor) la piastrella
till (cash desk) la cassa
(until) fino a
till 2 o'clock fino alle due
time il tempo
(of day) l'ora *f*
do you have the time? ha l'ora?
this time questa volta
what time is it? che ore sono?
timetable l'orario *m*
tin (can) la scatola di latta; la lattina
tinfoil la carta stagnola
tin-opener l'apriscatole *m*
tip (to waiter, etc) la mancia
to tip (waiter) dare la mancia
tired stanco(a)
tissues i fazzoletti di carta
to a
to London a Londra
to the airport all'aeroporto
toadstool il fungo velenoso
toast (to eat) il pane tostato
(raising glass) il brindisi
tobacco il tabacco
tobacconist's il tabaccaio
today oggi
toe il dito del piede
together insieme
toilet la toilette
toilet for disabled la toilette per i disabili
toilet brush lo spazzolino del gabinetto

toilet paper la carta igienica
toiletries gli articoli per l'igiene
token il gettone
toll (motorway) il pedaggio
tomato il pomodoro
a tin of tomatoes la scatola di pelati
peeled tomatoes i pelati
tomato juice il succo di pomodoro
tomato purée il concentrato di pomodoro
tomato sauce la salsa di pomodoro
tomorrow domani
tomorrow morning domani mattina
tomorrow afternoon domani pomeriggio
tomorrow evening domani sera
tongue la lingua
tonic water l'acqua tonica *f*
tonight stasera
tonsillitis la tonsillite
too (also) anche
too big troppo grande
too small troppo piccolo(a)
too hot troppo caldo(a)
too noisy troppo rumoroso(a)
tool l'attrezzo *m*
toolkit gli attrezzi
tooth il dente
toothache il mal di denti
toothbrush lo spazzolino da denti
toothpaste il dentifricio
toothpick lo stuzzicadenti
top: *the top floor* l'ultimo piano *m*
top la cima
(clothing) il top
on top of sopra di
topless in topless
torch (flashlight) la pila; la torcia elettrica
torn strappato(a)
total il totale
to touch toccare
tough (meat) duro(a)
tour il giro
guided tour la visita guidata
tour guide la guida turistica
tour operator l'operatore turistico *m*
tourist il/la turista

tourist information le informazioni turistiche
tourist office l'ufficio turistico *m*
tourist route l'itinerario turistico *m*
tourist ticket il biglietto turistico
to tow trainare
towbar la barra di traino
tow rope il cavo di traino
towel l'asciugamano *m*
tower la torre
town la città
town centre il centro città
town hall il municipio
town plan la piantina
toxic tossico(a)
toy il giocattolo
toy shop il negozio di giocattoli
track l'autodromo; la pista
tracksuit la tuta sportiva
traditional tradizionale
traffic il traffico
traffic jam l'ingorgo *m*
traffic lights il semaforo
traffic warden il vigile
trailer il rimorchio
train il treno
the first train il primo treno
the last train l'ultimo treno
the next train il prossimo treno
trainers le scarpe da ginnastica
tram il tram
tranquillizer il tranquillante
to transfer trasferire
to translate tradurre
translation la traduzione
to travel viaggiare
travel agent's l'agenzia di viaggi *f*
travel documents i documenti di viaggio
travel guide la guida
travel insurance l'assicurazione di viaggio *f*
travel sickness (sea) il mal di mare
(air) il mal d'aria
(car) il mal d'auto
traveller's cheques i traveller's (cheque)

tray il vassoio
trekking pole la racchetta da trekking
tree l'albero *m*
trip la gita; il viaggio
trolley il carrello
trouble i problemi
trousers i pantaloni
truck il camion
true vero(a)
trunk (luggage) il baule
trunks (swimming) i calzoncini da bagno
to try provare
to try on (clothes, etc) provare
t-shirt la maglietta
Tuesday il martedì
tumble dryer l'asciugatrice *f*
tunnel la galleria
Turin Torino
to turn (handle, wheel) girare
to turn around girarsi
to turn off (light, etc) spegnere
(tap) chiudere
to turn on (light, etc) accendere
(tap) aprire
turquoise (colour) turchese
tweezers le pinzette
twice due volte; il doppio
twin beds i letti gemelli
twins i gemelli
to type battere a macchina
typical tipico(a)
tyre la gomma; il pneumatico
tyre pressure la pressione delle gomme

U

ugly brutto(a)
ulcer (stomach) l'ulcera *f*
(mouth) l'afta *f*
umbrella l'ombrello *m*
(sunshade) l'ombrellone *m*
uncle lo zio
uncomfortable scomodo(a)
unconscious svenuto(a)
under sotto
undercooked poco cotto(a)

underground (metro) la metropolitana
underpants le mutande
underpass il sottopassaggio
to understand capire
do you understand? capisce?
I don't understand non capisco
underwear la biancheria intima
to undress spogliarsi
unemployed disoccupato(a)
to unfasten slacciare
United Kingdom il Regno Unito
United States gli Stati Uniti
university l'università f
unleaded petrol la benzina verde
unlikely improbabile
to unlock aprire
to unpack disfare la valigia
unpleasant sgradevole
to unplug staccare
to unscrew svitare
until fino a
unusual raro(a)

up: *to get up* alzarsi
upside down sottosopra
upstairs di sopra
urgent urgente
urine l'urina f
us ci; noi
USB flash drive (keydrive) la chiavetta USB
USB port la porta USB
to use usare
useful utile
username il nome utente
usual solito(a)
usually di solito
U-turn l'inversione a U f

V

vacancy (in hotel) la camera libera
vacant libero(a)
vacation la vacanza
vaccination la vaccinazione
vacuum cleaner l'aspirapolvere m
vagina la vagina
valid valido(a)

valley la valle
valuable di valore
valuables gli oggetti di valore
value il valore
valve la valvola
van il furgone
vase il vaso
VAT l'IVA f
vegan vegetaliano(a)
I'm vegan sono vegetaliano(a)
vegetables le verdure
vegetarian vegetariano(a)
I'm vegetarian sono vegetariano(a)
vehicle il veicolo
vein la vena
Velcro® il velcro®
vending machine il distributore automatico
venereal disease la malattia venerea
Venice Venezia
ventilator il ventilatore
very molto
vest la canottiera
vet il/la veterinario(a)
via passando per
to video (from TV) registrare su videocassetta
to make a video filmare
video il video
video camera la videocamera
video cassette/tape la videocassetta
video game il videogioco
video recorder il videoregistratore
view la vista
villa la villa
village il paese
vinegar l'aceto m
vineyard la vigna
viper la vipera
virus il virus
visa il visto
visit la visita
to visit visitare
visiting hours l'orario delle visite m
visitor il visitatore/la visitatrice
vitamin la vitamina
voice la voce

voicemail la casella vocale
volcano il vulcano
volleyball la pallavolo
voltage il voltaggio
volts i volt
to vomit vomitare
voucher il buono

W

wage il salario; la paga
waist la vita
waistcoat il gilè
to wait (for) aspettare
waiter/waitress il cameriere/
la cameriera
waiting room la sala d'aspetto
to wake up (someone) svegliare
(oneself) svegliarsi
Wales il Galles
walk la passeggiata
to walk andare a piedi
walking boots gli scarponcini
walking stick il bastone
wall il muro; la parete
wallet il portafoglio
to want volere
I want... voglio...
we want... vogliamo...
war la guerra
ward (hospital) il reparto
wardrobe l'armadio *m*
warm caldo(a)
it's warm fa caldo
to warm up (milk, etc) riscaldare
warning triangle il triangolo
d'emergenza
to wash lavare
(to wash oneself) lavarsi
wash and blow dry shampoo
e messa in piega
washbasin il lavandino
washing machine la lavatrice
washing powder il detersivo in
polvere
washing-up bowl la bacinella
washing-up liquid il detersivo
per i piatti

wasp la vespa
wasp sting la puntura di vespa
waste bin il bidone della spazzatura
watch l'orologio *m*
to watch guardare
watchstrap il cinturino dell'orologio
water l'acqua *f*
bottled water l'acqua in bottiglia *f*
drinking water l'acqua potabile
mineral water l'acqua minerale
slightly sparkling water l'acqua
leggermente frizzante
sparkling water l'acqua frizzante
still water l'acqua naturale
water heater lo scaldabagno
watermelon l'anguria *f*
waterproof impermeabile
to water-ski fare sci nautico
watersports gli sport acquatici
waterwings i braccioli salvagente
waves (on sea) le onde
waxing (hair removal) la ceretta
way in l'entrata *f*; l'ingresso *m*
way out l'uscita *f*
we noi
weak (person) debole
(tea, coffee, etc) leggero(a)
to wear portare
weather il tempo
weather forecast le previsioni del
tempo
website il sito web
wedding il matrimonio
wedding anniversary l'anniversario
di matrimonio *m*
wedding present il regalo di
matrimonio
wedding ring la fede
Wednesday mercoledì
week la settimana
during the week durante la settimana
last week la settimana scorsa
next week la prossima settimana
per week alla settimana
this week questa settimana
weekday il giorno feriale
weekend il fine settimana

next weekend il prossimo fine
  settimana
this weekend questo fine settimana
weekly settimanale
weekly pass l'abbonamento
  settimanale *m*
to weigh pesare
weight il peso
welcome benvenuto
well bene
(for water) il pozzo
well-done (steak) ben cotto(a)
wellington boots gli stivali di gomma
Welsh gallese
west ovest
wet bagnato(a)
wetsuit la muta
what cosa, quale, che
what is it? cos'è?
wheat il grano
wheel la ruota
wheelchair la sedia a rotelle
wheel clamp il ceppo bloccaruote
when quando
where dove
which qual/quale
while mentre
in a while fra poco
whipped cream la panna montata
whisky l'whisky *m*
white bianco(a)
who chi
whole tutto
wholemeal bread il pane integrale
whose: *whose is it?* di chi è?
why perché
wi-fi lo wi-fi *m*
wide largo(a); ampio(a)
widow la vedova
widower il vedovo
width la larghezza
wife la moglie
wig la parrucca
to win vincere
wind il vento
windbreak (camping) il frangivento
windmill il mulino a vento

window la finestra
(shop) la vetrina
(car) il finestrino
windscreen il parabrezza
windscreen wiper il tergicristallo
to windsurf fare il windsurf
windy: *it's windy* c'è vento
wine il vino
dry wine il vino secco
house wine il vino della casa
red wine il vino rosso
rosé wine il vino rosato
sparkling wine il vino frizzante
sweet wine il vino dolce
white wine il vino bianco
wine list la lista dei vini
wing (of bird) l'ala *f*
(of car) la fiancata
wing mirror lo specchietto laterale
winter l'inverno *m*
wire il filo
wireless internet il collegamento a
  internet senza fili
wireless wireless; senza fili
with con
with ice con ghiaccio
with milk con latte
with sugar con zucchero
without senza
without ice senza ghiaccio
without milk senza latte
without sugar senza zucchero
witness il/la testimone
woman la donna
wonderful meraviglioso(a)
wood (material) il legno
(forest) il bosco
wooden di legno
wool la lana
word la parola
work il lavoro
to work (person) lavorare
(machine, car, etc) funzionare
it doesn't work non funziona
work permit il premesso di lavoro
world il mondo
worried preoccupato(a)

worse peggio
worth (value) il valore
it's worth £5 (parcel) vale cinque sterline
to wrap up (parcel) incartare
wrapping paper la carta da regalo
wrinkles le rughe
wrist il polso
to write scrivere
please write it down lo scriva per favore
writing paper la carta da lettere
wrong sbagliato(a)
what's wrong? cosa c'è?
wrought iron il ferro battuto

X
x-ray la radiografia
to x-ray radiografare

Y
yacht lo yacht
year l'anno *m*
last year l'anno scorso
next year l'anno prossimo
this year quest'anno
yearly (every year) annualmente
yellow giallo(a)
Yellow Pages le pagine gialle®
yes sì
yesterday ieri
yet: *not yet* non ancora
yoghurt lo yogurt
low-fat yoghurt lo yogurt magro
plain yoghurt lo yogurt naturale
yolk il tuorlo
you tu; voi; lei
young giovane
your il/la suo(a); il/la tuo(a); il/la vostro(a)

Z
zebra crossing le strisce pedonali
zero lo zero
zip la cerniera
zone la zona
zoo lo zoo

Dictionary

● ●

A

a at; in
abbaglianti *mpl* full-beam headlights
abbiamo... we have...
non abbiamo... we don't have...
abbigliamento *m* clothes
abbonamento *m* subscription; season ticket
abbronzatura *f* suntan
abito *m* dress; man's suit
aborto *m* abortion
aborto spontaneo miscarriage
abuso *m* misuse
a.C. B.C.
accamparsi to camp
accanto (a) beside; next (to)
acceleratore *m* accelerator
accendere to turn on; to light
accendere i fari switch on your headlights
accendino *m* cigarette lighter
accensione *f* ignition
accento *m* accent *(pronunciation)*
acceso(a) on *(light, engine)*
accesso *m* access
divieto di accesso no access
accettazione *f* reception
accettazione bagagli check-in
accomodarsi to make oneself comfortable
si accomodi do take a seat
accompagnare to accompany
accordo *m* agreement
aceto *m* vinegar
acetone *m* nail polish remover
ACI *m* Automobile Association
acqua *f* water
acqua calda hot water
acqua corrente running water
acqua distillata distilled water
acqua gassata sparkling water
acqua leggermente frizzante slightly sparkling water

acqua minerale mineral water
acqua naturale still water
acqua potabile drinking water
acquisto *m* purchase
addetto(a) person in charge
adesso now
adulto(a) adult
aereo *m* plane; aircraft
aeroplano *m* airplane
aeroporto *m* airport
affari *mpl* business
per affari on business
affittare to rent; to let
affittasi for rent
affitto *m* lease; rent
affogare to drown
agenda *f* diary
agenzia *f* agency
agenzia di viaggi travel agent
agenzia immobiliare estate agent
aggredire to attack
aglio *m* garlic
ago *m* needle
ago ipodermico hypodermic needle
agosto *m* August
AIDS *m* AIDS
agriturismo holiday farm *(restaurant, rooms)*
aiutare to help
aiuto! help!
alba *f* dawn
albergo *m* hotel
albero *m* tree; mast
albicocca *f* apricot
alcolici *mpl* alcoholic drinks
alcolico(a) alcoholic
alcol *m* alcohol
alcuni(e) some; a few
alcuno(a) any; some
alimentari *mpl* groceries
aliscafo hydrofoil
allacciare to fasten *(seatbelt, etc)*
allarme *m* alarm

allarme antincendio fire alarm
allergia *f* allergy
allergico(a) a allergic to
alloggio *m* accommodation
alluvione *f* flood
Alpi *fpl* Alps
alpinismo *m* climbing
alt stop
altezza *f* height
alto(a) high; tall
alta stagione high season
alta marea high tide
altoparlante *m* loudspeaker
altro(a) other
altri passaporti other passports
alzarsi to get up; to stand up
amabile sweet *(wine)*
amare to love *(person)*
amarena *f* sour cherry
amaro(a) bitter *(taste)*
ambasciata *f* embassy
ambiente *m* environment
ambulanza *f* ambulance
ambulatorio *m* surgery; out-patients
America *f* America
americano(a) American
amico(a) *m/f* friend
ammalato(a) ill
amministratore delegato *m* CEO
ammontare *m* total amount
ammortizzatore *m* shock absorber
amo *m* hook
amore *m* love
analisi del sangue *f* blood test
analcolico *m* soft drink
analcolico(a) non-alcoholic
analgesico *m* painkiller
ananas *m* pineapple
anatra *f* duck
anca *f* hip
anche too; also; even
ancora still; yet; again
ancora un po'? a little more?
non ancora not yet
ancora *f* anchor
andare to go
andare a cavallo to ride a horse

andare a piedi to go on foot
andare bene to fit *(clothes)*
andare in macchina to go by car
andata: *andata e ritorno* return *(ticket)*
di (sola) andata single *(ticket)*
andiamo! let's go!
andiamo a... we're going to...
anestetico *m* anaesthetic
angina pectoris *f* angina
anguria *f* watermelon
anice *m* aniseed
animale *m* animal
animale domestico pet
annata *f* vintage; year
vino d'annata vintage wine
anniversario *m* anniversary
anno *m* year
buon anno! happy New Year!
annuale annual
annullamento *m* cancellation
annullare to cancel
annuncio *m* announcement; advert
l'antenna *f* aerial
antibiotico *m* antibiotic
anticipo *m* advance *(loan)*
in anticipo in advance; early
anticoncezionale *m* contraceptive
antifurto *m* burglar alarm
antigelo *m* antifreeze; de-icer
antipasto *m* starter; hors d'œuvre
antisettico *m* antiseptic
antistaminico *m* antihistamine
anziano(a) *m/f* senior citizen
ape *f* bee
aperitivo *m* apéritif
aperto(a) open
all'aperto open-air
appartamento *m* flat; apartment
appendicite *f* appendicitis
appuntamento *m* appointment; date
apribottiglie *m* bottle opener
aprile *m* April
aprire to open; to turn on *(tap)*
apriscatole *m* tin-opener
arachide *f* peanut
arancia *f* orange
aranciata *f* orangeade

arancione orange *(colour)*
area *f* area
area di servizio service area
argento *m* silver
aria condizionata *f* air-conditioning
armadio *m* cupboard; wardrobe
arrabbiato(a) angry
arredato(a) furnished
arrestare to arrest
arrivare to arrive
arrivederci goodbye
arrivo *m* arrival
arrivi internazionali international arrivals
arrivi nazionali domestic arrivals
arrosto *m* roast
arte *f* art; craft
articolo *m* article
articoli da dichiarare goods to declare
articoli da regalo gifts
artigiano(a) *m/f* craftsperson
artista *m/f* artist
artrite *f* arthritis
ascensore *m* lift; elevator
ascesso *m* abscess
asciugamano *m* towel
asciugare to dry
asciugatrice *f* tumble dryer
ASL local health centre
ascoltare to listen (to)
asma *f* asthma
asparagi *m* asparagus
aspettare to wait (for); to expect
aspirapolvere *m* vacuum cleaner
aspirina *f* aspirin
assaggiare to taste
asse *m* axle *(car)*
asse da stiro ironing board
assegno *m* cheque
assicurato(a) insured
assicurazione *f* insurance
assistente *m/f* assistant
assistenza *f* assistance; aid
associazione *f* association
assorbenti *mpl* sanitary towels
assorbenti interni tampons

attaccare to attach; to attack; to fasten
attacco *m* fit *(seizure)*
attacco cardiaco heart attack
attendere to wait for
attento(a) careful
attenzione *f* caution
fare attenzione to be careful
atterraggio *m* landing *(of plane)*
atterrare to land *(plane)*
attestare to declare
attore *m* actor
attracco *m* mooring; berth
attraente attractive
attraversare to cross
attraverso through
attrazione *f* attraction
attrezzatura *f* equipment
attrezzo *m* tool
attrice *f* actress
auguri! best wishes!
aumentare to increase
Australia *f* Australia
australiano(a) Australian
austriaco(a) Austrian
autentico(a) genuine
autista *m/f* driver
auto *f* car
autobus *m* bus
autofficina *f* garage *(for repairs)*
autonoleggio *m* car hire
autore *m* author
autoricambi *mpl* car parts and accessories
autorimessa *f* garage
autorizzazione *f* authorization
autostop *m* hitchhiking
autostrada *f* motorway
autunno *m* autumn
avanti in front; forward(s)
avanti! come in!
avere to have
avere bisogno di to need
avere fame to be hungry
avere sete to be thirsty
avvertire to warn
avvisare to inform; to warn

avviso *m* notice; advertisement
azienda *f* business; firm
azienda di soggiorno local tourist board
azzardo *m* risk; hazard
azzurro(a) light blue

B

babbo *m* daddy
Babbo Natale Father Christmas
baciare to kiss
bacinella *f* washing-up bowl
bacio *m* kiss
baci! love and kisses *(in letter)*
baffi *mpl* moustache
bagagli *mpl* luggage
bagagliaio *m* boot *(of car)*
bagaglio *m* luggage
bagaglio a mano hand luggage
bagnarsi to bathe; to get wet
bagnino *m* lifeguard
bagno *m* bath; bathroom
balcone *m* balcony
ballare to dance
balletto *m* ballet
ballo *m* dance
balneazione *f* bathing
divieto di balneazione no swimming
balsamo *m* hair conditioner
bambino(a) *m/f* child; baby
bambini *mpl* children
il seggiolino per bambini booster seat *(car)*
per bambini for children
bambola *f* doll
banana *f* banana
banca *f* bank
bancarella *f* stall; stand
banchina *f* platform; quay
banco *m* counter; desk
banco informazioni enquiry desk
Bancomat® *m* cash machine; ATM
banconota *f* banknote
banda larga *f* broadband
bandiera *f* flag
bar *m* bar; café
barattolo *m* tin; jar

barba *f* beard
barbiere *m* barber
barca *f* boat
barista *m/f* barman/barmaid
basso(a) low; short
bassa marea low tide
basta that's enough
battello *m* boat
batteria *f* battery *(car)*
batteria ricaricabile rechargeable
batteria scarica flat battery
baule *m* trunk *(luggage)*
bavaglino *m* bib
bello(a) beautiful; fine; lovely
benda *f* bandage
bene well; all right; OK
benvenuto welcome
benzina *f* petrol
fare benzina to get petrol
bere to drink
bevanda *f* drink
biancheria *f* linen *(for beds, table)*
biancheria intima underwear
bianco(a) white; blank
lasciate in bianco leave blank
biberon *m* baby's bottle
bibita *f* soft drink
bibite soft drinks
bicchiere *m* glass *(for drinking)*
bici *f* bike *(pushbike)*
bicicletta *f* bicycle
bidet *m* bidet
bidone *m* bin; dustbin; can
biglietteria *f* ticket office
biglietto *m* ticket; note; card
biglietto d'auguri greetings card
biglietto da visita business card
bin. *(abbreviation of)* **binario**
binario *m* platform
biologico(a) organic
biondo(a) blond *(person)*
biro *f* biro
birra *f* beer
birra alla spina draught beer
birra chiara lager
birra scura ale
birreria *f* bar; pub

biscotto *m* biscuit
bisogno *m* need
avere bisogno di to need
bistecca *f* steak
bloccare to block
bloccare un assegno to stop a cheque
blocchetto di biglietti *m* book of tickets
blocco *m* block; notepad
blu blue
blue jeans *mpl* jeans
boa *f* buoy
bocca *f* mouth
boccaglio *m* snorkel
bocce *fpl* bowls *(game)*
bolletta *f* bill
bollire to boil
bollitore *m* kettle
bomba *f* bomb
bombola del gas *f* gas cylinder
bombolone *m* doughnut
borotalco *m* talc
borsa *f* bag; handbag; briefcase
borsa termica cool-box *(for picnic)*
borseggiatore *m* pickpocket
borsellino *m* purse; wallet
borsa di plastica *f* plastic bag
bosco *m* wood; forest
bottega *f* shop
botteghino *m* box office
bottiglia *f* bottle
bottone *m* button
boxer *mpl* boxer shorts
braccialetto *m* bracelet
braccio *m* arm
braccioli *mpl* armbands *(swimming)*
braciola *f* steak; chop
brindisi *m* toast *(raising glass)*
brioche *f* croissant
britannico(a) *f* British
bronchite *f* bronchitis
bruciare to burn
bruciore di stomaco *m* heartburn
brutto(a) bad *(weather, news)*; ugly
buca delle lettere *f* postbox
bucato *m* washing; laundry
bucato a mano hand washing

bucato in lavatrice machine wash
buco *m* hole
buono(a) good
a buon mercato cheap
buon appetito! enjoy your meal!
buon compleanno! happy birthday!
buon giorno good morning/afternoon
buona notte good night
buona sera good afternoon/evening
buono *m* voucher; coupon; token
burattino *m* puppet
burrasca *f* storm
burro *m* butter
burro di cacao *m* lip salve
bussare to knock *(on door)*
busta *f* envelope
bustina di tè *f* tea bag
buttare via to throw away

C

cabina *f* beach hut; cabin
cabina telefonica phonebox
cacciavite *m* screwdriver
cadere to fall
caffè *m* coffee *(espresso)*
caffè corretto espresso with spirit such as grappa
caffè decaffeinato decaffeinated
caffè macchiato espresso with a little warm milk
caffè solubile instant coffee
caffellatte milky coffee
caffettiera *f* espresso-maker
calamita *f* magnet
calciatore *m* football player
calcio *m* football; kick
calcolatrice *f* calculator
caldo(a) hot
calendario *m* calendar
calle *f* street *(in Venice)*
callo *m* corn *(on foot)*
calmante *m* sedative
calmo(a) calm
calpestare to tread on
calvo(a) bald
calza *f* stocking; sock
calzamaglia *f* tights

calzature *fpl* shoes
calze *fpl* stockings; tights
calzini *mpl* socks
calzolaio *m* shoe mender
calzoleria *f* shoe mender's
calzoncini corti *mpl* shorts
calzoncini da bagno swimming trunks
cambiamento *m* change
cambiare to change
cambiare autobus/treno to change bus/train
cambiare soldi to change money
cambiarsi to change one's clothes
cambio *m* exchange; gearbox; transmission *(car)*
camera *f* room *(in house, hotel)*
camera da letto bedroom
camera doppia double room
camera libera vacancy *(in hotel)*
camera per famiglia family room
camera singola single room
cameriera *f* chambermaid
cameriere *m* waiter
camiceria *f* shirt shop
camicetta *f* blouse
camicia *f* shirt
camicia da notte nightdress
camion *m* lorry
camminare to walk
camoscio *m* chamois
campagna *f* countryside; campaign
campanello *m* bell
campeggiare to camp
campeggio *m* camping; campsite
campeggio libero free campsite
camping gas *m* gas da campeggio
campione *m* sample; champion
campo *m* field; court
campo da tennis tennis court
campo di calcio football pitch
campo di golf golf course
campo sportivo sports ground
camposanto *m* cemetery
Canada *m* Canada
canadese Canadian
canale *m* canal; channel

cancellare to erase; to cancel
cancellazione *f* cancellation
cancro *m* cancer
candeggina *f* bleach
candela *f* candle; spark plug
candida *f* thrush *(candida)*
cane *m* dog
canile *m* kennel
canna da pesca *f* fishing rod
cannuccia *f* straw *(for drinking)*
canoa *f* canoe
canottaggio *m* rowing
canottiera *f* vest
canotto *m* dinghy *(rubber)*
cantante *m/f* singer
cantare to sing
cantiere *m* building site; roadworks
cantina *f* cellar; wine cellar
canzone *f* song
capelli *mpl* hair
capire to understand
capisce? do you understand?
non capisco I don't understand
capitale *f* capital *(city)*
capitolo *m* chapter
capo *m* head; leader; boss
Capodanno *m* New Year's day
capogruppo *m* group leader
capolavoro *m* masterpiece
capolinea *m* terminus
capoluogo *m* county town
capotreno *m* guard *(on train)*
cappella *f* chapel
cappello *m* hat
cappotto *m* overcoat
cappuccino *m* cappuccino
capra *f* goat
carabiniere *m* policeman
caraffa *f* carafe
caramelle *fpl* sweets
carbone *m* coal; charcoal
carburante *m* fuel
carburatore *m* carburettor
carcere *m* prison
caricare to charge *(battery)*
devo ricaricare il telefonino I need to charge my phone

carico *m* load; shipment; cargo
carino(a) pretty; lovely; nice
carne *f* meat
carnevale *m* carnival
caro(a) dear; expensive
carote *fpl* carrots
carrello *m* trolley
carriera *f* career
carro *m* cart
carro attrezzi breakdown van
carrozza *f* carriage
carrozze cuccette couchettes
carrozza letto sleeper
carrozzeria *f* bodywork
carrozzina *f* pram
carta *f* paper; card; map
alla carta à la carte
carta assegni cheque card
carta d'argento senior citizen's rail card
carta di circolazione log book
carta di credito credit card
carta famiglia family rail card
carta d'identità identity card
carta d'imbarco boarding card
carta igienica toilet paper
carta stradale road map
carta verde green card
carte da gioco *fpl* playing cards
cartella *f* briefcase; folder
cartello *m* sign; signpost
cartine *fpl* cigarette papers
cartoccio *m* paper bag
cartoleria *f* stationer's
cartolina *f* postcard
casa *f* house; home
a casa at home
casalinga *f* housewife
casalinghi *mpl* household articles
cascata *f* waterfall
casco *m* helmet
casella postale *f* post-office box
casella vocale *f* voicemail
casinò *m* casino
caso: in caso di in case of
cassa *f* till; cash desk
cassa chiusa position closed

cassaforte *f* safe *(for valuables)*
cassetta *f* cassette
cassetta delle lettere letterbox
cassetto *m* drawer
cassiere(a) *m/f* cashier; teller
castello *m* castle
catena *f* chain; mountain range
catene (da neve) snow chains
cattedrale *f* cathedral
cattivo(a) bad; nasty; naughty
cattolico(a) Catholic
causa *f* cause; case *(lawsuit)*
a causa di because of
cavalcare to ride *(horse)*
cavallo *m* horse
cavatappi *m* corkscrew
cavo *m* cable
cavo da rimorchio tow rope
cavo della frizione clutch cable *(car)*
cavo del freno brake cable *(bicycle)*
cavolfiore *m* cauliflower
CD *m* CD
CD vuoto blank CD
c'è there is
cedro *m* cedar; lime *(fruit)*
celibe *m* single man *(not married)*
cellulare *m* mobile phone
cena *f* dinner *(evening meal)*
cenare to have dinner
cenone *m* New Year's Eve dinner
centesimo *m* cent *(euro)*
centimetro *m* centimetre
cento hundred
centrale central
centralino *m* switchboard
centro *m* centre
centro affari business centre
centro città city centre
centro commerciale shopping centre
centro storico old town
ceppo bloccaruote *m* wheel clamp
cera *f* wax *(for furniture)*
ceramica *f* ceramics; pottery
cercare to look for
ceretta *f* waxing *(hair removal)*
cerini *mpl* matches
cerniera *f* zip

cerotto *m* sticking plaster
certificato *m* certificate
certificato di nascita birth certificate
cervello *m* brain
cestino *m* basket; waste paper bin
cetriolo *m* cucumber
chatroom *m* chatroom *(internet)*
che what; which; that
che gusto? what flavour?
che ore sono? what time is it?
penso che sia ora I think that it's time
cherosene *m* paraffin
chi? who?
di chi è? whose is it?
chiamare to call
chiamare per telefono to phone
chiamarsi to be called *(name)*
come si chiama? what's your name?
chiamata *f* call *(telephone)*
chiave *f* key
chiave elettronica keycard
chiave inglese spanner
chiavetta di memoria *f* memory stick *(for camera, etc)*
chiavetta USB *f* USB flash drive
chiedere to ask; to ask for
chiesa *f* church
chilo *m* kilo
chilogrammo *m* kilogram
chilometraggio *m* mileage *(in km)*
chilometro *m* kilometre
chiodo *m* nail *(metal)*
chirurgia *f* surgery *(operations)*
chitarra *f* guitar
chiudere to close; to turn off *(tap)*
chiudere a chiave to lock
chiuso(a) closed
chiuso per turno closed for weekly day off
chiuso per ferie closed for holidays
chiusura centralizzata *f* central locking *(car)*
ciabatta *f* slipper; type of bread
ciao! hi!; bye!
cibo *m* food
cielo *m* sky
ciliegia *f* cherry

cinghia della ventola *f* fan belt
cintura *f* belt
cintura di sicurezza seatbelt
cinturino dell'orologio *m* watchstrap
cioccolato *m* chocolate
cipolla *f* onion
circo *m* circus
circolare to move *(traffic)*
circolazione *f* traffic
circonvallazione *f* ring road
cisterna *f* cistern; tank
cisti *f* cyst
cistite *f* cystitis
citofono *m* intercom
città *f* city; town
cittadinanza *f* citizenship
cittadino(a) citizen
classe *f* class
clavicola *f* collar bone
cliente *m/f* customer
climatizzato(a) air-conditioned
clinica *f* clinic
cocco *m* coconut
cocomero *m* watermelon
coda *f* tail; queue
codice *m* code
codice a barre barcode
codice postale postcode
codice stradale highway code
cofano *m* bonnet *(car)*
cognata *f* sister-in-law
cognato *m* brother-in-law
cognome *m* surname
di cognome mi chiamo... my surname is...
coincidenza *f* connection *(train, etc)*; coincidence
colazione *f* breakfast; lunch
collana *f* necklace
collant *mpl* tights
collega *m/f* colleague
collegamento a internet senza fili *m* wireless internet
colletto *m* collar
collina *f* hill
collo *m* neck; package

colluttorio m mouthwash
colomba f dove; Easter cake
colore m colour
Colosseo m Coliseum
colpa f fault
non è colpa mia it's not my fault
coltello m knife
combustibile m fuel
come like; as; how
come? how? *(in what way)*
come si chiama? what's your name?
come si pronuncia? how is it pronounced?
come si scrive? how is it spelt?
come sta? how are you?
come va? how's it going?
cominciare to begin
commesso(a) m/f assistant; clerk
commissariato m police station
commozione cerebrale f concussion
comodo(a) comfortable
compagnia f company
compagnia aerea airline
compilare to fill in *(form)*
compleanno m birthday
completo(a) no vacancies; full
completo m outfit
comporre to dial *(number)*
comprare to buy
compreso(a) included
compressa f tablet
computer m computer
computer palmare palmtop
computer portatile laptop
comune m town hall; commune
con with
con bagno with bathroom
con filtro filter-tipped
con ghiaccio with ice
concerto m concert
conchiglia f seashell
condimento m seasoning; dressing *(for food)*
conducente m/f driver *(taxi, bus)*
confermare to confirm
confine m boundary; border
congelatore m freezer

congratulazioni! congratulations!
congresso m conference
cono m cone
cono gelato ice-cream cone
conoscere to know *(to be acquainted with)*
consegna f consignment; delivery
conservante m preservative
consigliare to advise
consiglio m advice
consumare to use up
da consumarsi entro best before
consumazione f drink
contanti mpl cash
pagare in contanti to pay cash
contatore m electricity meter
contento(a) happy
continuare to continue
conto m account; bill
conto corrente current account
conto dettagliato itemised bill
conto in banca bank account
contorno m vegetable side dish
contrabbando m smuggling
contratto m contract
contravvenzione f fine
contro against; versus
controllare to check
controllo m check; control
controllo passaporti passport control
controllore m ticket collector
convalida f date stamp
convalidare to validate *(ticket)*
convincere to persuade
coperta f blanket
coperto m place setting; cover charge
copertura f cover *(insurance)*
coppa gelato f ice cream served in goblet/tub
coppia f couple *(two people)*
copriletto m bedspread
coraggioso(a) brave
corda f rope
cordless m cordless phone
cornetto m ice cream cone
corpo m body
corrente f current *(electric, water)*

corrente d'aria draught
correre to run
corridoio *m* corridor
corriere *m* courier
corsa *f* race; journey
corsa semplice single fare
corsia *f* lane; hospital ward; route
corsia di emergenza hard shoulder
corsia di sorpasso outside lane
corso *m* course; avenue
corso dei cambi exchange rates
corso intensivo crash course
cortile *m* courtyard
corto(a) short
cos'è? what is it?
cos'è successo? what happened?
cosa *f* thing
cosa? what?
coscia *f* thigh
così so; thus *(in this way)*
cosmetici *mpl* cosmetics
costa *f* coast
Costa Azzurra French Riviera
costare to cost
costoletta *f* chop
costoso(a) expensive
costruire to build
costume *m* custom; costume
costume da bagno swimsuit
cotone *m* cotton
cotone idrofilo cotton wool
cotto(a) cooked
poco cotto(a) medium rare *(steak)*
cotton fioc® *m* cotton bud
crampi *mpl* cramps
cravatta *f* tie
credere to believe
credito *m* credit
carta di credito credit card
non si fa credito no credit given
crema *f* cream; custard
crema da barba shaving cream
crema solare suncream
crescere to grow
crespella *f* fried pastry twist
cric *m* jack *(for car)*
crisi epilettica *f* epileptic fit

cristallo *m* crystal
di cristallo made of crystal
croccante *f* crisp
croce *f* cross
crocevia *m* crossroads
crociera *f* cruise
crollo *m* collapse
cronaca *f* news
cruciverba *m* crossword puzzle
crudo(a) raw
cuccetta *f* couchette; sleeper
cucchiaino *m* teaspoon
cucchiaio *m* spoon; tablespoon
cucina *f* cooker; kitchen; cooking
cucina a gas gas cooker
cucinare to cook
cucire to sew
cuffia *f* bathing cap
cuffie *fpl* earphones
cugino(a) *m/f* cousin
culla *f* cradle
cuocere to cook
cuocere a vapore to steam
cuocere alla griglia to grill
cuoco *m* cook
cuoio *m* leather
cuore *m* heart
cupola *f* dome
curva *f* bend; corner
cuscino *m* cushion
custode *m* caretaker
custodia *f* case; holder
cyber-café *m* internet cafe

D

da from; by; worth
da asporto take-away
dall'America from England
dalla Scozia from Scotland
da vedere worth seeing
da 100 euro worth 100 euros
dadi *m* stock cubes
danneggiare to spoil; to damage
danno *m* damage
dappertutto everywhere
dare to give
dare da mangiare to feed

dare la mancia to tip *(waiter, etc)*
dare la precedenza give way
dare su to overlook; to give onto
data *f* date
data di nascita date of birth
data di scadenza sell-by date
dati *mpl* data
dattero *m* date *(fruit)*
davanti a in front of; opposite
dazio *m* customs duty
d.C. A.D.
debito *m* debt
decaffeinato(a) decaffeinated
decollare to take-off
decollo *m* takeoff
delizioso(a) delicious
dente *m* tooth
dentiera *f* dentures
dentifricio *m* toothpaste
dentro in; indoors; inside
deodorante *m* deodorant
deodorante per ambienti air freshener
deposito bagagli *m* left-luggage
descrivere to describe
descrizione *f* description
desiderare to want; to desire
destinazione *f* destination
destra *f* right
detergente *m* cleanser
detersivo *m* detergent
detersivo in polvere soap powder
detersivo per i piatti washing-up liquid
detrazione *f* deduction
dettagli *mpl* details
deviazione *f* detour; diversion
di of; some
di cristallo/plastica made of crystal/plastic
di Giovanni Giovanni's
di lusso luxury *(hotel, etc)*
di mattina in the morning
di moda fashionable
di notte at night
di pomeriggio in the afternoon
di stagione in season

di valore of value; valuable
diabete *m* diabetes
diabetico(a) diabetic
diaframma *m* cap *(diaphragm)*
dialetto *m* dialect
diamante *m* diamond
diapositiva *f* slide *(photo)*
diarrea *f* diarrhoea
dicembre *m* December
dichiarare to declare
dichiarazione *f* declaration
dieta *f* diet
essere a dieta to be on a diet
dietro behind; after
dietro di me behind me
difetto *m* fault
difficile difficult
diga *f* dam; dyke
digerire to digest
digestivo *m* after-dinner liqueur
dimenticare to forget
Dio *m* God
dipinto(a) painted; painting
diramazione *f* fork *(in road)*
dire to say; to tell
diretto(a) direct
in diretta live *(TV programme, etc)*
treno diretto through train
direttore *m* manager; director
direzione *f* management; direction
dirigere to manage *(be in charge of)*
diritto(a) straight
sempre diritto straight on
disabile disabled *(person)*
disastro *m* disaster
disco *m* disk; record
disco orario parking disk
discoteca *f* disco
disdire to cancel
disegno *m* drawing
disfare la valigia to unpack
disinfettante *m* disinfectant
disoccupato(a) unemployed
dispiacere: *mi dispiace* I'm sorry
disponibile available
distaccare to detach; to unplug
distante far; distant

distanza *f* distance
distorsione *f* sprain
distributore *m* dispenser
distributore di benzina petrol station
disturbare to disturb
disturbo *m* trouble
dito *m* finger
dito del piede toe
ditta *f* firm; company
diurno(a) day(time)
divano *m* sofa; divan
divano letto sofa bed
diversi(e) several; various
diverso(a) different
divertente funny *(amusing)*
divertimento *m* entertainment; fun
divertirsi to enjoy oneself
dividere to share
divieto forbidden; not allowed
divieto di sorpasso no overtaking
divieto di sosta no parking
divisa *f* uniform
divorziato(a) divorced
dizionario *m* dictionary
DOC *(abbreviation of)*
denominazione di origine
 controllata *(guarantee of wine quality)*
doccia *f* shower
docente *m/f* lecturer
DOCG *(abbreviation of)*
denominazione di origine
 controllata e garantita *(guarantee of wine quality)*
documenti *mpl* papers *(passport)*
dogana *f* customs
dolce sweet *(not savoury)*; mild
dolce *m* sweet; dessert; cake
dolcificante *m* sweetener
dolciumi *mpl* sweets
dollari *mpl* dollars
dolore *m* pain; grief
doloroso(a) painful
domanda *f* question
domandare to ask *(a question)*
domani tomorrow
domani mattina tomorrow morning
domani pomeriggio tomorrow

afternoon
domani sera tomorrow evening/night
domattina tomorrow morning
domenica Sunday
donna *f* woman
donne ladies; women
dopo after; afterward(s)
dopobarba *m* aftershave
dopodomani the day after tomorrow
doppio(a) double
dormire to sleep
dove? where?
dovere to have to
droga *f* drugs *(narcotics)*
drogheria *f* grocery shop
duepezzi *m* two-piece suit; bikini
duomo *m* cathedral
durante during
durare to last
duro(a) hard; tough; harsh
DVD *m* DVD
lettore DVD DVD player

E

e and
E *(abbreviation)* east
è is (to be)
ebreo(a) Jewish
ecc. etc.
eccedenza *f* excess; surplus
eccesso *m* excess
eccesso di velocità speeding
eccezionale exceptional
eccezione *f* exception
ecco here is/are
ecologico(a) ecological
economico(a) cheap
ecoturismo *m* eco-tourism
edicola *f* newsstand; kiosk
edificio *m* building
effetto *m* effect
effetti personali belongings
egregio(a) dear *(in formal letter)*
elastico *m* rubber band
elenco *m* list
elenco telefonico phone directory
elettricista *m/f* electrician

elettricità f electricity
elettrico(a) electric(al)
elettrodomestici mpl electrical goods
elettronico(a) electronic
agenda elettronica electronic organizer
elisoccorso m air ambulance
emergenza f emergency
emicrania f migraine
emorroidi fpl haemorrhoids
enoteca f wine shop; wine bar
ente m corporation; body
entrambi(e) both
entrare to come/go in; to enter
entrata f entrance
entrata abbonati season ticket
 holders' entrance
entrata libera free admission
epatite f hepatitis
epilessia f epilepsy
epilettico(a) epileptic
equitazione f horse-riding
erba f grass
ernia f hernia
errore m mistake
esame m examination
esatto(a) exact; accurate
esaurimento nervoso m nervous
 breakdown
esaurito(a) exhausted; out of print
tutto esaurito sold out
esca m fishing bait
escluso(a) excluding
escursione f excursion
esente exempt
esente da dogana duty-free
esempio example
per esempio for example
esercizio m exercise; business
esigenza f requirement
esperto(a) expert; experienced
esplosione f explosion
esportare to export
esposto(a) exposed
esposto(a) a nord north-facing
espresso m express train; coffee
espresso(a) express (parcel, etc)
essere to be

essere assicurato(a) to be insured
essere capace (di) to be able (to)
essere d'accordo to agree
essere nato(a) to be born
est m east
estate f summer
esterno(a) outside; external
estero(a) foreign
all'estero abroad
estintore m fire extinguisher
estivo(a) summer
età f age
etichetta f luggage tag; label
euro euro
euro cent m centesimo
Europa f Europe
eventuale possible
evitare to avoid

F

fa ago
un anno fa a year ago
fabbrica f factory
fabbricare to manufacture
faccia f face
facile easy
fagiano m pheasant
fagiolini m runner beans
fai da te m DIY
fallire to fail
fallito(a) bankrupt
fallo m foul (football)
falso(a) fake
fame f hunger
avere fame to be hungry
famiglia f family
familiare family; familiar
famoso(a) famous
fanale m light
fanalino dello stop m brake light
fango m mud
farcito(a) stuffed; filled
fare to do; to make
fare attenzione to be careful
fare la spesa to go shopping
fare la spesa su internet to shop
 online

farfalla *f* butterfly
fari *mpl* headlights
farina *f* flour
farmacia *f* chemist's; pharmacy
farmacie di turno duty chemists
farmacista pharmacist
farmaco *m* drug *(medicine)*
faro *m* headlight; lighthouse
fascia *f* band; bandage
fastidio: *non mi dà fastidio* I don't mind
fatto a mano hand-made
fatto di... made of...
fattoria *f* farm; farmhouse
fattura *f* invoice
favore *m* favour
per favore please
fax *m* fax
fazzoletto *m* handkerchief
fazzoletto di carta tissue
febbraio February
febbre *f* fever
avere la febbre to have a temperature
febbre da fieno hay fever
fede *f* wedding ring; faith
federa *f* pillowcase
fegato *m* liver
felice happy
felpa *f* sweatshirt
femmina *f* female
feriale workday *(Monday-Saturday)*
ferie *fpl* holiday(s)
essere in ferie to be on holiday
ferire to injure
ferita *f* wound; injury; cut
ferito(a) injured
fermare to stop
fermata *f* stop
fermata dell'autobus bus stop
fermo(a) still; off *(machine)*
stare fermo to stay still
ferro da stiro *m* iron *(for clothes)*
ferrovia *f* railway
festa *f* festival; holiday; party
festa nazionale public holiday
festivo(a) sundays/public holiday
fetta *f* slice

fiamma *f* flame
fiammifero *m* match
fico *m* fig
fidanzato(a) engaged *(to marry)*
fieno *m* hay
fiera *f* fair *(trade)*
fiera dell'artigianato craft fair
figlia *f* daughter
figlio *m* son
fila *f* line *(row, queue)*
fare la fila to queue
filiale *f* branch; subsidiary
film *m* film *(at cinema)*
filo *m* thread; wire
filo interdentale dental floss
filtro *m* filter
filtro dell'olio oil filter
finanza *f* finance
Guardia di finanza Customs and Excise
fine *f* end
fine settimana weekend
fine stagione end of season
fine elegant; fine
finestra *f* window
finestrino *m* window *(car, train)*
finire to finish
finito(a) finished
fino a until; as far as
fino alle due till 2 o'clock
fior di latte *m* cream *(ice cream flavour)*
fiori *mpl* flowers
fiorista *m/f* florist
Firenze Florence
firma *f* signature
firmare to sign
firmare il registro to sign the register
fiume *m* river
focaccia *f* flat salted bread
foglia *f* leaf *(of tree, etc)*
fogna *f* sewer; drain
folla *f* crowd
folle mad
in folle in neutral *(car)*
fon *m* hairdryer
fondo *m* back *(of room)*; bottom
fontana *f* fountain

fonte f source
foratura f puncture
forbici fpl scissors
forbicine nail scissors
forchetta f fork *(for eating)*
foresta f forest
forfora f dandruff
formaggio m cheese
fornaio m baker
fornello m stove; hotplate
fornitore m supplier
forno m oven
forno a microonde microwave
forse perhaps
forte strong; loud; high *(speed)*
fortunato(a) lucky
forza f strength; force
foto f photo
fotocamera digitale f digital camera
fotocopia f photocopy
fotocopiare to photocopy
fotocopiatrice f photocopier
fototessera f passport-type photo
foulard m headscarf
fra between; among(st)
fra 2 giorni in 2 days
fra poco in a while
fragile breakable
fragola f strawberry
frana f landslide
francese French
francese m French *(language)*
Francia f France
francobollo m stamp
frappé m milk shake
fratello m brother
frattura f fracture
frazione f village
freccia f indicator *(car)*; arrow
freddo(a) cold
frenare to brake
freno m brake
freno a mano handbrake
frequente frequent
fretta f hurry
avere fretta to be in a hurry
friggere to fry

frigorifero m refrigerator
frittata f omelette
fritto(a) fried
frizione f clutch *(car)*
frizzante fizzy; sparkling
fronte f forehead; front
di fronte a facing; opposite
frontiera f frontier; border
frullato m milkshake
frutta f fruit
frutta secca dried fruit
frutti di mare mpl seafood
fruttivendolo m greengrocer
FS Italian State Railways
fuga f escape; leak *(gas)*
fuggire to escape
fulmine m lightning
fumare to smoke
non fumo I don't smoke
fumatori smokers
fumo m smoke
funerale m funeral
funghi mpl mushrooms
funghi porcini boletus mushrooms
funghi secchi dried mushrooms
funicolare f funicular railway
funzionare to work *(mechanism)*
non funziona it doesn't work
fuoco m fire; focus
fuochi d'artificio fireworks
fuori outside; out
fuori servizio out of order
furgone m van
furto m theft
fuseaux mpl leggings
fusibile m fuse
futuro m future

G

gabinetto m lavatory
gabinetto biologico chemical toilet
gabinetto medico doctor's surgery
galleria f tunnel; gallery; arcade; circle
  (theatre)
galleria d'arte art gallery
Galles m Wales
gallese Welsh

gamba f leg
gara f race (sport)
garanzia f guarantee; warranty
gas m gas
gasolio m diesel
gassato(a) fizzy
gassosa f lemonade
gastrite f gastritis
gatto m cat
gay gay (person)
gel per capelli m hair gel
gelateria f ice-cream shop
gelatina f jelly
gelato m ice cream
gelo m frost
geloso(a) jealous
gemelli mpl twins; cufflinks
genere m kind (type); gender
genero m son-in-law
genitori mpl parents
Genova f Genoa
gentile kind (person)
Germania f Germany
gesso m chalk; plaster (for limb)
gettare to throw
non gettare rifiuti no dumping
gettone m token
gettone di presenza attendance fee
ghiaccio m ice
ghiacciolo m ice lolly
giacca f jacket
giallo m thriller (book or film)
giallo(a) yellow; amber (light)
giardiniere m gardener
giardino m garden
gilè m waistcoat
gin m gin
gin tonic gin and tonic
ginecologo/a m/f gynaecologist
ginocchio m knee
giocare to play; to gamble
giocattolo m toy
gioco m game
gioco a quiz quiz show
gioielleria f jeweller's
gioielli mpl jewellery
gioielliere m jeweller

giornalaio m newsagent
giornale m newspaper
giornalista m/f journalist
giornata f day
giorno m day
giorni feriali Monday-Saturday
giorni festivi Sundays/holidays
giovane young
giovedì m Thursday
girare to turn; to spin
girarsi to turn around
girasole m sunflower
giro m tour; turn
fare un giro a piedi to go for a stroll
giro turistico sightseeing tour
gita f trip; excursion
gita in barca boat trip
gita in pullman coach trip
giù down; downstairs
giubbino fluorescente m fluorescent
  waistcoat
giubbotto salvagente m life jacket
giudice m judge
giugno m June
giusto(a) fair; right (correct)
gli the; to him/it
globale inclusive (costs)
glutine glutin
goccia f drop (of liquid); drip
gola f throat; gorge
golfo m gulf
gomito m elbow
gomma f rubber; tyre
gomma a terra flat tyre
gomma da cancellare eraser
gommone m dinghy (inflatable)
gonfiare to inflate
gonfio(a) swollen
gonfiore m lump (swelling)
gonna f skirt
Gps m GPS (global positioning system)
gradazione f content (of alcohol)
gradevole pleasant
gradino m step; stair
Gran Bretagna f Great Britain
grana f parmesan cheese
granaio m barn

granchio m crab
grande large; great; big
grande magazzino m department store
grandine f hail
granita f water ice (flavoured)
grappa f strong spirit (often drunk with coffee)
grasso(a) fat; greasy
gratis free of charge
grattacielo m skyscraper
grattugia f grater
grattugiato(a) grated
gratuito(a) free of charge
il servizio è gratuito service included
grave serious
grazie thank you
gridare to shout
grigio(a) grey
griglia f grill
alla griglia grilled
grissini mpl breadsticks
grosso(a) big; thick
grucce fpl crutches
gruccia f coat hanger
gruppo m group
gruppo sanguigno blood group
guadagnare to earn
guanciale m pillow
guanto m glove
guanti di gomma rubber gloves
guanto da forno oven glove
guanto di spugna facecloth
guardacoste m coastguard
guardare to look (at); to watch
guardaroba m cloakroom
guardia f guard
Guardia di finanza Customs and Excise
guasto out of order
guerra f war
guida f guide (person or book); directory
guida a sinistra left-hand drive
guida telefonica telephone directory
guida turistica tour guide
guidare to drive; to steer
guidatore m driver

guinzaglio m lead (for dog)
gustare to taste; to enjoy
gusto m flavour

H

ha...? do you have...?
ha l'ora? do you have the time?
hamburger m burger
herpes m cold sore; herpes
ho... I have...
ho ... anni I'm ... years old
ho bisogno di... I need...
ho fame I'm hungry
ho fretta I'm in a hurry
ho sete I'm thirsty
hostess f stewardess

I

i the (plural)
identificare to identify
idratante m moisturizer
idraulico m plumber
ieri yesterday
il the (singular)
imbarcarsi to embark
imbarcazione f boat
imbarco m boarding
carta d'imbarco boarding card
imbottigliato(a) bottled
imbucare to post (letter, etc)
immediatamente at once
immergere to dip (into liquid)
immersioni subacquee fpl scuba diving
immobilizzatore m immobilizer (on car)
immondizie fpl rubbish
immunizzazione f immunisation
impanato coated in breadcrumbs
imparare to learn
impasto m mixture
imperatore m emperor
impermeabile m raincoat
impero m empire
impiego m use; employment
impiegato(a) m/f employee; white-collar worker

184

importante important
importare to import; to matter
non importa it doesn't matter
importo m amount
impossibile impossible
imposta f tax *(on income)*; shutter
imposta sul valore aggiunto (IVA) value-added tax (VAT)
improbabile unlikely
in in; to
in Spagna to Spain
in vacanza on holiday
inalatore m inhaler
inadempienza f negligence
incantevole charming
incaricarsi di to take charge of
incartare to wrap up *(parcel)*
incassare to cash *(a cheque)*
incendio m fire
inchiostro m ink
incidente m accident
incinta pregnant
incluso(a) included; enclosed
incontrare to meet
incontro m meeting *(by chance)*
incrocio m crossroads; junction
indicatore m indicator; gauge
indicatore del livello dell'olio oil gauge
indicazioni fpl directions
indice m index; contents
indietro backwards; behind
indirizzo m address
infarto m heart attack
infatti in fact; actually
infermeria f infirmary
infermiera f nurse
infezione f infection
infiammabile inflammable
infiammazione f inflammation
influenza f flu
informare to inform
informarsi (di) to inquire (about)
informazioni fpl information
infuso di erbe f herbal tea
ingessatura f plaster cast
Inghilterra f England

inghiottire to swallow
inglese English
ingorgato(a) blocked *(pipe, sink)*
ingorgo m blockage; hold-up
ingorgo stradale traffic jam
ingresso m entry/entrance
ingresso gratuito free entry
iniezione f injection
inizio m start
innocuo(a) harmless
inondazione m flood
inoltre besides
inquinato(a) polluted
insalata f salad
insalata di patate potato salad
insalata di pomodori tomato salad
insalata mista mixed salad
insalata verde green salad
insegnante m/f teacher
insegnare to teach
inserire to insert
inserire le banconote una per volta insert banknotes one at a time
insettifugo m insect repellent
insetto m insect
insieme together
insolazione f sunstroke
insulina f insulin
interessante interesting
internazionale international
internet f internet
collegamento a internet senza fili wireless internet
sei collegato a internet? do you have internet access?
interno m inside; extension *(phone)*
intero(a) whole
interpretazione f interpretation
interprete m/f interpreter
interruttore m switch
intervallo m half-time; interval
intervento m operation
inversione f U-turn
intervista f interview
intestato(a) a registered in the name of
intimi donna mpl ladies' underwear

185

intorno around
intossicazione alimentare f food-poisoning
introdurre to introduce
inutile unnecessary; useless
invalido(a) disabled; invalid
invece di instead of
invernale winter
inverno m winter
investire to knock down (car)
inviare to send
invitare to invite
invito m invitation
io I
ipermercato m hypermarket
ipermetrope long-sighted
iPod m iPod
Irlanda f Ireland
Irlanda del Nord Northern Ireland
irlandese Irish
iscritto m member
per iscritto in writing
iscriversi a to join (club)
iscrizione f inscription; enrolment
isola f island
istituto m institute
istruttore(trice) m/f instructor
istruzioni fpl instructions
Italia f Italy
italiano(a) Italian
itinerario m route
itinerario turistico scenic route
itterizia f jaundice
IVA f VAT

J

jolly m joker (cards)

L

la the; her; it; you
là there
per di là that way
labbra fpl lips
lacca f lacquer; hair spray
ladro m thief
lago m lake
lamette fpl razor blades

lampada f lamp
lampadina f lightbulb
lampone m raspberry
lana f wool
largo(a) wide; broad
lasciare to leave; to let (allow)
lassativo m laxative
lassù up there
latte m milk
latte a lunga conservazione long-life milk
latte di capra goat milk
latte di soia soya milk
latte fresco fresh milk
latte in polvere powdered milk
latte intero whole milk
latte parzialmente scremato semi-skimmed milk
latte scremato skimmed milk
lattuga f lettuce
lavabile washable
lavaggio m washing
lavaggio auto car wash
per lavaggi frequenti for frequent use
lavanderia f laundry (place)
lavanderia automatica launderette
lavandino m sink; washbasin
lavare to wash
lavare a secco to dry-clean
lavarsi to wash (oneself)
lavasecco m dry-cleaner's
lavastoviglie f dishwasher
lavatrice f washing machine
lavorare to work (person)
lavoro m job; occupation; work
lavori stradali road works
lavori in corso road works
le the; them; to her; to you
legge f law
leggere to read
leggero(a) light (not heavy); weak
legno m wood (material)
lei she; her; you
lentamente slowly
lente f lens (of glasses)
lente d'ingrandimento magnifying glass

lenti a contatto contact lenses
lento slow
lenzuolo m sheet *(bed)*
lesbica lesbian
lesione f injury
lettera f letter
lettera raccomandata registered letter
lettino m cot
letto m bed
letti a castello bunk beds
letto a una piazza single bed
letto matrimoniale double bed
letti gemelli twin beds
lettore CD m CD player
lettore di MP3 MP3 player
lì there *(over there)*
libero(a) free/vacant
libreria f bookshop
libretto m booklet; log book *(for car)*
libretto degli assegni cheque book
libro m book
licenza f licence; permit
licenza di caccia hunting permit
licenza di pesca fishing permit
limetta per le unghie f nail file
limite m limit; boundary
limite di velocità speed limit
limone m lemon
linea f line; route
linea aerea airline
lingua f language; tongue
lino m linen
liquido m liquid
liquido dei freni brake fluid
liquido lavavetri screen wash
liquido per lenti a contatto contact lens solution
liquore m liqueur
liquori mpl spirits *(alcohol)*
liscio(a) smooth; straight; plain
lista f list
lista dei vini wine list
listino prezzi m price list
litro m litre
livello m level
lo him; it

locale local
locale m room; place; local train
locale notturno nightclub
località di vacanza f resort
locanda f inn
Londra f London
lontano(a) far
lozione f lotion
lozione solare suntan lotion
lucchetto m padlock
lucchetto della bici bike lock
luce f flight
lucertola f lizard
luglio m July
lui him
lumaca f snail
luna f moon
luna di miele honeymoon
luna park m funfair
lunedì m Monday
lunghezza f length
lungo(a) long
lungo la strada along the street
a lungo for a long time
lungomare m promenade; seafront
luogo m place
luogo di nascita place of birth
lupo m wolf
lusso m luxury
di lusso luxury *(hotel, etc)*

M
ma but
macchia f stain; mark
macchina f car; machine
fotocamera digitale digital camera
macchina a noleggio hire car
macchina fotografica camera
macchina sportiva sports car
macedonia f fruit salad
macellaio m butcher's
macinato(a) ground *(coffee, meat)*
madre f mother
magazzino m warehouse
maggio m May
maggiore larger; greater; older; largest; greatest; oldest

maglietta *f* t-shirt
maglione *m* jumper; sweater
magro(a) thin *(person)*; low-fat; lean *(meat)*
mai never; ever
maiale *m* pig; pork
maionese *f* mayonnaise
mal *see* **male**
malato(a) ill; sick
malattia *f* disease
malattia venerea venereal disease
male badly *(not well)*
male *m* pain; ache
mal d'aria air sickness
mal d'auto car sickness
mal d'orecchi earache
mal di denti toothache
mal di gola sore throat
mal di mare sea sickness
mal di pancia stomachache
mal di testa headache
maltempo *m* bad weather
mamma *f* mum(my)
mancia *f* tip *(to waiter, etc)*
mandare to send
mandare per fax to fax
mandare un sms to text
mango *m* mango
mangiare to eat
mangiare fuori to eat out
manica *f* sleeve
la Manica the English Channel
manicure *m* manicure
mano *f* hand
fatto(a) a mano handmade
Mantova *f* Mantua
manuale di conversazione *m* phrase book
manzo *m* beef
marca *f* brand *(make)*
marcia *f* gear *(car)*; march
marciapiede *m* pavement
mare *m* sea; seaside
Mare del Nord North Sea
margarina *f* margarine
margherita *f* daisy
marina *f* navy

marito *m* husband
marmellata *f* jam
marmellata d'arance marmalade
marrone *m* brown; chestnut
marsupio *m* bumbag; money belt
martedì *m* Tuesday
martedì grasso Shrove Tuesday
martello *m* hammer
marzo *m* March
maschera *f* mask; fancy dress
maschile masculine; male
massaggio *m* massage
massimo(a) maximum
masticare to chew
masterizzare to burn a CD
materassino *m* airbed; lilo
materasso *m* mattress
materiale *m* material
matrigna *f* stepmother
matrimonio *m* wedding
mattina *f* morning
di mattina in the morning
matto(a) mad
mazza *f* mallet
mazze da golf golf clubs
meccanico *m* mechanic; repair shop
medicina *f* medicine
medico *m* doctor
Mediterraneo *m* Mediterranean
medusa *f* jellyfish
megabyte *m* megabyte (Mb)
meglio better; best
meglio di better than
mela *f* apple
melanzana *f* aubergine; eggplant
melone *m* melon
membro *m* member
meningite *f* meningitis
meno less; minus
mensa *f* canteen
mensile monthly
mensilmente monthly
mensola *f* shelf
menta *f* mint
mento *m* chin
mentre while; whereas
menù *m* menu

menù a prezzo fisso set-price menu
menù alla carta à la carte menu
menù turistico set menu
meraviglioso(a) wonderful
mercatino dell'usato *m* flea market
mercato *m* market
merce *f* goods
merci *fpl* freight; goods
mercoledì *m* Wednesday
merenda *f* snack
meridionale southern
mese *m* month
messa *f* mass *(in church)*
messaggio *m* message
messaggio SMS SMS message
mestruazioni *fpl* period *(menstrual)*
metà *f* half
metà prezzo half-price
metro *m* metre
metro a nastro tape measure
metropolitana *f* underground; metro
mettere to put; to put on *(clothes)*
mettersi in contatto con to contact
mezzanotte *f* midnight
mezzi *mpl* means; transport
mezzo *m* middle
mezzo(a) half
mezza pensione half board
mezzogiorno *m* midday; noon
il Mezzogiorno the south of Italy
mezz'ora *f* half an hour
mi me; to me; myself
mia my
microfono *m* microphone
miele *m* honey
migliorare to improve
migliore better; best
Milano Milan
miliardo *m* billion
milione *m* million
mille thousand
millimetro *m* millimetre
minestra *f* soup
minidisk *m* minidisk
minimo *m* minimum
ministro *m* minister *(political)*
minorenne underage

minori *mpl* minors
minuto *m* minute
mio my
miscela *f* blend
misto(a) mixed
mittente *m/f* sender
mobili *mpl* furniture
moda *f* fashion
moderno(a) modern
modo *m* way; manner
modulo *m* form *(document)*
modulo d'iscrizione registration form
moglie *f* wife
molletta *f* clothes peg
molletta per capelli hairgrip
molo *m* jetty; quay; pier
molti(e) many
molte grazie thanks very much
molto much; a lot; very
molta gente lots of people
molto tempo for a long time
monastero *m* monastery
moneta *f* coin; currency
montagna *f* mountain
monumento *m* monument
mordere to bite
morire to die
morsicare to bite
morsicato(a) bitten
morso *m* bite
morso(a) bitten
morto(a) dead
mosca *f* fly
moscerino *m* midge; gnat
moschea *f* mosque
mosso(a) rough *(sea)*; ruffled
mostra *f* exhibition
mostrare to show
moto *f* motorbike
motore *m* engine; motor
motorino *m* moped
motorino d'avviamento *m* starter
 motor
multa *f* fine *(to be paid)*
municipio *m* town hall
muro *m* wall
museo *m* museum

musica f music
muta f wetsuit
mutande fpl underpants
mutandine fpl knickers; panties

N

N north (abbreviation)
nafta f diesel
Napoli Naples
nascita f birth
naso m nose
nastro m tape; ribbon
nato(a) born
nauseato(a) nauseous
nave f ship
navigatore satellitare m satellite
navigation system (for car)
nave-traghetto f ferry
nazionale national; domestic (flight)
nazionalità f nationality
nazione f nation
né ... né neither ... nor
nebbia f fog

necessario(a) necessary
negativo m negative (photo)
negozio m shop
nero(a) black
nessuno(a) no; nobody; none
netto m net
al netto di IVA net of VAT
neve f snow
nevicare to snow
niente nothing
niente da dichiarare nothing to
declare
nipote m/f nephew/niece;
grandson/granddaughter
noce f walnut
nocivo(a) harmful
nodo m knot; bow
nodo ferroviario junction (railway)
noi we
noleggiare to hire
noleggio m hire
noleggio auto car hire
noleggio barche boat hire
noleggio bici bike hire

noleggio sci ski hire
nolo m hire
nome m name; first name
nome da ragazza maiden name
nome utente username
non not
non ancora not yet
non c'è there isn't
non funziona it doesn't work
non capisco I don't understand
non pericoloso(a) safe
non-fumatore m/f non-smoker
nonna f grandmother
nonno m grandfather
nord m north
nostro(a) our
notare to notice
notizie fpl news
notte f night
notte di San Silvestro New Year's Eve
di notte at night
novembre m November
nubile single (woman)
nulla nothing; anything
nullo(a) void (contract)
numero m number; size (of shoe)
numero del conto account number
numero di camera room number
numero di cellulare mobile number
numero di telefono phone number
nuora f daughter-in-law
nuotare to swim
Nuova Zelanda f New Zealand
nuovo(a) new
di nuovo again
nuvoloso(a) cloudy

O

o or
O (abbreviation for Ovest) west
obbligatorio(a) compulsory
oceano m ocean
occasione f opportunity; bargain
occhiali mpl glasses
occhiali da sci skiing goggles
occhiali da sole sunglasses
occhio m eye

occupato(a) busy/engaged
odore *m* smell
offerta *f* offer
officina *f* workshop; repair shop
oggetto *m* object
oggi today
OGM (privo(a) di organismi geneticamente modificati) GM-free
ogni each; every
ogni giorno every day; daily
ogni quanto? how often?
ogni tanto occasionally
olio *m* oil
olio solare suntan oil
olio di girasole sunflower oil
olio d'oliva olive oil
olive *fpl* olives
oltre beyond; besides
ombra *f* shade
all'ombra in the shade
ombrello *m* umbrella
ombrellone *m* sun umbrella
ombretto *m* eye shadow
omeopatico(a) *m/f* homeopathic *(remedy)*
omeopatia homeopathy
omogeneizzati *mpl* baby food
omosessuale homosexual
onde *fpl* waves
onestà *f* honesty
onesto(a) honest
opera *f* opera
operatore turistico *m* tour operator
operazione *f* operation *(surgical)*
opuscolo *m* brochure
ora now
ora *f* hour
che ore sono? what's the time?
ora di punta rush hour
orario *m* timetable
in orario on time
orario di apertura opening hours
orario di cassa banking hours
orario visite visiting hours
ordinare to order; to prescribe
ordine *f* order *(in restaurant)*

ordinato(a) tidy
orecchini *mpl* earrings
orecchio *m* ear
orecchioni *mpl* mumps
oreficeria *f* jeweller's
ormeggiare to moor
ormeggio *m* mooring
oro *m* gold
placcato oro gold-plated
orologeria *m* watchmaker's
orologio *m* clock; watch
orticaria *f* rash *(skin)*
ortografia *f* spelling
ospedale *m* hospital
ospite *m/f* guest; host/hostess
osso *m* bone
ostello *m* hostel
ostello della gioventù youth hostel
osteria *f* inn
ottenere to get; obtain
ottenere la linea to get through *(on phone)*
ottimo(a) excellent
ottobre *m* October
otturazione *f* filling *(in tooth)*
ovest *m* west

P

pacchetto *m* packet
pacco *m* package; parcel
padella *f* frying-pan
Padova Padua
padre *m* father
padrone(a) *m/f* owner
paesaggio *m* scenery; countryside
paese *m* country *(nation)*; village
pagare to pay; to pay for
pagato(a) paid
pagina *f* page
paio *m* pair
palazzo *m* building; block of flats; palace
palestra *f* gym
palla *f* ball
pallina *f* ball *(small)*
pallina da golf golf ball
pallina da tennis tennis ball

pallone *m* football
pandoro *m* Italian Christmas cake
pane *m* bread; loaf
pane integrale wholemeal bread
pane carré sandwich bread
pane e coperto cover charge
pane di segale rye bread
panettone *m* Italian Christmas cake
panetteria *f* baker's
pangrattato *m* breadcrumbs
panificio *m* bakery
panino *m* bread roll
panino imbottito sandwich
paninoteca *f* sandwich bar
panna *f* cream
panno *m* cloth; fabric
pannolini *mpl* nappies
pantaloni *mpl* trousers
pantaloni corti shorts
pantofole *fpl* slippers
papa *m* pope
papà *m* daddy
parabrezza *m* windscreen
paramedico *m* paramedic
paraurti *m* bumper *(on car)*
parcheggiare to park
parcheggio *m* car park
parcheggio custodito supervised car park
parcheggio libero free parking
parcheggio sotterraneo underground car park
parchimetro *m* parking meter
parco *m* park
parco nazionale national park
parente *m/f* relation; relative
Parigi *f* Paris
parlare to speak; to talk
parmigiano *m* parmesan
parmigiano grattugiato grated parmesan
parola *f* word
parola d'ordine password
parolaccia *f* swear word
parrucchiere(a) *m/f* hairdresser
parte *f* share; part; side
partenza *f* departures

partenze internazionali international departures
partenze nazionali domestic departures
partire to depart; to leave
partita *f* match; game
partita di calcio football match
passaggio *m* passage; lift *(in car)*
dare un passaggio to give a lift
passaporto *m* passport
passeggiata *f* walk; stroll
passeggino *m* pushchair
passo *m* pace; pass *(mountain)*
fare quattro passi to go for a stroll
passo carrabile keep clear
passo chiuso pass closed
pasticcino *m* cake *(small, fancy)*
pastiglia *f* tablet *(pill)*
pasto *m* meal
pastorizzato pasteurised
patata *f* potato
patatine *fpl* crisps
patatine fritte chips
patente *f* permit; driving licence
patrigno *m* stepfather
pavimento *m* floor
paziente *m/f* patient
pecora *f* sheep
pedaggio *m* toll *(motorway)*
pedale *m* pedal
pedalò *m* pedalboat
pedicure *m* chiropodist
pedoni *mpl* pedestrians
peggio worse
pelati *mpl* tinned tomatoes
pelle *f* skin; hide; leather
pellegrino *m* pilgrim
pelletterie *fpl* leather goods
pellicola *f* film *(for camera)*
pellicola a colori colour film
pellicola in bianco e nero black and white film
pelo *m* fur
pene *m* penis
penicillina *f* penicillin
penisola *f* peninsula
penna *f* pen

pensare to think
pensione *f* guesthouse
mezza pensione half board
pensione completa full board
pentola *f* saucepan
pepe *m* pepper *(spice)*
peperoncino *m* chilli
peperone *m* pepper (vegetable)
per for; per; in order to
per esempio for example
per favore please
per via aerea air mail
pera *f* pear
perché why; because; so that
percorso *m* walk; journey; route
percorso panoramico scenic route
perdere to lose; to miss *(train, etc)*
perdita *f* leak *(of gas, liquid)*
pericolante unsafe
pericolo *m* danger
pericoloso(a) dangerous
non pericoloso(a) safe
periferia *f* outskirts; suburbs
permanente continua parking
  restrictions still apply
permanenza *f* stay; residency
permesso *m* licence; permit
permesso! excuse me! *(to get by)*
permesso di soggiorno residence
  permit
permettere to allow
perso(a) lost *(object)*; missed *(train, plane, etc)*
persona *f* person
le persone con esigenze particolari
  people with special needs
personale *m* staff
pesante heavy
pesare to weigh
pesca *f* angling; fishing; peach
divieto di pesca no fishing
pescare to fish
pesce *m* fish
pesche *m* peaches
pescivendolo *m* fishmonger's
peso *m* weight
pettine *m* comb

petto *m* chest; breast
petto di pollo chicken breast
pezzo *m* piece; bit; cut *(of meat)*
piacere to please
le piace? do you like it?
piacere! pleased to meet you!
piangere to cry *(weep)*
piano slowly; quietly
piano *m* floor *(of building)*; plan
pianta *f* map; plan; plant
pianterreno *m* ground floor
piantina *f* street map
piatto *m* dish; course; plate
primo piatto first course
piazza *f* square *(in town)*
piazzale *m* large square
piazzola (di sosta) *f* lay-by
piccante spicy; hot; strong *(cheese)*
picchetto *m* tent peg
piccolo(a) little; small
piede *m* foot
a piedi on foot
pieno(a) full
pietra *f* stone
pigiama *m* pyjamas
pigro(a) lazy
pila *f* battery; torch
pillola *f* pill
pinne *fpl* flippers
pino *m* pine
pinze *fpl* pliers
pinzette *fpl* tweezers
pioggia *f* rain
piombo *m* lead *(metal)*
piovere to rain
piscina *f* swimming pool
piscina per bambini paddling pool
piselli *m* peas
pista *f* track; race track
pista da ballo dance floor
pista da sci ski run
più more; most; plus
più di more than
più economico(a) cheaper
più tardi later
piumino *m* duvet
pizzeria *m* pizza restaurant

pizzico *m* pinch; sting
pizzo *m* lace
plastica *f* plastic
di plastica made of plastic
pneumatico *m* tyre
pochi(e) few
poco(a) little; not much
un po' *(shortened form of poco)* a little
podologo *m* chiropodist
poi then
polizia *f* police
polizia stradale traffic police
poliziotto *m* policeman
polizza *f* policy
pollo *m* chicken
polmone *m* lung
poltrona *f* armchair; seat in stalls
pomata *f* ointment
pomeriggio *m* afternoon
di pomeriggio in the afternoon
pomodoro *m* tomato
pompa *f* pump
pompa da bicicleta bicycle pump
pompelmo *m* grapefruit
ponte *m* bridge; deck
ponte macchine car deck
pontile *m* jetty; pier
porcellana *f* china
porri *m* leeks
porta *f* door; gate; goal
porta di sicurezza emergency exit
portabagagli *m* luggage rack; porter *(at airport, station, etc)*
portacenere *m* ashtray
portafoglio *m* wallet
portare to carry/bring; to wear
portiere *m* porter *(doorkeeper)*; goalkeeper
portineria *f* caretaker's lodge
porto *m* port; harbour
porto di scalo port of call
Portogallo *m* Portugal
porzione *f* portion; helping
posate *fpl* cutlery
posologia *f* dosage
possiamo we can
non possiamo we cannot

posso I can
non posso I cannot
posta *f* post office; mail
posta elettronica e-mail
posta raccomandata registered mail
posteggio *m* car park
posteggio taxi taxi rank
posto *m* place; job; seat
posti a sedere seating capacity
posti in piedi standing room
posti prenotati reserved seats
potabile ok to drink
potere to be able
pranzo *m* lunch
pré-maman *m* maternity dress
preavviso *m* advance notice
precotto(a) ready-cooked
predeterminare l'importo desiderato select required amount
preferire to prefer
preferito(a) favourite
prefisso *m* prefix; area code
prefisso telefonico dialling code
pregare to pray
si prega... please...
prego don't mention it!
prelievo *m* collection; sample
premere to push; to press
premio *m* prize
prendere to take; to catch *(bus, etc)*
prendere il sole to sunbathe
prendere in prestito to borrow
prenotare to book; to reserve
prenotato(a) reserved
prenotazione *f* reservation
preoccupato(a) worried
preparare to prepare; to get ready
presa *f* socket *(electric)*
preservativo *m* condom
pressione del sangue *f* blood pressure
prestare to lend
presto early; soon
prete *m* priest
previsione *f* forecast
previsioni del tempo weather forecast

previsto(a) scheduled; expected
come previsto as expected
prezzo *m* price
prezzo al dettaglio retail price
prezzo al minuto retail price
prezzo di catalogo list price
prezzo d'ingresso entrance fee
prezzo fisso set price
prima di before
primavera *f* spring *(season)*
primo(a) first; top; early
primo piano first floor
primo piatto first course
principale main
principiante *m/f* beginner
privato(a) private
problema *m* problem
professione *f* profession
professore *m/f* teacher; professor
profondità *f* depth
profondo(a) deep
profumeria *f* perfume shop
progettare to plan
programma *m* programme; syllabus; schedule
proibire to ban; to prohibit
proibito(a) forbidden; prohibited
prolunga *f* extension *(electrical)*
promettere to promise
pronto(a) ready
pronto! hello! *(on telephone)*
pronto soccorso casualty
proprietario(a) *m/f* owner
proprio(a) own
prosciutto cotto *m* ham *(cooked)*
prosciutto crudo *m* ham *(cured)*
prossimamente coming soon
prossimo(a) next
proteggislip *m* panty liner
protesi dell'anca *f* hip replacement
protestante Protestant
provare to try; to test *(try out)*; to try on *(clothes)*
provvisorio(a) temporary
prugna *f* plum
pubblicità *f* advertisement
pubblico *m* audience; public

pulce *f* flea
pulito(a) clean
pulizia *f* cleaning
pulizia del viso facial
pullman *m* coach
pulmino *m* minibus
punteggio *m* score
puntine *fpl* points
punto *m* point; stitch; full stop
punto d'incontro meeting place
puntura *f* bite; sting; injection
puzzle *m* jigsaw
puzza *f* bad smell

Q

qua here
quaderno *m* exercise book
quadro *m* picture; painting
qual(e) what; which; which one
qualche some
qualche volta sometimes
qualcosa something; anything
qualcuno someone; somebody
qualificato(a) qualified
qualità *f* quality
qualsiasi any
qualunque any
quando? when?
quanto(a)? how much?
quanti(e)? how many?
quartiere *m* district
quarto *m* quarter
quarto d'ora quarter of an hour
quattro four
quei those; those ones
quel(la) that; that one
quelli(e) those; those ones
quello(a) that; that one
questi(e) these; these ones
questo(a) this; this one
questura *f* police station
qui here
quindi then; therefore
quindici giorni fortnight
quotidiano *m* daily (paper)
quotidiano(a) daily

R

rabarbaro *m* rhubarb
rabbia *f* anger; rabies
racchetta *f* racket; bat
racchetta da neve snowshoe
racchetta da sci ski pole
racchetta da trekking trekking pole
raccomandare to recommend
racconto *m* story
radiatore *m* radiator
radio *f* radio
radiografia *f* x-ray
raffreddore *m* cold *(illness)*
raffreddore da fieno hay fever
ragazza *f* young woman; girlfriend
ragazza alla pari au pair
ragazzo *m* young man; boyfriend
RAI *f* Italian State Broadcasting
rallentare to slow down
rapido *m* express train
rapido(a) high-speed; quick
rasoio *m* razor
rasoio elettrico electric razor
reato *m* crime
recarsi alla cassa pay at cash desk
recentemente recently
reclamo *m* complaint
recupero monete returned coins
regalo *m* present; gift
reggiseno *m* bra
regione *f* region; district; area
registrare to record
registratore *m* cassette player
registro *m* register
Regno Unito *m* United Kingdom
regolamento *m* regulation
regolare regular; steady
remare to row *(boat)*
rendersi conto di to realize
rene *m* kidney
reparto *m* department; ward
restare to stay; to remain
restituire to return; to give back
restituzione *f* return; repayment
resto *m* remainder; change *(money)*
restringersi to shrink
rete *f* net; goal

rete portabagagli rack *(luggage)*
retro *m* back
vedi retro please turn over
retromarcia *f* reverse gear
reumatismo *m* rheumatism
ricambio *m* spare part; refill
ricaricare to recharge *(battery)*
caricatelefono *m* recharger *(mobile)*;
   caricabatterie (battery)
ricetta *f* prescription; recipe
ricevere to receive; to welcome
ricevitore *m* receiver *(phone)*
ricevuta *f* receipt
richiedere to require
richiesta *f* request
riciclare to recycle
riconoscere to recognize
riconoscimento *m* identification
ricordare to remember
non mi ricordo I don't remember
ricordo *m* souvenir; memory
ricorrere a to resort to
ricoverare to admit *(to hospital)*
recovero per auto *m* car port
ridere to laugh
ridurre to reduce
riduttore *m* adaptor
riduzione *f* reduction
riempire to fill
rientro *m* return; return home
rifare to do again; to repair
rifiutare to refuse
rifiuti *mpl* rubbish; waste
rifugio *m* mountain inn; shelter
righello *m* ruler *(for measuring)*
rigore *m* penalty *(football)*
riguardo *m* care; respect
riguardo a... regarding...
rilasciato(a) a issued at
rimandare to postpone
rimanere to stay; to remain
rimborsare to reimburse
rimborso *m* refund
rimessa *f* remittance; garage
rimettere to put back
rimettersi to recover *(from illness)*
rimorchiare to tow

rimorchio *m* trailer
a rimorchio on tow
rimozione *f* removal; towing away
Rinascimento *m* Renaissance
rinfreschi *mpl* refreshments
ringraziare to thank
rinnovare to renew
rinunciare to give up
riparare to repair
riparato(a) sheltered; repaired
riparazione *f* repair
ripetere to repeat
ripido(a) steep
ripiegare to fold
ripieno *m* stuffing
riposarsi to rest
riposo *m* rest *(repose)*
risalita *f* reascent
risarcimento *m* compensation
riscaldamento *m* heating
riscaldare to heat up *(food)*
rischio *m* risk
risciacquare to rinse
riscuotere to collect; to cash
riserva *f* reserve; reservation
riserva di caccia private hunting
riserva naturale nature reserve
riservare to reserve
riservato(a) reserved
riso *m* rice; laugh
risotto *m* rice cooked in stock
risparmiare to save *(money)*
rispondere to answer; to reply
risposta *f* answer
ristorante *m* restaurant
ritardo *m* delay
ritirare to withdraw
ritiro *m* retirement; withdrawal
ritiro bagagli baggage reclaim
ritornare to return *(go back)*
ritorno *m* return
riunione *f* meeting
riuscita *f* result; outcome
riva *f* bank; shore
riviera *f* riviera
rivista *f* magazine; revue
rivolgersi a to refer to *(for info)*

roba *f* stuff; belongings
roccia *f* rock
rognoni *mpl* kidneys
romanico(a) Romanesque
romanzo *m* novel
romanzo rosa romantic novel
rompere to break
rondine *f* swallow *(bird)*
rosa pink
rosa *f* rose
rosmarino *m* rosemary
rosolia *f* German measles; rubella
rossetto *m* lipstick
rosso(a) red
rosticceria *f* shop selling cooked food
rotonda *f* roundabout
rotondo(a) round
rotto(a) broken
roulotte *f* caravan
rovesciare to spill; to knock over
rovine *fpl* ruins
rtd *(abbreviation for **ritardo**)*, delay
rubare to steal
rubinetto *m* tap
rubrica *f* address book
ruggine *f* rust
rughe *fpl* wrinkles
rullino *m* roll of film
rum *m* rum
rumore *m* noise
rumoroso(a) noisy
ruota *f* wheel
ruota di scorta spare wheel
rupe *f* mountain cliff
ruscello *m* stream
russare to snore

S

S *(abbreviation)* south
sabato Saturday
sabbia *f* sand
saccarina *f* saccharin
sacchetto *m* small bag
sacchetto di carta paper bag
sacchetto di plastica plastic bag
sacco *m* large bag
sacco a pelo sleeping bag

sacco della spazzatura bin bag
sacerdote m priest
sagra f local food festival
sala f hall; auditorium
sala da pranzo dining room
sala d'aspetto waiting room
sala partenze departure lounge
salame m salami
salario m wage
salato(a) salted; savoury
saldare to settle *(bill)*; to weld
saldi sale
saldo m payment; balance
sale m salt
salire to rise; to go up
salire in to get in *(vehicle)*
salita f climb; slope
in salita uphill
salmone m salmon
salmone affumicato smoked salmon
salone m lounge; salon
salotto m living room; lounge
salsa f sauce
salsiccia f sausage
saltare to jump
saltato(a) sautéed
salumeria f delicatessen
salumi mpl cured pork meats
salute f health
salute! cheers!
saluto m greeting
salvagente m life belt
salvare to rescue; to save *(life)*
salvavita m circuit breaker
salve! hello!
salvia f sage *(herb)*
salvietta f serviette
salviettine per bambini fpl baby
  wipes
salvo except; unless
sandali mpl sandals
sangue m blood
al sangue rare *(steak)*
sanguinare to bleed
sapere to know
sapone m soap
sapore m flavour; taste

saporito(a) tasty
Sardegna f Sardinia
sarto m tailor
sartoria f tailor's; dressmaker's
sasso m stone
sauna f sauna
sbagliato(a) wrong
sbaglio m mistake
sbandare to skid
sbandata f skid
sbarco m landing *(boat)*
sbrigare to hurry
scadente low *(standard, quality)*
scadenza f expiry
scadere to expire *(ticket, etc)*
scaduto(a) out-of-date; expired
scala f scale; ladder; staircase
scala anticendio fire escape
scala mobile escalator
scalare to climb
scaldabagno m water heater
scaldare to heat up
scale fpl stairs
scalino m step
scalo m stopover
scaloppina f veal escalope
scannerizzare to scan
lo scanner scanner
scarico(a) flat *(battery)*
scarpa f shoe
scarpe da ginnastica trainers
scarponcini mpl walking boots
scarponi da sci mpl ski boots
scatola f box; tin
scatola di pelati tinned tomatoes
scegliere to choose
scelta f range; selection; choice
scendere to go down
scendere da to get off *(bus, etc)*
scheda f slip *(of paper)*; card
scheda telefonica phonecard
schiena f back *(of body)*
sci m ski; skiing
sci di fondo cross-country skiing
sci nautico water-skiing
scialuppa di salvataggio f lifeboat
sciare to ski

sciarpa f scarf
sciogliere to melt
sciopero m strike
sciovia f ski-lift
scivolare to slip
scomodo(a) inconvenient; uncomfortable
scomparire to disappear
scompartimento m compartment
scongelare to defrost
sconto m discount
sconti reductions
scontrino m ticket; receipt; chit
scopa f broom *(brush)*
scoppio (di pneumatico) m blowout *(of tyre)*
scorso(a) last
scossa f shock *(electric)*
scottatura f burn
scottatura solare sunburn
Scozia f Scotland
scozzese Scottish
scrivania f desk
scrivere to write; to spell
scultura f sculpture
scuola f school
scuola di sci ski school
scuola materna nursery school
scuro(a) dark *(colour)*
scusare to excuse; to forgive
scusarsi to apologise
scusi? pardon?
se if; whether
sé oneself
seconda f second gear
secondo m second *(time)*; main course *(meal)*; according to
secondo(a) second
seconda classe second class
di seconda mano secondhand
sedano m celery
sede f head office
sedersi to sit down
sedia f chair
sedia a rotelle wheelchair
sedia a sdraio deckchair
sedile per bambini m babyseat *(car)*

il seggiolino per bambini booster seat *(car)*
seggiolone m highchair
seggiovia f chair-lift
segnale m signal; road sign
segnare to score *(goal)*
segreteria telefonica f answering machine
seguente following
seguire to follow; to continue
sella f saddle
selvatico(a) wild
semaforo m traffic lights
semifreddo m dessert made with ice cream
seminterrato basement
semplice plain; simple
sempre always; ever
per sempre for ever
senape f mustard
senso unico one-way street
senso vietato no entry
sentiero m path; footpath
sentire to hear
sentirsi to feel
senza without
separato(a) separated
sera f evening
serbatoio m tank *(car)*
serbatoio dell'acqua cistern
serio serious *(not funny)*
serpente m snake
serratura f flock
servire to serve
servizio m service; report *(in press)*
servizio al tavolo waiter service
servizio compreso service included
servizi mpl facilities; bathroom
sesso m sex
seta f silk
sete f thirst
avere sete to be thirsty
settembre m September
settentrionale northern
settimana f week
settimana bianca week's skiing holiday

settimanale weekly
sfida *f* challenge
sfuso(a) loose; on tap *(wine)*
sganciare to lift receiver
sì yes
Sicilia *f* Sicily
sicurezza *f* safety; security
controllo di sicurezza security check
sicuro(a) sure
sidro *m* cider
Sig. Mr *abbreviation of* **Signor**
Sig.ra Mrs/Ms *abbreviation of* **Signora**
sigaretta *f* cigarette
sigaro *m* cigar
Sig.na Miss *abbreviation of* **Signorina**
Signor: *il Signor Grandi* Mr Grandi
signora *f* lady; madam; Mrs; Ms
signore ladies
signore *m* gentleman; sir
signori gents
signorina *f* young woman; Miss
silenzio *m* silence
SIM *f* SIM card
simile a similar to
simpatico(a) pleasant; nice
sindacato *m* trade union
sindaco *m* mayor
singolo(a) single
sinistra *f* left
sistemare to arrange
sito *m* site
sito web website
skipass *m* skipass
slacciare to unfasten; to undo
slavina *f* snowslide; landslide
slegato(a) loose *(not fastened)*
slittata *f* skid
slogatura *f* sprain
smarrito(a) missing *(thing)*
smettere to stop doing something
soccorso *m* assistance; help
soccorso alpino mountain rescue
socio *m* associate; member
soggiorno *m* stay; sitting room
soldi *mpl* money
sole *m* sun; sunshine
solito: *di solito* usually

sollevare to raise; to relieve
sollievo *m* relief
solo(a) alone; only
solubile soluble
caffè solubile instant coffee
sonnifero *m* sleeping pill
sono I am (to be)
sopra on; above; over
di sopra upstairs
sopracciglia *fpl* eyebrows
sopravvivere to survive
sorella *f* sister
sorpassare to overtake *(in car)*
sorpresa *f* surprise
sorridere to smile
sorriso *m* smile
sospeso(a) suspended; postponed
sosta *f* stop
divieto di sosta no parking
sott'acqua underwater
sotterraneo(a) underground
sotto underneath; under; below
Spagna *f* Spain
spagnolo(a) Spanish
spalla *f* shoulder
sparire to disappear
spazzatura *f* rubbish
spazzola *f* brush
spazzola per capelli hairbrush
spazzolino da denti toothbrush
speciale special
specialità *f* speciality
specialmente especially
spedire to send; to dispatch
spegnere to turn off; to put out
spendere to spend *(money)*
spento(a) turned off; out *(light, etc)*
sperare to hope
spese *fpl* shopping; expenses
spesso often
spettacolo *m* show; performance
spezzatino *m* stew
spiaggia *f* beach; shore
spiaggia privata private beach
spiccioli *mpl* small coins; change
non ho spiccioli I've no change
spiegare to explain

spina f bone (of fish); plug (electric)
spinaci m spinach
spingere to push
spirale f coil (IUD)
spogliatoio m dressing room
sporco(a) dirty
sportello m counter; door (train, car)
sportivo(a) informal (clothes)
sposarsi to get married
sposato(a) married
non sposato(a) single
spremuta f freshly squeezed juice
spugna f sponge
spuma f hair mousse
spumante m sparkling wine
spuntino m snack
squadra f team
squillare to ring (phone)
Srl Ltd
stabilimento m factory
stadio m stadium
stagione f season
di stagione in season
stalla f stable
stampata f printout
stampatello m block letters
stanco(a) tired
stanza f room
stanza da bagno bathroom
stanza dei giochi playroom
stare to be; to keep
come sta? how are you?
stare attento(a) a... beware of..
stare bene to be well
stare in piedi to stand
stai zitto! keep quiet!
stasera tonight; this evening
Stati Uniti mpl United States
stazione f station; resort
stazione balneare seaside resort
stazione dell'autobus bus station
stazione di servizio petrol station
stazione ferroviaria train station
stella f star
sterlina f sterling; pound
stesso(a) same
stirare to iron

stitichezza f constipation
stitico(a) constipated
stivali mpl boots
storia f history
storico(a) historic(al)
centro storico old town
strada f road; street
strada chiusa road closed
strada panoramica scenic route
strada sbarrata road closed
strada senza uscita no through road
strada statale main road
stradina f lane
straniero(a) foreign; foreigner
strano(a) strange
stupido(a) stupid
su on; onto; over; about; up
sua his; her(s); its; your(s) (with f sing)
subito at once; immediately
succedere to happen
succo m juice
succo d'arancia orange juice
succo di frutta fruit juice
succo di mela apple juice
succo di pomodoro tomato juice
succursale m branch (of bank, etc)
sud m south
sue his; her(s); its; your(s) (with fpl)
suo(i) his; her(s); its; your(s) (with mpl)
suocera f mother-in-law
suocero m father-in-law
suola f sole (of foot, shoe)
suonare to ring; to play
suono m sound
superare to exceed; to overtake
supermercato m supermarket
supplemento m supplement
supposta f suppository
surf m surf
surgelato(a) frozen
sveglia f alarm clock/call
svegliare to wake up
svenire to faint
sviluppare to develop (photos)
Svizzera f Switzerland
svizzero(a) Swiss
svolta f turn

T

tabaccaio *m* tobacconist's
tacco *m* heel
tachimetro *m* speedometer
taglia *f* size (of clothes)
tagliare to cut
tailleur *m* women's suit
tallone *m* heel
tangenziale *f* ring road
tanti(e) so many
tanto(a) so much; so
tappo *m* cork; plug; cap
tappo del serbatoio petrol cap
tardi late
targa *f* numberplate (car)
tariffa *f* tariff; rate
tariffa economica cheap rate
tariffa festiva rate on holidays
tariffa ore di punta peak rate
tartufo *m* truffle
tasca *f* pocket
tassa *f* tax
tasso *m* rate
tasso di cambio exchange rate
tavola *f* table; plank; board
tavola calda hot snacks
tavola da surf surfboard
taxi *m* taxi
tazza *f* cup
tè *m* tea
tè al latte tea with milk
tè al limone lemon tea
tè freddo iced tea
teatro *m* theatre; drama
tedesco(a) German
telecomando *m* remote control
telefonare to (tele)phone
telefonata *f* phone call
telefonino *m* mobile phone
telefono *m* telephone
telefono pubblico payphone
televisione *f* television
telone impermeabile *m*
 groundsheet
temperatura *f* temperature
temperino *m* penknife
tempesta *f* storm

tempio *m* temple
tempo *m* weather; time
temporale *m* thunderstorm
tenda *f* curtain; tent
tendalino *m* awning (for caravan etc.)
tendine *m* tendon
tenere to keep; to hold
tenore *m* tenor (singer)
tenore alcolico *m* alcohol content
tergicristallo *m* windscreen wiper
terminal *m* terminal (airport)
termometro *m* thermometer
termosifone *m* heater
terra *f* earth; ground
terrazza *f* terrace
terremoto *m* earthquake
terza *f* third gear
terzi *mpl* third party
terzo(a) third
tessera *f* pass; season ticket; card
tessuto *m* fabric
testa *f* head
testicoli *mpl* testicles
tettarella *f* dummy (for baby)
tetto *m* roof
tettuccio apribile *m* sunroof (car)
Tevere *m* Tiber
thermos *m* thermos flask
thriller *m* thriller
timone *m* rudder
tirare to pull
toccare to touch; to feel
non toccare do not touch
togliere to remove; to take away
toilette *f* toilet
tonno *m* tuna
topo *m* mouse
Torino *f* Turin
tornare to return; to come/go back
torneo *m* tournament
toro *m* bull
torre *f* tower
torrone *m* nougat
torta *f* cake; tart; pie
Toscana *f* Tuscany
tosse *f* cough
tossico(a) toxic

tossire to cough
totale *m* total *(amount)*
tovaglia *f* tablecloth
tovagliolo *m* napkin
tra between; among(st); in
tradizionale traditional
tradurre to translate
traduzione *f* translation
traffico *m* traffic
traghetto *m* ferry
tramezzino *m* sandwich
trampolino *m* diving board; ski jump
tranquillante *m* tranquillizer
tranquillo(a) quiet *(place)*
trasferire to transfer
trasporto *m* transport
trattoria *f* restaurant
traveller's cheque *mpl* traveller's
  cheque
traversata *f* crossing
treno *m* train
treno merci goods train
triangolo d'emergenza *m* warning
  triangle
tribuna *f* stand *(stadium)*
tribunale *m* law court
trimestre *m* term *(school)*
triste sad
tritare to mince; to chop
troppi(e) too many
troppo too much; too
trovare to find
trucco *m* make-up
tu you *(familiar)*
tubo *m* pipe; tube
tubo di scappamento exhaust
tuffarsi to dive
turno *m* turn; shift
di turno on duty
tuta sportiva *f* tracksuit
tutti (e) all; everybody
tutte le direzioni all routes
tutto everything; all

U

ubriaco(a) drunk
uccello *m* bird

uccidere to kill
UE Unione Europea EU European
  Union
ufficio *m* office; church service
ufficio informazioni information
  bureau
ufficio oggetti smarriti lost property
  office
ufficio postale post office
ufficio turistico tourist office
uguale equal; even
ulcera *f* ulcer
ultimo(a) last
un a; an; one
unghia *f* nail *(finger, toe)*
unione *f* union
università *f* university
uno(a) a; an; one
uomo *m* man
uomini gents
uova *mpl* eggs
uovo *m* egg
uovo di Pasqua Easter egg
uova di polli ruspanti free range eggs
uovo sodo hard-boiled egg
urina *f* urine
uragano *m* hurricane
urgente urgent
usare to use
uscire to go/come out
uscita *f* exit/gate
uscita di sicurezza emergency exit
uso *m* use
utile useful
uva *f* grapes

V

va bene all right *(agreed)*
vacanza *f* holiday(s)
vacanze estive summer holidays
vaccinazione *f* vaccination
vagina *f* vagina
vaglia *m* money order
vagone *m* carriage; wagon
vagone letto sleeper
vagone ristorante restaurant car
valanga *f* avalanche

valico m pass *(mountain)*
valido(a) valid
valido fino a... valid until...
valigia f suitcase
valore m value; worth
di valore valuable
valuta f currency
valvola f valve
varicella f chickenpox
vasetto m jar
vaso m vase
vassoio m tray
vecchio(a) old
vedere to see
vedova f widow
vedovo m widower
vegetaliano(a) vegan
vegetariano(a) vegetarian
veicolo m vehicle
vela f sail; sailing
veleno m poison
velenoso(a) poisonous
veloce quick

velocemente quickly
velocità f speed
vena f vein
vendere to sell
vendesi for sale
vendita f sale
vendita a rate hire purchase
vendita al minuto retail
venerdì m Friday
venerdì santo m Good Friday
Venezia f Venice
venire to come
ventaglio m fan *(hand-held)*
ventilatore m electric fan
vento m wind
verde green
verdura f vegetables
verde green
vergine blank *(disk, tape)*
vermut m vermouth
vernice f paint
verniciare to paint
vero(a) true; real; genuine
versamento m payment; deposit

versare to pour
vertice m summit
vescica f blister
vespa f wasp
vestaglia f dressing gown
vestirsi to get dressed
vestiti mpl clothes
vestito m dress
vetrina f shop window
vetro m glass *(substance)*
via f street; by *(via)*
per via aerea by air mail
viaggiare to travel
viaggiatore m traveller
viaggio m journey; trip; drive
viaggio d'affari business trip
viaggio organizzato package tour
viale m avenue
vicino (a) near; close by
vicolo m alley; lane
vicolo cieco cul-de-sac
videocamera f videocamera
videocassetta f videocassette
videofonino m camera phone
videogioco m computer game
videoregistratore m video recorder
vietato forbidden
vietato accendere fuochi do not light fires
vietato fumare no smoking
vietato l'ingresso no entry
vietato ingresso veicoli no entry for vehicles
vietato scendere no exit
vigili del fuoco fire brigade
vigilia f eve
Vigilia di Natale Christmas Eve
vigna f vineyard
vincere to win
vino m wine
vini da pasto table wines
vino da tavola table wine
vini pregiati quality wines
vino bianco white wine
vino rosso red wine
violentare to rape
virus m virus

visita *f* visit
visite guidate guided tours
visitare to visit
vista *f* view
visto *m* visa
vita *f* life; waist
vita notturna night life
vitamina *f* vitamin
vite *f* vine; screw
vivavoce *m* hands-free kit *(for phone)*
vivere to live
vivo(a) live; alive
voce *f* voice
volante *m* steering wheel
volare to fly
voler dire to mean *(signify)*
volere to want
volo *m* flight
volo charter charter flight
volo di linea scheduled flight
volta *f* time

una volta once
due volte twice
voltaggio *m* voltage
vomitare to vomit
vongola *f* clam
vostro(a) your; yours
vulcano *m* volcano
vuoto(a) empty; blank *(disk, tape)*

Z

zanzara *f* mosquito
zanzariera *f* mosquito net
zia *f* aunt
zio *m* uncle
zona *f* zone
zona blu restricted parking zone
zona pedonale pedestrian
zucchero *m* sugar
zucchini *mpl* courgettes
zuppa *f* soup
zuppa inglese type of trifle

Further titles in Collins' phrasebook range
Collins Gem Phrasebook

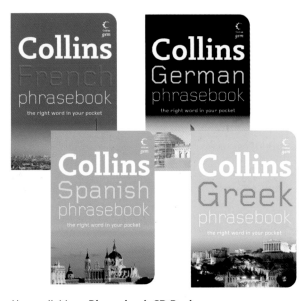

Also available as **Phrasebook CD Pack**

Other titles in the series

Afrikaans	Japanese	Russian
Arabic	Korean	Thai
Cantonese	Latin American	Turkish
Croatian	Spanish	Vietnamese
Czech	Mandarin	Xhosa
Dutch	Polish	Zulu
Italian	Portuguese	